Thoughtful Fundraising

Fundraising is a maturing profession, but one that is increasingly controversial. Media reports of poor practice have contributed to concerns about the integrity of fundraisers and the uses which have been made of the resources they raise. As a result, a consensus now exists among senior figures in the industry about the changes that are required. Technique is no longer enough. Many more of the next generation of practitioners must be capable of considered reflection, organizational and inter-organizational strategic thinking, and value-based leadership. A global drive to raise standards in the profession and to benchmark these through the establishment of accredited qualifications is underway.

The Institute of Fundraising in the UK is in the vanguard of these developments – and this book is designed to support them. Its readings move the thinking in the profession beyond its familiar formulae and assumptions, opening up critical debate about the nature, contribution and limitations of fundraising in its various forms and contexts. Many of the readings were commissioned for this book by experts in the field, others have been selected and edited from diverse sources. Together they are essential reading for anyone who aspires to work at senior levels in fundraising or is currently engaged in studying this challenging area.

Jill Mordaunt is Senior Lecturer in Social Enterprise at the OU Business School.

Professor Rob Paton is a senior figure in the OU Business School where he set up the Centre for Public Leadership and Social Enterprise (PuLSE).

The OU Business School

The OU Business School is the business faculty of The Open University, Europe's largest university and the only UK university dedicated to distance learning.

The OU Business School offers a three-tier ladder of opportunity for managers at different stages of their careers: the Professional Certificate in Management; the Professional Diploma in Management; and the Masters Programme.

This Reader is the prescribed Course Reader for the course Winning Resources and Support which is part of the Undergraduate Programme at The Open University Business School. Opinions expressed in this Reader are not necessarily those of the Course Team or of The Open University.

Further information on OU Business School courses and qualifications may be obtained from the OU Business School, PO Box 197, Walton Hall, Milton Keynes MK7 6BJ, United Kingdom; tel. OU Business School Information Line: +44 (0) 8700 100311.

Alternatively, much useful course information can be obtained from the OU Business School's website at http://www.oubs.open.ac.uk.

Thoughtful Fundraising

Concepts, issues and perspectives

Edited by

Jill Mordaunt and Rob Paton

Routledge
Taylor & Francis Group

LONDON AND NEW YORK

OU
Business
School

Institute of
Fundraising

First Published 2007
by Routledge
2 Park Square, Milton Park, Abingdon, Oxon OX14 4RN

Simultaneously published in the USA and Canada
by Routledge
270 Madison Ave, New York, NY 10016

Routledge is an imprint of the Taylor & Francis Group, an informa business

Typeset in Perpetua by
Florence Production Ltd, Stoodleigh, Devon
Printed and bound in Great Britain by
TJ International, Padstow, Cornwall

British Library Cataloguing in Publication Data
A catalogue record for this book is available from the British Library

Library of Congress Cataloging in Publication Data
Thoughtful fundraising: concepts, issues and perspectives/
    edited by Jill Mordaunt and Rob Paton.
        p. cm.
    Includes bibliographical references and index.
    1. Fund raising.   I. Mordaunt, Jill.   II. Paton, Rob.
    HG177.T473 2007
    658.15′224—dc22   2006022005

ISBN10: 0–415–39429–5 (hbk)
ISBN10: 0–415–39428–7 (pbk)

ISBN13: 978–0–415–39429–1 (hbk)
ISBN13: 978–0–415–39428–4 (pbk)

Contents

Notes on contributors

John Baguley is a speaker and writer on management and fundraising worldwide. Director of the International Fundraising Consultancy and the author of *Successful Fundraising* (Bibliotek, 2000), he has been the Fundraising Director of the Medical Foundation, Amnesty International and Friends of the Earth. He was the first Director of International Fundraising for Amnesty's International Secretariat and the first Director of the Soil Association. He has extensive overseas experience, and recent research interests include the globalization of NGOs.

Richard Brewster is Visiting Senior Research Fellow at the Open University Business School in the United Kingdom and Executive Director of the National Center on Nonprofit Enterprise (NCNE), based in Arlington, North Virginia, USA. From 1995 to 2003, Richard was Chief Executive of Scope, the national disability charity and one of the UK's largest non-profits. Prior to this, he was Scope's Director of Marketing, responsible for fundraising, PR and campaigning.

Sue Douthwaite is Senior Visiting Research Fellow and Academic Leader of the MSc in Charity Fundraising and Marketing, in the Centre for Charity Effectiveness, Cass Business School, City University, UK. As an independent consultant, she brings extensive experience of fundraising and governance. A previous Honorary Secretary of the UK's Institute of Fundraising, she is active at board level in international women's organizations and disability grant-making. Her research interests include board governance and regulation in charities.

Marilyn Fischer is Professor of Philosophy at the University of Dayton, in Dayton, Ohio, USA. For many years she chaired the Ethics Education Committee of the local chapter of AFP (Association of Fundraising Professionals). She has authored *Ethical Decision Making in Fund Raising* (John Wiley, 2000), *On Addams* (Wadsworth, 2004) and many scholarly articles on professional ethics and political philosophy. She is currently writing a book on Jane Addams's theory of cosmopolitan pacifism.

Jenny Harrow is Professor of Voluntary Sector Management in the Centre for Charity Effectiveness, Cass Business School, City University, UK, where she leads the Centre's research. She has a research focus on government–voluntary sector relations, governance, regulation and grant-making, with interests in collaborative research. She holds board member roles in community development and grant-making and is currently Secretary of the 'Pracademics' Special Interest Group of the (US-based) Association for Research in Nonprofit and Voluntary Action.

Warren F. Ilchman is Director of the Indiana University Center on Philanthropy.

Elaine Jay has over sixteen years' experience as a fundraiser in a number of UK charities, including the RSPCA, where she headed Individuals Fundraising. She has also held several agency-side roles, at Amherst Direct Marketing, WWAV Rapp Collins and Personal Fundraising Partnership. A specialist in individuals fundraising and fundraising planning since 2001, Elaine has worked as a consultant. She is co-author of *Building Donor Loyalty* (Jossey Bass, 2004) and *Fundraising Management* (Routledge, 2004).

Mark Juergensmeyer is Director of Global and International Studies and Professor of Sociology and Religious Studies at the University of California, Santa Barbara. He is an expert on religious violence, conflict resolution and South Asian religion and politics. His book on Gandhian conflict resolution has recently been reprinted as *Gandhi's Way* (University of California Press, updated edition, 2005). His most recent work is an edited volume, *Global Religions* (Oxford University Press, 2003).

Stanley N. Katz is Director of the Center for Arts and Cultural Policy Studies at the Woodrow Wilson School of Public and International Affairs at Princeton University, and past President of the American Council of Learned Societies.

Gregory C. Kozlowski was Professor of History at DePaul University until his death in 2002. A scholar of South Asian and Islamic history, he was an international authority on Muslim philanthropic endowments in both British India and modern Pakistan and India. He cultivated a lifelong interest in the Muslim world. In his scholarship and teaching, he linked European philosophy and Christian theology with Muslim philosophy and theology.

Diana Leat is an independent consultant and Visiting Professor at the Centre for Charity Effectiveness, Cass Business School, City University, UK. She has held research and teaching posts in a number of universities and research centres in the UK, the USA and Australia. Her most recent publications include an analysis of risk in grant-making, a study of creative philanthropy in action and a study of UK foundations' roles and visions.

Adele Lindenmeyr is Chairperson and Professor of History at Villanova University in Pennsylvania. A specialist on Russian social and women's history, she has published widely on the history of charity, social welfare and civil society. Her 1996 book *Poverty Is Not a Vice: Charity, Society, and the State in Imperial Russia* (Princeton University Press) received the Heldt Prize for the Best Book Published by a Woman in Slavic Studies, in 1996.

Darrin M. McMahon is the Ben Weider Professor of History at Florida State University. He is the author of *Enemies of the Enlightenment* (Oxford University Press, 2001) and *Happiness: A History* (Atlantic Monthly Press, 2006), and co-editor with Florence Lotterie of *Les Lumières européennes dans leurs relations avec les autres grandes cultures et religions du XVIIIe siècle* (Paris: Honoré Champion, 2002).

Jill Mordaunt is Senior Lecturer in Social Enterprise at the Open University where she was extensively involved in the development of specialist courses for public and non-profit organizations. She has research interests in the role of institutional funding in shaping non-profit activity, and more recently her main work has focused on issues of organizational failure, turnaround and recovery in public and non-profit organizations. She is currently evaluating the impact of consultancy interventions in organizational development.

Redmond Mullin is Chairman of Redmond Mullin Ltd. He has a varied background, having been a Jesuit, in research at Masius, in advertising at J. Walter Thompson, in fundraising with Wells, a director at Charities Aid Foundation. He was a founder of the ICFM, a non-executive director of the London Philharmonic Orchestra, Chairman of the Advisory Committee for the Open University Voluntary Sector Management Programme and of ICFM's Fellows Working Party.

Francie Ostrower is a Professor in the Center on Nonprofits and Philanthropy at the Urban Institute in Washington.

Rob Paton is Professor of Social Enterprise at the Open University where he pioneered the use of distance learning for management, professional and leadership development. He is currently working with nine chief executives on the 'inside story' of their working lives. His recent publications include *Managing and Measuring Social Enterprises* (Sage, 2003), *The Handbook of Corporate University Development: Managing Strategic Learning Initiatives in Public and Private Domains* (Gower, 2005) and *Making Policy Happen* (Routledge, 2006).

Cathy Pharoah was Director of Research at the Charities Aid Foundation until 2006, responsible for annual publications such as *Charity Trends* which monitors trends in the income and expenditure of the top fundraising charities, and the amounts donated by the general public. She is a Fellow of the RSA, a member of the editorial boards of Nonprofit and Voluntary Sector Marketing and Voluntary Action, and a committee member of the Social Research Association.

Edward L. Queen II is Director of the Ethics and Servant Leadership Program at the Center for Ethics, Emory University, Atlanta.

Adrian Sargeant is the Robert F. Hartsook Professor of Fundraising at the Center on Philanthropy at Indiana University. He is also Visiting Professor of Philanthropy at the Centre for Philanthropy and Nonprofit Studies at Queensland University of Technology, Brisbane, Australia. He is Editor of the *International Journal of Nonprofit and Voluntary Sector Marketing* and the author of *Marketing Management for Nonprofit Organizations* (Oxford University Press, 2004).

Anja Schaefer works as a lecturer in corporate social responsibility at The Open University, UK. Prior to that she worked as a lecturer in management at King's College London and as an ESRC research associate at Manchester Business School. She has taught a variety of courses in corporate social responsibility, marketing and business strategy. Her main research interests are in the areas of environmental management and business sustainability.

Nikki van der Gaag is a freelance writer specializing in development issues. She has worked for the Minority Rights Group, the World Council of Churches, Oxfam, New Internationalist and the Panos Institute. With Cathy Midwinter, she was part of an FAO project looking at images of Africa in both European and African countries at the end of the 1980s and has been interested in the debate on the use of images ever since.

Tina Wallace has been a researcher, university teacher, NGO worker and a consultant in Africa and the UK for over thirty years, focusing especially on gender, education, water and refugees, as well as on organizational issues – strategic thinking, learning, monitoring and evaluation. She has published widely: her publications include *Changing Perceptions* (Oxfam, 1991), *New Roles and Relevance* (Kumarian Press, 2000), *Gender, Water and Development* (Berg, 2005) and *The Aid Chain* (ITDG, 2006).

Foreword

Fundraising is among the most modern and flexible career choices. On one level it creates the opportunity for all of us to use our wealth to make a difference and to change the world around us. You cannot get much more socially responsible than that. On another level the core skills that are inherent in a good fundraiser are those commonly called the 'life skills'. These include good interpersonal skills, listening, empathy, and excellent communicational ability. However, it is not enough just to possess these skills, and when they are combined with excellent training and knowledge the results can be transformational.

The Winning Resources and Support course at the Open University brings the Institute's professional qualifications within reach of a wide audience. This reader is a vital support tool to those having the foresight and professionalism to get qualified just as fundraising reaches ever greater recognition as a serious and worthwhile profession.

Lindsay Boswell
Institute of Fundraising

Acknowledgements

We are very grateful to all who have contributed to the creation of this book, especially those from whom we have commissioned articles, for their forbearance and patience with our feedback, critical comments, and for their willingness to redraft pieces in a timely fashion. We hope that they are as satisfied with the result as we are.

We would also like to thank Terry O'Sullivan (Chair of Winning Resources and Support) for his critical comments on the concept of the book; Barry Jones for his reliable and efficient administrative support; Sue Treacy for managing the formatting and handover drafts of the material, and Gill Gowans in OU Publishing and Francesca Heslop and Emma Joyes at Routledge for their patience.

The publishers would like to thank the following for permission to reprint material.

Mullin, R. (1995) *Foundations for fundraising*, pp. 1–17. Hemel Hempstead: ICAS Publishing.

Ilchman, W. F., Katz, S. and Queen II, E. L. (eds) (2006) *Philanthropy in the World's Traditions*, pp. 197–214, 263–278, 279–308, 309–331, © 2006 Indiana University Press. Reprinted by permission of Indiana University Press.

Paton, R. (1995) 'What's different about nonprofit and voluntary sector marketing? A research agenda', *International Journal of Non-profit and Voluntary Sector Marketing*, 1: 1, pp. 23–31, © 1995 John Wiley & Sons Limited. Reproduced with permission.

Ostrower, F. (1995) 'Why the wealthy give: the culture of elite philanthropy', in *Trustees of Culture*, pp. 32–38, 58–59, 64–89, 94–101, © 1995 The University of Chicago Press. Reprinted by permission of the publisher.

Sargeant, A. and Jay, E. (2004) 'Donor development', in A. Sargeant, *Fundraising Management*, Chapter 7, © 2004 Routledge. Reproduced by permission of Taylor & Francis Books UK.

Paton, R. (1999) 'Performance comparisons in fundraising: the case of Fundratios', *International Journal of Non-profit and Voluntary Sector Marketing*, 4: 4, pp. 287–299, © 1999 John Wiley & Sons Limited. Reproduced with permission.

Fischer, M. (2000) 'Conceptual tools for ethical decision making', in *Ethical Decision Making in Fund Raising*, Chapter 1, © 2000 John Wiley & Sons, Inc. Reproduced with permission.

Introduction to Book

THE CHALLENGE OF SUSTAINABLE FUNDING – now a major pre-occupation for non-profit organizations – is not new. Historically, small and medium-sized charities used the contributions of dedicated supporters and volunteers, and wherever possible sought larger contributions, through church or other connections, from more wealthy individuals. But throughout the last half century, the number of paid fundraisers has been increasing steadily. Fundraising is now a profession.

The Association of Fundraising Professionals was founded in the USA in the 1960s, and the UK followed in 1983 with the formation of what is now the Institute of Fundraising (originally the Institute of Charity Fundraising Managers). For several years the Resource Alliance has been running professional training courses for fundraisers in Africa and many parts of Asia. In addition, the European Fundraising Association was established in 2004, marking a significant step in the professionalization of fundraising in seventeen European countries. This seeks among other things to raise the level both of debate and of professional standards of fundraisers across Europe. The scale of the fundraising endeavour is now truly enormous. In the UK the Institute of Fundraising (Ramrayka 2004) found that there were over 12,000 fundraisers employed in the top 500 charities in the UK, between them raising over £8.6 billion in 2002 to 2003, as well as many more people in smaller organizations who have a fundraising remit in the job description.

What factors are driving this burgeoning professionalization? First, the role that voluntary and non-profit organizations play in society has changed. There has been a shift from supplementing state services to taking a much larger role in provision (along with the private sector) from a state that sees itself mainly as a commissioner rather than a provider of services. This has been an important factor in the huge growth in the number of non-profit organizations of various kinds. By 2004, Wilding *et al.* (2006)

found that there are around 169,000 general charities in the UK with a combined income of £26.3 billion. This represented an increase from 98,000 organizations in 1991 with growth in income concentrated in the largest. It is also clear that giving is a significant part of life for many people – almost three-fifths of the population in the UK give to charity in a typical month (Wilding op.cit.).

This increase in the size of the sector, and in the 'market' for donations, has led to increased competition to raise money for the cause. One of Wilding's findings is that although there is more money raised in the UK overall by the charity sector, most of that increase has been in the larger charities (i.e. those most likely to be employing professional fundraisers), while the income of smaller charities has at best remained static. Every organization has to work increasingly hard to gain the attention of donors and to stand out from many others who espouse similar causes. Thus more and more organizations are turning to professional fundraisers either as employees or as consultants to assist them with devising their strategy and persuading donors to give.

The professionalization of fundraising is also part of a general trend in the sector towards more businesslike management in general. This has been a concomitant of more institutional funding, particularly from state sources. Another long-term trend has been in calls for transparency and accountability, with questions sometimes being raised about performance and effectiveness in the use of donated monies. At the same time, there have been a few, but highly visible, scandals about the misappropriation of funds. Many people operating in small organizations have tales to tell of campaigns in which the expenses of the fundraising have exceeded the monies raised or, worse, monies have been diverted to non-charitable purposes. Occasionally, blatant corruption such as funding cars and personal expenses for employees or trustees has taken place (Charity Commission 2006). All this has led to demands to improve training and standards for all engaged with fundraising, and the Institute of Fundraising and other professional bodies have been at the forefront in seeking to maintain the good name of the profession.

The activities of fundraisers now touch virtually every part of civil society. Their ambit ranges from the arts to zoological societies and does not only include what is generally considered the charitable sector but also draws in religious, environmental, development and human rights organizations, political parties, as well as many parts of the public sector such as educational bodies (from nursery schools to universities), and the health service. They also involve huge numbers of volunteers participating in organizing the many activities that fundraisers undertake to raise funds.

As the professionalization has increased there has also been increased special-ization within the profession itself. Most large organizations have a huge range of different posts which will include people who focus on particular aspects of fundraising such as big gifts or legacies, developing members to become more committed donors, and specialists in trading such as retailing, selling charity Christmas cards and so on, as well as fundraising directors who focus on the overall strategy.

Alongside this, the methods adopted by fundraisers have increasingly drawn on ideas from commercial marketing. Most significant has been the development of direct marketing techniques involving large databases of potential donors and the use of direct mail shots targeted at those who fit particular profiles. The major direct marketing agencies compete eagerly for the contracts of major charities and campaigning groups. Many larger organizations' fundraising strategies now include hard-sell techniques such as cold-calling, door-to-door sales of goods and subscriptions, and latterly what some have come to call 'chuggers' – charity muggers – people employed on a commission basis to sell subscriptions to people in the street.

This has had two implications for the industry. First, there is a large growth in the number of private sector professionals playing both central and ancillary roles in professional fundraising. Besides a huge army of freelance consultants, there are those who run call centres, design database management systems, advertising and image designers, IT specialists for websites and online giving, and so on. Fundraising has become big business.

Second, there is a constant drive to be innovative as tried and trusted techniques become 'old hat'. This has led to healthy questioning and debate within the profession. On the one hand, some observers of the fundraising world – for example, Joe Saxton, quoted in *The Guardian* (Shifrin 2006) – argues that there is 'no such thing as donor fatigue – only marketing fatigue'. This puts the emphasis on finding novel ways of presenting the case and capturing attention. The danger is that this creates an accelerating treadmill of constant innovation. Fundraisers can then become obsessed with technique, with any new idea rapidly becoming a fashion, imitated aggressively across the field. The sheer volume of unsolicited mail that arrives through the public's letter-boxes stands as testimony to this – complete with its free Biros, questionable questionnaires, coloured ribbons, slogan-bearing wristbands and, more recently, metal tags.

Others contend that much of this activity is of doubtful effectiveness, short-sighted and wastes money. It degenerates into a pursuit of novelty in attracting attention and coaxing particular responses. Crucially, it loses sight of a much bolder opportunity and challenge – finding innovative ways for concerned individuals gradually to expand their lives and their social involvement, and to make a continuing difference in the world on the issues that they care about. From this perspective, the most significant developments in fundraising in recent years have been those that link donors directly with activists on the ground (e.g. Peace Direct) or beneficiaries (as in sponsorship schemes of one sort or another).

Long may such debates continue. What is clear is that many more of the next generation of senior fundraising practitioners must be capable of considered reflection, organizational and inter-organizational strategic thinking, and value-based leadership. This book is intended to contribute to that development.

Although prepared with professional fundraisers in mind, it is intended also for two other audiences. First, senior figures in small organizations that have fundraising as part of their brief may find that it provides an overview of the field, complementing the many useful 'how-to-do-it' books that offer detailed recipes for specific practices or techniques. Second, we hope it will be useful for a wider audience of senior leaders in charities and non-profits – those who work closely with senior fundraisers, and to whom fundraisers may report. They need to understand their fundraising colleagues, the better to engage with them in discussion of results and future strategy. Arguably, one part of the problem with fundraising is that too often it is left to the fundraisers – this is a bit like leaving marketing to the sales force in a commercial organization.

Responsibility for resource mobilization runs right through the organization. It depends on the activities of senior managers and trustees in bringing contacts and awareness of new opportunities to the organization, the role of grassroots staff and beneficiaries in feeding back on issues and emerging needs – as well as fundraisers' ability to identify new ways of attracting support. Indeed, it may be particularly important for those aspiring charity managers who feel no great affinity for their more commercially minded colleagues in the fundraising department that they read this book!

The book is divided into four parts which together give an overview of the central concepts and issues in fundraising. Part One, 'Perspectives on fundraising', deliberately stands right back, setting this practice in a historical and cross-cultural context, before exploring one of the central issues in the profession – its relationship to the very visible and powerful marketing profession.

Part Two, 'Fundamental concepts and techniques', offers a brisk but authoritative tour of the ideas and techniques that are currently fundamental to fundraising practice. These include the ways in which fundraisers research, test and *motivate* existing and potential donors, and use *relationships* and *social networks* to lever donations. The various approaches to *fundraising campaigns* and their associated risks are also examined, along with the key ideas underpinning prospect research techniques.

Part Three, 'Environments for fundraising', explores some of the ways in which these ideas and approaches are played out in the four main types of fundraising, and the issues that may arise. The readings cover the implications of seeking resources from *individual donors* (are the demographics of giving changing?), from *corporations* (what is in it for them, and what issues do they pose for the recipients?), from *foundations* (how do they go about making decisions on their grants?), and finally from *public bodies* (what will be the implications of engaging with public policy in this way?).

Part Four, 'Challenges for senior professionals and trustees', sets out some of the challenges that face the profession but also charities and non-profits more broadly. These concern the difficulties in judging the performance of fundraising programmes and schemes, the regulation of fundraising activities, ethical issues in fundraising, the controversy over images used in fundraising, and the strategic issues which many charities face around the composition of a revenue portfolio.

References

Charity Commission (2006) *Inquiry Reports* http://www.charity-commission.gov.uk/investigations/inquiryreports/inqreps.asp.

Ramrayka, L. (2004) *Working in Fundraising,* London: Guardian Books.

Schifrin, T. (2006) 'Dedicated followers of compassion', *Guardian,* 24 April.

Wilding, K., Clark, J., Griffith, M., Jochum, V. and Wainwright, S. (2006) *The UK Voluntary Sector Almanac 2006: The State of the Sector,* London: NCVO.

PART ONE

Perspectives on fundraising

INTRODUCTION

WHAT IS FUNDRAISING? Anyone who thinks the answer is obvious, or amenable to some 'essentialist' definition, should find this section enlightening. Rather, the current concept of fundraising is a loose and still contested bundle of practices and ideas peculiar to Western society at this time. Some of them are new and some go back a long way; some are universal and some will not travel well to other societies. The construction and institutionalization of 'fundraising' is a work in progress – and one that is unlikely to be completed so long as society keeps changing.

The first chapter, by Mullin, outlines the Judaeo-Christian roots of modern Western fundraising, tracing its origins in religious injunctions to care for the poor and to achieve salvation by good works. These included the building and maintenance of cathedrals; and Mullin reveals that, while some of the causes for which funds are now raised may have changed, the general means and motives have not changed so radically. Today's fundraiser would be comfortable with donors' desires for immortalizing their names, gaining standing and respect in the community as well as altruistic gifts and also with some of the fundraising instruments: collection boxes, matched funding, high-society fundraising events, patrons, charity trading, the use of direct mail and sponsored events. Equally, the trends towards corruption also emerged early on, with the need to regulate and maintain ethical standards evident as early as the Middle Ages.

Chapter 2 (Ilchman *et al.*) shows that giving is not unique to Western cultures, but that its meaning and institutional forms vary widely. While the Hindu religion emphasizes the importance of gifts to worthy recipients, it was the teaching of Gandhi that transformed these ideas into the modern context. In Islamic societies, the author counsels against overly simplistic and blanket interpretations of motivations, and suggests the need to look at the differences between different Muslim states – important points also for multicultural societies. One thing that distinguishes Russia from the other two examples is the amount of aid that has poured into the country from former 'enemies of the USSR', with much of the funding going to Russian NGOs rather than to the state to create a 'civil society'. This has aroused suspicions on the part of the Russians particularly of US motives, as well as creating a sense of humiliation at going from superpower to beggar nation. This is not helped by the weakness of regulation of the charitable sector and its propensity to being self-serving and even corrupt. Thus, although philanthropy has religious underpinnings in all of these contexts, it is also important to understand the socio-political contexts. This is one reason why there are significantly fewer international brands in fundraising than there are in other sectors.

One of the most powerful influences on the emergent profession is the marketing discipline – within which many fundraisers have been trained and pursued careers at one time or another. It is hardly surprising that many people view fundraising through a marketing lens – and will argue that *really* it is just a special case of marketing. In Chapter 3, Paton challenges casual thinking on this issue – both for and against. He argues against conflating the concepts and draws out key distinctions. The similarities are strongest where commercial concepts and strategies have clear parallels – in the area of mass fundraising. Here, commercial marketing and fundraising are similar (consider, for example, the development of brands in the 'lifestyle' charities in environmental and development work). Nevertheless, he argues that the fundraising role in charities is only *one part* of a more distributed and complex marketing function within non-profit organizations. The trick is to manage the integration of these different elements.

Chapter 1

Redmond Mullin

TWO THOUSAND YEARS OF DISREPUTABLE HISTORY

Edited from: Mullin, R. (1995) *Foundations of fundraising*, pp. 1–17, Hemel Hempstead: ICAS Publishing.

Summary

CHARITIES AND THE FUNDRAISING that supports their activities have been established for over 2,000 years. Both originally drew on Jewish and Graeco-Roman traditions. Fundraising throughout its history has depended on leaders, volunteers and a range of methods segmented in relation to target supporters. The principles have remained constant although activity has been affected by circumstances and by the means available – pulpit or television. It seems there have almost always been professional fundraisers and that criticism of them has remained fairly constant, hence 2,000 years of regulation and licensing. Today we are in a period of extraordinary competition, with national and international regulation a crucial topic.

Fundraising in Late Antiquity

There is famine in Palestine; give your support. I am sending Titus to receive the money you promised and have told people how generous you will be. Every week before he arrives, set aside a considered sum, calculated according to your means. It must be ready before I get there, so that there is no fund-raising during my visit. If you are not as generous as you promised to be, I and you will be shamed. There were previous complaints about the handling of funds, so please appoint trustees to account for the money and take it to Jerusalem. If you like, I will go with them.

That is a paraphrase of part of Paul's letters to the Corinthians, promoting famine relief to Palestine, written less than thirty years after the Crucifixion.[1]

Paul's is a remarkable precedent for fundraising letters. It is also part of one of the greatest world traditions of fundraising and community care. These early Christians were continuing Jewish tradition which survives today. Then it was common practice for the Jews of the diaspora to send funds to Jerusalem, even after its destruction in AD 70. As late as the third century, fundraisers were being appointed to organise this activity.[2]

That was only one aspect of Jewish fundraising and charity. There were people in each community assigned to fundraising; others to the distribution of food, clothes and funds. Rabbi Jose Ben Halafta prayed for the job of fundraiser to avoid the distributor's hard choices. Rabbi Akiba said: 'It is a greater virtue to cause another to give than to give yourself', blessing fundraisers. Giving was assessed proportionately to means (as Paul suggests) with the object that no member of the community and no visiting Jew should be in need.[3] Care embraced the *ger*, the gentile resident, the non-Jew.[4] As we have seen, it included relief and alms for Jerusalem. The tradition continued and developed over the following centuries.

The European fundraising tradition was already drawing on established structures and practice from its beginning. It drew on the traditions – Roman and Greek – of the Roman Empire as well as on Judaism. Much in that sophisticated world seems familiar. The rich man of Gytheion who, in AD 161–9, gave oils for the baths, did so on condition that three marble pillars publicising his philanthropy be set up at the prominent places in town. So, in the twelfth century, Bubwith of Wells provided 160 craftsmen's salaries on condition that the north tower be named after him.[5] So, today, the name on the building or facility can clinch a gift. Indeed, in the ancient world the funding of public works and social service by the very rich sometimes took the place of taxation. Private gifts often funded civil works, public buildings, poor relief and even the fleet, as well as circuses and public display.[6]

It seems that the early Christian communities provided for themselves and generously for others. They made donations through a kind of community chest from which everyone, especially the poorest, benefited.[7] In 373 Basil (Bishop of Caesarea), a knowing manipulator of the state system, who had set up a large hostel and hospice outside Caesarea about a year before, wrote to the Imperial Prefect's Assistant: 'have the kindness to inspect the home for the poor and exempt it entirely from taxation to make the small property of the poor immune from assessment'.[8] It was an important (and corrupting) moment for the new religion when Constantine removed distribution of poor relief – in bread and corn doles – from pagan to Christian priests. Even by Basil's time, founding donors' names and portraits were appearing on Christian buildings and by 321 there was a large flow of legacies to the Christian church and its causes. Peter Brown writes: 'the ancient search for personal fame through well-publicised giving, had entered the church in a peculiarly blatant form'.[9]

The fundraising and giving of the Christian churches reached far away: in 253 Cyprian in Carthage sent 100,000 sesterces to devastated Numidia; and the church in Rome cared for 1,500 indigent people, many of them refugees. Ambrose in Milan sent ransoms for prisoners in the Balkans (selling his Arian enemies' memorial patens and chalices to pay for this).[10] Support of the poor through its charity was to give the strengthening church distinctive influence as the late Roman Empire (East and West) christianised itself. The poor, disregarded by non-Christian communities, became a special factor for the churches', and particularly their bishops', successful bid for power. Among the poor, then as now, lone parents and the homeless were particularly abandoned. The poor without status were a threat in the growing cities. The bishops and churches embraced them, thus offering security to the state and securing their own statutory position. As numbers of the indigent grew, the church listed the approved poor and, after the Council of Chalcedon, issued under a bishop's signature their licences for begging – a practice that was to become familiar again in pre- and post-Reformation Europe.[11]

Much of that early fundraising was managed by people within the Christian (or Jewish) community assigned to this task. Were there professionals as well as volunteers? Perhaps. In the *Ecclesiastical History*, by Eusebius (260–340), the heretic Montanus is criticised because 'It is he who appointed collectors of money, who organised the receiving of gifts under the name of offerings'.[12] If this is the professionals' first appearance in history, it is in a hostile text – something you will be used to by the end of this chapter.

Fundraising in the Middle Ages

The Middle Ages were a definitive time for charities. It was during this period that trust law was established in Britain. During the thirteenth century, the Franciscan order was founded. Its elected poverty prevented not just its members, but also the order itself from ownership of property. To allow gifts to reach the friars, a 'spiritual friend' outside the order owned and managed property on the friars' behalf. This was the origin of our trust law.[13]

This was also the period during which the 'heads of charity' from the English 1601 Act were gradually formulated. During the Middle Ages they were a statement of priorities for benevolent action and for funding, to which spiritual benefits would be attached as an incentive. They identified the private and communal issues toward which voluntary funding should be directed. Langland (poet laureate for the poor and disabled), writing between 1360 and 1370, cites as objects for charity hospitals, the unfortunate, the sick, bad roads, broken bridges, help for maidens, the bedridden poor, prisoners, sending young children to school and the endowment of religion.

This was also a high period for fundraising. In 1174, when the monastery of St Evurtius, just outside the walls of Orleans, had been sacked by the Normans,

Table 1.1 Milan Cathedral fundraising, 1386–91

Source	Method and purpose	Motivations
Very rich individual	Request for marker gift To ask and be model for the rich	Memorial Salvation

Rich individuals
  (nobles, soldiers,
  lawyers, doctors)
	Request for major support
	Pressure from Court
	Legacies
	Sons' volunteer labour
	Committee membership
		Memorials
		Salvation
		Peer esteem

Prosperous individuals	Through confraternities Sponsor craftsmen, navvies Gifts in kind Legacies Committee membership	(Memorial) Salvation Peer group Citizenship
Ordinary people	House-to-house collections Street collections Fundraising events and functions Jumble sales Volunteer labour	Salvation Peer group Citizenship
Young	Schools fundraising	

Bishop Stephan sent out two fundraising letters, parts of which I paraphrase: 'Standing in the smoking ashes of our church among the scorched timbers of its walls, soon to rise again, we are forced to approach the general public and shamelessly to ask for support from outside gifts'.[14]

For a more detailed description of medieval fundraising, Table 1.1 shows the segmentation of giving between sources, methods used and motivations for the building of Milan Cathedral between 1386 and 1391. That remarkable campaign was described in an article published by Edmund Bishop at Downside in 1899. He describes how the community came together productively at every level to achieve their cathedral. It was a few individuals who started the street and house-to-house collections. It was civic rivalry between guilds and fraternities and between other classes and groups in Milan which brought out the volunteer teams. The fundraising was managed by a committee. There really were jumble sales and school fundraising. There was also an admirable attempt at major support fundraising.

There was uniformity, apparently, in fundraising around Europe in the Middle Ages. These were some of the ways in which the funds were raised:

- Indulgences were effective: in June 1390 the Milan fabric fund raised 2,398 lira; in June 1391, with a Jubilee indulgence, it raised 24,858 lira.
- Collection boxes, common since antiquity, occur everywhere. Poor Friar Elias, succeeding St Francis and cast as a Judas figure, is criticised for installing

one on the site of the basilica he was building in Assisi, in 1230, to hold the saint's body.

- It was very usual for there to be matching funding between bishop and chapter for building their cathedral, the chapter perhaps pledging 50 per cent of the bishop's commitment (as, for example, at Exeter and Chartres).
- There was high-society fundraising: at New Sarum, in 1220, noblemen and noblewomen could lay a foundation stone, then covenant a seven-year subscription to the fabric fund.
- There were many major patrons. Bishop Thoresby (between 1352 and 1373) at York funded 650 salaries for the Minster. Bishop Grandisson at Exeter was helping to fund both his cathedral and his bridge (still visible) about 1328. There were foundations by kings and queens. Henry III and Henry VII made major foundations. Nobles such as Henry de Blois were involved: he set up one of England's most ancient charities at St Cross, Winchester. There were merchants such as Gervase of Southampton, who founded God's House and endowed it as a hospital for poor folk there.
- There was endowment through income-earning assets such as shops, markets, mineral assets, fisheries and mills (cf. current charity trading). Thus in the twelfth century the cathedral chapter was co-owner of the Great Quay in Amiens. Dues levied on Jewish families and enterprises might be transferred to a church or monastery. In Barcelona in the fourteenth century income from the mills was intended to secure income for the hospital there, relieving it of dependence on small-scale fundraising.
- There were even records of sponsored bell-ringing at Rouen and in other places.[15]

The guilds were powerful vehicles for medieval, communal philanthropy. They were formed for various purposes: for piety, to mount miracle plays, and most enduringly as mutual-help associations within a craft or trade. That last form of association has survived in the City of London and other livery companies. More pious types of guild were abolished at the Reformation. Guilds were the original community-chest bodies. There were real wooden iron-bound chests, often with strong double locks, which could only be opened by two aldermen with separate keys. Guildsmen looked after each other and their families, visiting the sick (perhaps with a bottle from the guild's ale store) and providing grants and pensions. There was assistance with grants and loans at times of financial difficulty. All guilds had benevolent objects written into their statutes and looked for contributions, sometimes apportioned according to means, from members. The statutes of a York guild declared: 'Vain is the gathering of the faithful unless some work of kindliness is done'. Most guilds were also committed to works of mercy for non-members and to altruistic objects: poor, sick and handicapped people; travellers; schools and schoolmasters: roads, bridges and causeways.[16] We have seen how the guilds of a city might rally to the building of their cathedral. In Strasburg, the guilds had crucial welfare roles. There was overlap across Europe between guild activity and the systematisation of relief and statutory limitation to a community's responsibility for relief. In Britain the 1536 Beggars Act threatened penalties for unsystematic philanthropy:

No manner of person . . . shall give any ready money in alms, otherwise than to the common boxes and common gatherings . . . upon pain to lose and forfeit ten times the value of all such ready money as shall be given in alms contrary to the tenor and purport of [the Act].

This was an early attempt at the control of giving and of relief.[17]

Medieval fundraisers were conspicuously successful, hence the real corruption and the criticism. The 1215 Lateran Council decreed that *quaestores eleemosynarii*, as they were called, could only operate under licence from their bishop or from the Pope, a formula already guaranteed to stir strife where papal demands for funds were unwelcome. Despite the regulations, the *quaestores'* success attracted fraud. False fundraisers (sometimes brought in by the chapter) would mount appeals, for their own and sometimes the chapter's gain.

Fraud and personal gain were, perhaps, the least damaging criticisms of the *quaestores*. What they offered was the purchase of salvation. It was salvation purchased through gifts that these medieval fundraisers offered, to their own, their licence-givers' and notionally the donors' gains. They bore relics and were probably the first laymen allowed into Christian pulpits. They drew wrath from reformers as well as satire from poets. They could work for a variety of causes. Chaucer's swindling, prospering pardoner raised funds for the hospital of the Blessed Mary of Rouncivalle near Charing Cross.

Fundraising after the Reformation

On 31 October 1517 the Pope's arch fundraiser, the Dominican John Tetzel, came to sell indulgences near Wittenberg. He was raising money for building St Peter's in Rome and to help pay off a huge debt owed by Prince Bishop Albert of Brandenburg to the Fuggers, who were massive money-lenders. The family still has charitable foundations in Europe. At Wittenberg, Prince Frederick the Wise of Saxony had built up his own collection of relics, from which he wanted to see profits. Far more potently, Martin Luther was Professor of Scripture there. When the Saxons flooded across the border to hear Tetzel preach and to pay for pardons and remissions, Luther protested against such purchase of paradise by publishing his ninety-five theses. His was the cause of salvation by faith alone.

Of course the criticism did not begin with Luther; nor did the debate end with him. Yet it was the *quaestor* or fundraiser Tetzel who sparked the Reformation. (In recognition, the American *Philanthropy Monthly* makes its annual Tetzel Award to the most discreditable fundraising performance each year.)

Roman indulgences were peddled on into our own time; but what was left for the Protestant world? With promises of salvation abandoned, the main elements of technique and leadership could stay in place. In England during the sixteenth and seventeenth centuries the pulpit was a medium through which most people could be reached, week by week. It had been the medium for the pardoners before the Reformation. Now it was used as potently. In 1536, the year in which he issued his Act Against Papal Authority, Henry VIII also decreed in his Beggars Act that 'every preacher, parson, vicar, curate of the realm' should use sermons and all other means to 'exhort, move, stir and provoke people to be liberal and bountifully to extend their alms and contributions toward the comfort and relief of poor, impotent, decrepit, indigent and needy people'.[18]

Henry VIII did not give the first example. Henry III, among others, had been there before him. Reformed monarchs became regular fundraisers for such causes as the Society for the Propagation of the Gospel. Queen Anne, George I, George II, George III, George IV, William IV and Queen Victoria all wrote appeal letters on its behalf. George III, for example, decreed: 'upon this occasion, Ministers in each parish [are to] effectually excite their parishioners to a liberal contribution' which would be collected at their homes during the following week by the church wardens and overseers for the poor.[19]

Royal patronage and the pulpit were only one aspect of fundraising in England after Henry VIII. Printing was a main instrument of Reformation. Print and literacy increased in influence. Here is a direct marketing appeal by the Quaker John Bellers in his *Proposals for Raising a College of Industry* (the origin of the Saffron Walden Boarding School) in 1696. He is itemising the needs in what looks like an excellent appeal:

> For every 300 persons, the raising of:
> £10,000 to buy an Estate in Land of £500 p.a.
> £2,000 to Stock the Land
> £3,000 to prepare Necessaries to Set the Several Trades to Work
> £3,000 for New-building or Repairing Old
> In all 18,000 pound
> A hundred pound a year in such a College, I suppose will maintain ten times
>   as many people as £100 a year in alms-houses.[20]

By 1712 the Society for Promoting Christian Knowledge (SPCK) and others were beginning to build their residing and subscribing members' lists, their databases of supporters. Restrictions such as licensing persisted. In 1718 'a little contingent' from St Anne's, Aldersgate, arrived without licence to raise funds in Chislehurst. They were brought before the High Sheriff. He demanded: 'By what right are you strolling and begging through the country without a licence?' One of the trustees was sent to gaol.[21]

All the time, social leadership dominated large segments of English fundraising. Hogarth and Handel devotedly raised funds for the Foundling Hospital – Handel was anxious for those children even on his death bed.[22] There was a great concern and generosity – and vulgarity: 'Find a Duchess, flatter her and get £500' was the motto of the *Press Bazaar News* late in the nineteenth century.[23]

Where were the 'professionals'? As usual, they emerge in criticism because of the percentage that professional companies were taking. In the eighteenth and nineteenth centuries, companies like Robert Hodgson & Byrd and Hall & Stevenson were taking 5–7.5 per cent of the sums raised.[24]

Modern fundraising

Professionally designed and managed fundraising probably started about 1883, in the United States, for the Young Men's Christian Association (YMCA). That was the beginning of a new style of professionalism. In 1919, Ward, Hill, Pierce & Wells became the first professional fundraising company of its kind, Wells having previously worked for the YMCA. From their activity emerged two other main fundraising companies, Craigmyle and Hooker. From these came a highly trained generation of professionals.

During the late 1950s and early 1960s, about the time that the Wells company was transforming some aspects of fundraising, a revolution emerged. Before then, Third World causes had a relatively weak impact, except for occasional appeals, often associated with church missionary initiatives, and sometimes combining Christian with imperial expansion.[25] Then independence for North African nations, World Refugee Year and famine in Biafra and the Congo created an impetus which gave their cause priority. Photographs of starving children and adults in the poor world shocked our rich world into its response. For the rest of the century, Oxfam, War on Want, Save the Children, Christian Aid and the Catholic Fund for Overseas Development (CAFOD) would make their powerful arguments for attention, action and funding support. Simultaneously, prosperity in the West increased and a new age of consumption began in the Western democracies.

Such developments also contributed to the competition for funds which became acute from the mid-1980s onwards. Several factors created this competition. In the United Kingdom, there was rapid increase both in new charity registrations and in the number and scale of appeals launched. The full range of marketing techniques had been brought into the more sophisticated charities' fundraising repertory. They competed through highly segmented direct marketing, sometimes controversially through telephone solicitation, and through television advertising, when this was permitted after 1990. Before the mid-1980s, major support fundraising had largely been confined to capital appeals for universities, schools, hospitals and major arts enterprises. After the success of the National Society for the Prevention of Cruelty to Children (NSPCC), many more charities added this segment of support and style of fundraising to their strategies. For example, there was the remarkable Wishing Well Appeal for the hospital for sick children at Great Ormond Street.[26] There were at the same time massive exercises that powerfully reached other, sometimes younger segments of the world for support: Band Aid, the Telethon and Charity Projects' Comic Relief. Camelot and the National Lottery added billions of pounds to the resources available. The result was that virtually everyone was receiving better-designed, higher-pitched propositions for support more frequently and from more petitioners for funds than ever before.

Meanwhile, the government has liberalised our tax regime so that it encourages more widespread and higher levels of giving. Give As You Earn encourages employees to give routinely through their payrolls. Gift Aid allows tax concessions on one-off gifts, introducing an equivalent to the US tax deduction system for UK charities and donors. For charities that have used them these have had very positive impacts on fundraising here. Government policies and provisions also increased demand from not-for-profit bodies of all kinds – from the arts, old and emergent universities and new hospital trusts. Oxford and Cambridge responded with unprecedented appeals, their targets above £250 million.

Charities responded by intensifying their fundraising. Improvement in the quality and standards of charity personnel has been a crucial issue. There has been much to encourage this since 1980. Standards of recruitment have been raised. There have been some increases in remuneration. Training and educational provision for the sector have greatly improved. Numbers of skilled people, particularly in the 30–45 age group, have grown significantly. There are signs that the sector will be able to offer sound internal career progression and also some exchange with related commercial sectors. The Institute of Fundraising has had a crucial role in this. It has pioneered accredited training for charity personnel and has introduced Codes of Conduct for a number of fundraising activities encouraging self-regulation in this field. It has had a positive impact on UK government and EU legislation and regulation; it attracts several hundred people to its annual convention. Above all, it has created a sense of professionalism in the sector.

Over the past twenty years, economic shifts, external to fundraising, became opportunities for it. Huge increases in new private wealth have created fortunes, at their highest levels matching, or excelling, those of the established, philanthropic individuals and families. Many of those established fortunes have also grown. At lower levels a new tier of prospects for fundraising, recently prosperous, has emerged. These are people earning above, say, £250,000 yearly who can be caused to give £100,000 or more by using our benevolent tax regime for gifts and flexibly spreading the gifts over time. Many of these new philanthropists are in their thirties or forties when they engage in giving. Exploitation of these opportunities has been hesitant, patchy. Have too many fundraisers still been so timid, lacking in understanding, too sceptical, unskilled to identify and motivate such new prospects at levels appropriate to them? A recent study of *Trends in Charitable Giving for the 21st Century* has no chapter on modern major support fundraising. The Giving Campaign hardly touched it. There has been substantial consequent loss for charitable enterprise. The NSPCC, through its Full Stop appeal, did exploit the opportunities. Full Stop has been a total appeal, targeted at the whole population. At its highest financial levels, it has pursued appropriate targets for those richest prospects. Its top 43 units of support have yielded some £66 million. They mounted a successful prosperous – 'Patrons' – programme. Its top 25 units of support have delivered above £5 million. The appeal total is now approaching £200 million. Full Stop has demonstrated that it is not just the great universities and other major institutions which can raise such sums – in total and in their constituent units of support. The opportunities are there for the great welfare organisations also, if only they grasp them.

Notes

1   Corinthians 16.1–4; 2 Corinthians 8.16–21.
2   Cf. Emil Schurer, *The Jewish People in the Time of Jesus*, Schocken, New York, 1961, p. 288.

3   Cf. Peah 8.7, etc., *The Mishnah*, trans. Herbert Danby, Oxford University Press, 1933; *The Talmud*, trans. H. Polano, Warne, London and New York, 1978, p. 243; C. G. Montefiore and H. Loewe (eds), *A Rabinic Anthology*, Schocken, New York, 1974, pp.174–6.

4   *The Talmud*, p. 198; Gittin 5.9, *The Mishnah*, trans. Danby, p. 314; Montefiore and Loewe, *A Rabbinic Anthology*, p. 424.

5   Inscription AD 161–9, in A. R. Hands, *Charities and Social Aid in Greece and Rome*, Thames & Hudson, London 1968, p. 206.

6   Cf. Paul Veyne, *Bread and Circuses*, Allen Lane, London, 1990, pp. 88, 89 and *passim*.

7   Justin, *Apology*, XVII.6.

8   Basil, *Letters*, Loeb, 1928, CXLII and CXLIII.

9   Cf. Hilary Feldman, *Some Aspects of the Christian Reaction to the Tradition of Classical Munificence with Particular Reference to the Works of John Chrysostom and Libanius*, Oxford M.Litt thesis, 1980, pp. 270f.; Henry Chadwick, *The Early Christian Church*, Penguin, 1967, p. 58; Peter Brown, *Power and Persuasion in Late Antiquity*, University of Wisconsin Press, 1992, p. 95.

10   Eusebius, *Ecclesiastical History*, Loeb, 1926 and 1932, IV.XXIII; Cyprian, Ep. 62, in J. P. Migne (ed.), *Patrologiae latinae cursus completus*, 221 vols, Paris, 1844–64; Brown, *Power and Persuasion*, p. 96.

11   Brown, *Power and Persuasion*, *passim*.

12   Eusebius, *Ecclesiastical History*, V.XVIII.

13   F. W. Maitland, *Equity*, Cambridge University Press, 1932, pp. 23 and 25; and *Constitutional History of England*, Cambridge University Press, 1098, pp. 223ff.

14   Bishop Stephan, E. VIII and IX, Migne, *Patrologiae latinae*.

15   For cathedral fundraising cf. especially Murray, *Building of Troyes Cathedral*; 'Church-building in the Middle Ages', C. R. Cheney, *Medieval Texts and Studies*, Oxford University Press, 1973, pp. 346ff.; Roland Recht (ed.), *Les Bâisseurs des Cathédrales Gothiques*, Editions les Musées de la Ville de Strasbourg, 1989, esp. Wilhelmus Hermanus Vroom, 'La Construction des Cathédrales au Moyen Age: Une Performance Economique', pp. 81ff.; Henry Kraus, *Gold Was the Mortar*, Routledge & Kegan Paul, London, 1979, *passim*. For other medieval fundraising mentioned, cf. Rotha Mary Cray, *The Mediaeval Hospitals of England*, Cass, London, 1966; Center for Medieval and Renaissance Studies, *The Dawn of Modern Banking*, University of California, Yale, 1979, esp. p. 146; and R. Mullin, *Wealth of Christians*, Orbis, London, 1984.

16   Cf. Toulmin Smith with Lujo Brentano, *English Guilds: The Original Ordinances of More Than One Hundred Early English Guilds*, Early English Text Society/Oxford University Press, 1870, reprinted 1963, *passim*; W. E. Tate, *The Parish Chest*, Cambridge University Press, 1946, *passim*.

17   J. R. Tanner, *Tudor Constitutional Documents, AD 1485–1603*, Cambridge University Press, 1930, pp. 480f.

18   Tanner, *Tudor Documents*, p. 480.

19   C. F. Pascoe, *Two Hundred Years of the SPG 1701–1900*, SPG, London, 1901, pp. 53, 649, 742, 483, 824; cf. Cray, *Mediaeval Hospitals*, p. 180.

20   John Bellers, 'Proposals for Raising a College of Industry 1696', collected in Hugh Barbour and Arthur O. Roberts, *Early Quaker Writings 1650–1700*, Eerdmans, Grand Rapids, MI, 1973 pp. 451f.

21   Owen, *English Philanthropy*, p. 48.

22   See the paintings and *Messiah* manuscript held by the Thomas Coram Foundation, which is heir to the Foundling Hospital.

23   Quoted in F. K. Prochaska, *Women and Philanthropy in 19th Century England*, Oxford University Press, 1980, p. 60. The Press Bazaar was a fundraising initiative for the London Hospital which published its own newspaper and used the quoted text as its motto.

24   Owen, *English Philanthropy*, pp. 480f.

25   Cf. Pascoe, *SPG*, pp. x, 195, etc.; Robert T. A. Hardy, *A History of the Churches in the United States and Canada*, Oxford University Press, 1976, pp. 278f.; Mullin, *Wealth of Christians*, pp. 115ff. and 147ff.

26   Cf. Marion Allford, *Charity Appeals: The Complete Guide to Success*, Dent, 1992.

Chapter 2

Warren F. Ilchman, Stanley N. Katz and Edward L. Queen II

DIFFERENT TRADITIONS OF PHILANTHROPY

Edited extracts from: Ilchman, W. F., Katz, S. N. and Queen II, E. L. (eds) (2006) *Philanthropy in the World's Traditions*, Indiana University Press.

Introduction

IN THIS CHAPTER a variety of specialists turn their attention to the role of philanthropy – of giving and sharing beyond the family – in the life of particular culture(s). Something called 'philanthropy' rooted in ethical notions of giving and serving to those (in the wider community) probably existed in most cultures and in most historical periods, and this was often driven by religious traditions.

These extracts show that philanthropy does not simply reflect a culture but the struggles and contexts in which a culture finds itself and of struggles between cultures. Like many other arenas it becomes a location where cultural values and norms are contested. The way philanthropy is done, the way it is structured, and its preferred objects often become battlegrounds for other issues.

Hindu philanthropy

Mark Juergensmeyer and Darrin M. McMahon

The act of giving a gift – *dana* (in Sanskrit) or *dan* (in Hindi) – is one of the oldest and most important aspects of Hindu religiosity. It is a central concept in the

Rg Veda, which dates back at least three millennia. The *Laws of Mann* explains that each of the four great ages in the cycles of cosmic time has its own chief duty. In the first, it is the performance of austerities; in the second, knowledge; in the third, sacrifice; and in the fourth – an age of so enormous a span of time that it includes all of recorded history – 'making gifts' is the highest duty that humans can achieve.

Classically, there were six elements of *dana*: the donor, the donee, the charitable attitude, the subject of the gift (which must have been acquired by the donor in a proper way), appropriate time, and appropriate place. For each of these there were variations. Not only Brahmans, but also ordinary – albeit 'worthy' – persons might be recipients of a gift, depending on the time and circumstance.

Central to the Vedas is the notion of *ista-purta,* which translates roughly as the 'cumulative spiritual result or merit due to one's performance of sacrifices and charitable acts'. Spiritual merit, in other words, accrued as a function of giving. And although donations flowed most directly from kings, lords, and other prosperous figures to those who enjoyed the special privilege of *prati-'grrah* (acceptance of gifts) – the Brahmans – it is important to note that from quite early on giving in a more general sense took on positive religious connotations. Giving to others was also extolled as an exemplary religious act.

Are these Vedic concepts still prevalent in Indian society? Some scholars claim that they are. Gonda concludes his study of *dan* in the *Dharmasastra* with a brief discussion of Gandhian movements in modern India to show that the 'ancient traditions have not been broken off'.

The idea of service as a form of giving owes its origins to a development in Hinduism later than *dan,* the Vedas, and the *Dharmasastra.* This development was the practice of giving time and menial duties to the maintenance of temple deities, an activity known as *seva,* 'service'. The difference between *seva* and *dan* was not solely a difference between material gifts and gifts of service. In the *bhakti* understanding of *seva,* there was also a difference of motivation: *seva* was a reflexive act of love, whereas *dan* had been an expression of obligation. In *bhakti* Hinduism, God was often experienced through one's teacher, or *guru,* who in many cases became the object of loving service. Still, acts of kindness and generosity to other people counted as *seva* to the *guru,* for they allowed one to share the guru's love and indirectly return it. As with *dan,* the reward for *seva* was *karmic* merit. Whereas the notion of *dan* tends to center on things – gifts – and therefore privileges those economically able to make material donations, *seva* emphasizes gestures and acts.

In modern India *seva* is the dominant form of worship in many movements based on the teachings of the medieval *gurus* and their descendants. For example, in the Radhasoami faith, a modern-day North Indian *bhakti* movement, everyone regardless of class or station must perform the most menial tasks of *seva.* Thousands of followers – rich and poor – trek through the dust, moving earth with wicker baskets on their heads as a way of furthering Radhasoami construction projects and of learning something about submission, humility, and service. There is also, however, 'money *seva*' and large social service projects that are *seva* to society undertaken on the master's behalf. Members provide time as well as money, and many become officially recognized as *sevadars* (providers of service) who staff and take part in enterprises such as food distribution, village clinics, eye-care camps, and hospitals.

It is unlikely that many of India's traditional concepts of giving and service would have been accepted as easily into modern society had it not been for the efforts of that remarkable Indian leader who brought so many aspects of Hindu culture into the modern world: Mohandas Gandhi. The notions of *dan* and *seva* were a significant part of Gandhi's thinking, but he gave them his own interpretation. Gandhi had a habit of taking traditional Hindu religious terms and transforming them in a social and political way, stripping them of sectarian religious affiliation. For instance, the notion of ascetic renunciation, *tapasya,* was transformed by Gandhi into the idea of disciplined political action; and the great battles of the *Bhagavad Gita* were interpreted as metaphors for the moral struggles of daily life.

Likewise, Gandhi construed the gifts and service implied by *dan* and *seva* as social ones. This marked a turning point in the pattern of generosity in India, for Gandhi's social interpretation of ritual offerings made it possible for wealthy Indians to think of such offerings not just as 'gifting' tributes aimed at enhancing the giver's power but as philanthropy, support for the general welfare of all. Gandhi also made it possible for Hindus to think of this general social welfare as fulfilling Hindu tradition: for in Gandhi's interpretation of Hindu mythology the great epoch of God *(Ram Raja)* was not at the mythical limits of cosmic time but something possible within one's own lifetime. Gandhi's *Ram Raja* was an ideal civil society — a *dharmic* social order that humans created by tapping the spiritual resources within them, especially the divine qualities of love, generosity, giving, and service that lay in the human heart. Gandhi's notions of philanthropy and social service retained some of the essential features of *dan* and *seva,* however: like these concepts, Gandhian ideas of social service included an insistence on purity of the act, the giver, and the receiver, and the benefit of the transaction for the ultimate transformation of the world.

These ideas of Gandhi, and the example set by Gandhi himself, made a great impact on the thinking of many young leaders involved in India's independence movement. . . .

The involvement of merchant-caste people in philanthropic activities was not entirely due to Gandhi, however. As early as the eighteenth century there already were movements throughout India in which newly wealthy groups attempted to increase their status and political influence through strategic acts of giving. In the nineteenth century, middle-class Hindu organizations, such as the *Arya Samaj,* established their own schools and hospitals in order to compete with Christian missionary institutions. Today the Indian tax code recognizes these groups as worthy, tax-exempt objects of generosity.

Still, the example and ideas of Gandhi brought such acts of generosity into the realm of modern philanthropy. Gandhi came from the same caste, class, and upbringing as many of India's most influential businessmen, so it was understandable that he would make an impact on their lives. . . and [those he influenced] shared with Gandhi a number of fundamental conceptions: a committed Indian nationalism, a bitter distaste of the workings of caste and caste discrimination, and above all, a profound belief in the importance of religion as a motivating factor in daily life.

Religious authority, reform, and philanthropy in the contemporary Muslim world

Gregory C. Kozlowski

The *Holy Qur'an* contains many injunctions to believers to take care of the poor. Giving to the orphan, the widow, the wayfarer, and the needy is a duty which all believers owe to God. Formalized as one of the 'five pillars' of Islam, *zakat* is often interpreted as a kind of tax requiring that the prosperous give annually a certain portion of their total wealth not merely a part of their income, to support the poor.

Many of Islam's counsels demonstrate a strong egalitarian bent and a fear of the hierarchies that wealth generates. To the present day, Muslim religious thinkers emphasize that the poor have an inherent right to their sustenance and an Islamic state ought to guarantee that right. Thus, 'charity' carries no connotation of being a redistribution of wealth to people who do not deserve it. In its strictest sense, *zakat* is not philanthropy – something which arises from a human concern for the disadvantaged segments of humanity. Rather it is a divine command: part of Islam's moral imperative. One must give, because God has ordered it. Making such donations brings the individual closer to God.

Just as in Euro-American philanthropy, complicated webs of intention and activity appear in Muslim benefactions. While the genuinely pious motives of individuals must be considered, placing charitable activity in a social context requires attention to the many economic, cultural, and political exchanges which necessarily accompany any attempt to distribute great wealth to worthwhile causes.

Endowments (*awqaf*) became, by the fourteenth or fifteenth centuries (CE), the Islamic world's most familiar philanthropic institutions. 'Religious and charitable trust' is a common textbook definition of a *waqf*. In practice, endowments were much more than that. Personal, familial, and religious concerns mixed easily in all *awqaf*. Some percentage of the endowed income customarily did go to support a mosque, religious school (*madrasah*), and shrine or to a ceremony such as the commemoration of the birthday of the Holy Prophet. Yet, with the appointment of a custodian – often the donor him/herself or some close relative – and the assignment of some of the proceeds to family members or dependants, the endowment bore certain resemblances to Anglo-American testamentary arrangements, such as entailments or trusts. The legal fluidity of *awqaf*, despite their proven inability to grant fiscal or social stability, made them a favoured instrument for settling the estates of people belonging to the higher and middling ranks of society.

Europeans and Americans have cast the recent history of the Muslim world primarily in terms of religion and its presumed, usually negative, political consequences. They pay little, if any, attention to the ways in which Islam's institutional complexion has changed over the past fifty years. Muslim philanthropic institutions, most notably endowments, *awqaf* (the singular is *waqf*), have altered their aims and style of management in dramatic as well as subtle ways. Those transformations have been much more than simple responses to the stimuli provided by a supposedly innovative and politically aggressive 'West'. Since the eighteenth century, at least, currents of change within the Muslim world have affected the shape of philanthropic activity probably as much as the examples set by the Ford or Rockefeller foundations. Contemporary philanthropic institutions in the Islamic world have merged, separated and reconfigured both external and indigenous forms. Old and new have blended, sometimes almost imperceptibly, in any given organization. Muslim philanthropy in the context of global history since 1945, therefore, displays a series of unresolved tensions. On the religious level, 'scripturalist' approaches to Islam, especially those employing the Oneness of God (*tawhid*) to dismiss 'popular' beliefs, such as the efficacy of praying to saints (*autzja*) to intercede with the Almighty, exert considerable international appeal.

Religious reformers of the eighteenth century, among both the Sunni and Shia, in some sense reinvented purificationist approaches that reshaped contemporary readings of the Islamic past. In the late twentieth century, scholars and journalists have usually described that understanding of the faith and its history as 'fundamentalist' – though 'revivalist' or 'reformist' might better suit the character of what are really several different movements. Muslim and non-Muslim observers alike have tended to assume that the fundamentalists have succeeded. If the commentators' opinions can be trusted, fundamentalists have acquired a monopoly on determining Islam's future.

By whatever name, neither revivalists nor fundamentalists have been as successful as the trend spotters have imagined. 'Popular' styles of piety within Islam – often apolitical in their acceptance of the intercession of saints or displaying a certain eagerness to admit that miracles do happen, have survived nearly two centuries of preaching by self-assured reformers. The persistence of those popular inclinations among believers *is* partly explainable because the beliefs and practices, scorned by the revivalists/reformists, are anchored in tens of thousands of locally controlled endowed/philanthropic institutions.

Because some individual Muslims, as well as groups of Muslims, eschew the most divisive consequences of implicit or explicit confrontations between cosmopolitan and local versions of Islam, Euro-Americans often miss the anxieties which emerge between one set of believers and another. No single trend or movement, whether scripturalist or popular, currently dominates all Muslims in every place in the world.

Muslim philanthropic organizations in the modern world reflect religious tensions and compromises in several ways. An Iranian 'foundation' (*bunyad*) might emphasize that Islam is the only religion which genuinely espouses social protest by the poor. A Saudi Arabian 'trust' stresses that wealth bestowed on the few meets the highest ethical standards of Islam, so long as a significant portion of the abundance finds its way into the hands of the needy. Both Iranian and Saudi Arabian organizations advance one or another reformist line, which appears contradictory, but countless other institutions hold close to the popular practices of the localities in which most of their activities take place. In the face of bold contrarieties, whether between one or another style of reformism, and both in conflict with populist customs, another set of institutions seeks to avoid all doctrinal as well as doctrinaire wrangling.

The global prominence which Islam has achieved because of such dramatic political events as the Iranian Revolution, the rapid rise in the fortunes of a very few oil-rich states, or the Persian Gulf War, carries with it another knot of uncertainties. While it may be an error to overemphasize the connections of Islam to politics, the interaction between the two should be considered. The melding of religion and politics presents a variety of aspirations. On the one hand, Islam seems to some believers to be returning to the central place in world history it occupied from the sixth until the eighteenth century. Both wealth and revolution engender prominence. At the same time, highly visible Muslim movements must defend themselves against the opprobrium that Euro-Americans almost invariably heap on all things Islamic. Elation over apparent victories stands alongside a persistent fear of imminent defeat. Many philanthropic organizations manifest that fluctuation between bright confidence and a nagging sense of impending catastrophe.

Islamdom's philanthropic institutions operate within international and local environments too rich to be described within the narrow boundaries of a single essay. Muslims live within economies that include very rich nations – Abu Dhabi or Saudi Arabia – and very poor ones – Bangladesh and Sudan. Turkey, Pakistan, India, and Malaysia aspire to industrial prosperity and political power. The middle economic tier, comprising Turkey, India, and Pakistan, already possess sophisticated technological resources in their universities, laboratories, and factories, but still must contend with majority populations directly engaged in agriculture. Nations like Afghanistan still have 'internal frontiers' dominated by nomadic or seminomadic groups. Moreover, with a Muslim population exceeding some 6 million, the United States of America must now be reckoned a significant part of the Muslim world.

The reinvention of charity in post-communist Russia

Adele Lindenmeyer

Given the fate of private philanthropy and voluntarism between 1917 and 1985 – reviled, persecuted, and manipulated – their revival in the first years of the *perestroika* era greatly surprised most observers. In the upsurge of voluntarism that swept the country after 1985, thousands of new charitable and mutual aid organizations, foundations, and similar initiatives sprang up. For the first time since 1922, foreign philanthropic organizations were officially allowed to operate on Soviet soil.

Under President Mikhail Gorbachev's policy of openness, or *glasnost'*, newspapers, magazines, and television programs were filled with sympathetic reports of new philanthropic initiatives and discussions of the meaning and importance of private giving.

The reasons behind this renaissance of philanthropy are complex and require much further research. A few tentative explanations may be offered here, however. First of all, neither philanthropy nor voluntarism ever entirely disappeared from the Soviet Union. The unrecorded acts of kindness Soviet citizens performed toward their neighbors can never be calculated. One group that played an especially important role in preserving the idea of compassion and the practice of giving during the Brezhnev period was dissident human rights activists. Soviet authorities punished dissidents with lengthy prison terms, arrest, and loss of employment. Their spouses and children also suffered impoverishment and persecution. Faced with these hardships and no other recourse, members of the dissident community provided each other with significant material and moral support, and kept alive a spirit of compassion and a tradition of mutual aid.

A second factor behind the revival of philanthropy under Gorbachev was the rehabilitation of religion and the great increase in freedom for various faiths. The Orthodox Church, which celebrated with great fanfare one thousand years of Russian Christianity in 1988, was a particular beneficiary of the new policy. Long persecuted and criticized, the Church as an institution, along with figures from its past such as Father Ioann of Kronstadt, now received praise from officials and the press for emphasizing love for one's neighbor and for their charitable works. In press interviews, clergymen pointed to a great upsurge in volunteer social service work by congregations and believers of various faiths, and called for the abolition of laws that prohibited religious groups from engaging in charity.

Third, social problems and needs greatly increased, especially after the Soviet Union broke up in late 1991. Disabled veterans from Afghanistan, refugees from ethnic wars around the former USSR, elderly people subsisting on pensions, military officers and their families returning from Eastern Europe to homelessness and joblessness in Russia – these are just a few of the new problems that arose.

In addition, poverty became visible again. Once found primarily around the few churches still operating under Soviet rule, beggars now returned to the streets in large numbers, often identifying themselves as war victims or impoverished pensioners. As censorship steadily decreased after 1985, articles about crime, poverty, homelessness, and other social problems on the one hand, and appalling conditions in state welfare institutions on the other, began to fill the press. Soviet citizens experienced the shock of suddenly learning some of the true dimensions of domestic problems whose existence had long been denied. As they discovered poverty and need in their own midst, many began to look for ways to help. In addition, disasters of incredible proportions, especially the accident at the Chernobyl nuclear power plant in 1986 and the Armenian earthquake in 1988, received extensive media coverage and added to the misery and shock. Reports of these disasters prompted an unprecedented, spontaneous outpouring of donations from Soviet citizens.

As it had in the early postrevolutionary years, but not under Stalin, Khrushchev, or Brezhnev, the Soviet government under Gorbachev decided not to suppress these charitable impulses. Why? A faltering economy and revelations of huge state budget deficits left the state ill-equipped to deal alone with so many problems of such magnitude. In addition, the state could no longer control or orchestrate all public activities from above; as the processes of *glasnost'* and *perestroika* gained their own momentum, the initiative to organize for philanthropic purposes swelled from below.

The charitable movement of the postcommunist period is a synthesis of old and new. Many organizations and activities that emerged after 1985 consciously modeled themselves after prerevolutionary forms or ideals of giving. In St. Petersburg and Moscow, for example, the Orthodox Church revived the nineteenth-century idea of parish charitable brotherhoods. As new books and exhibits recalled the extraordinary philanthropy of prerevolutionary Moscow industrialists and merchants, some of the country's new entrepreneurs and private businesses began to contribute to education, the arts, and charity.

Alongside organizations that recall charitable traditions are new kinds of organizations that emphasize self-help, advocacy, or empowerment of the needy. This trend may be found, for example, in the many new societies founded by and for handicapped people in the former USSR, like the All-Russian Society of the Disabled (established in 1989), with more than a thousand businesses employing over 19,000 disabled people. A coalition composed of this society, war veterans, retired army and law enforcement officers, and the Chernobyl Alliance created a political party in 1993, called Dignity and Mercy, and ran fifty-eight candidates in the parliamentary elections of December 1993. Support groups for parents of mentally retarded or hearing-impaired children, refuges for battered women, and counselling for the terminally ill – these are additional examples of new directions taken by postcommunist philanthropy.

One of the most notable factors in the revival of philanthropy is the involvement of foreign organizations on a scale unprecedented in Russian history. At least since the 1988 Armenian earthquake, assistance from foreign governments and non-governmental organizations has poured into the USSR and the Commonwealth of Independent States from Germany, Japan, the United States, and other countries. International organizations such as Care, Project Hope, United Way, and many others now have offices in Moscow and other cities and extensive operations throughout the CIS. Since the breakup of the USSR in late 1991, foreign humanitarian organizations have turned increasingly away from working with government agencies and toward establishing partnerships with non-governmental organizations, in an effort to help indigenous philanthropic organizations eventually become self-sustaining. Since 1985 the flow of funds to the Commonwealth of Independent States from abroad, accompanied by advice and assistance on everything from computer networking to fundraising techniques, has unquestionably ameliorated the lives of countless individuals in need and strengthened the voluntary sector.

The return of philanthropy has been less smooth than occasional glowing reports in the Russian or foreign press suggest, however. The drafting and implementation of much-needed new laws on non-profit public associations, on charities and foundations, and on charitable gifts have been very slow. Hyperinflation, corruption, and other aspects of the unstable political and economic situations of the postcommunist era greatly complicate the tasks of fundraising, management, and disbursement. Perhaps most important, Russians must overcome the effects of decades of official condemnation of philanthropy.

American and other foreign aid has become a special focus of Russians' skepticism about philanthropy. As in the 1920s, questions have been raised about the 'real' motives behind foreign humanitarian aid. Rumors or press reports about rancid butter or expired oral contraceptives shipped as 'aid' from the United States to the CIS feed resentment at having been reduced from a superpower to a 'beggar' nation. However good the intentions on both sides, partnerships between American and Russian non-governmental organizations have often been rocky. Cultural differences contribute to miscommunication and frustration on both sides. As Americans and other foreigners rush to do good, they overlook or discount the capabilities of their Russian partners. According to one American participant in these exchanges,

> Perhaps the most often heard complaint from local partners has to do with attitude. The leaders of the emerging third sector in the [CIS] are highly educated, proud people. Many started their work at a time when 'private' organizations were still unpopular and even illegal. They are rightfully proud of what they have accomplished on their own under difficult and, even, dangerous circumstances. They are resentful when an American organization comes in with the attitude that nothing of value existed before its arrival and treats the local organization as a 'client' rather than a partner.

Irina Kozyreva, a leader in philanthropic assistance to displaced military families and the wife of the former Russian foreign minister, has also criticized the inequity intrinsic to partnerships between wealthy American and struggling Russian humanitarian organizations, while acknowledging that the latter can learn much from their American counterparts.

The humiliation of receiving aid from former enemies of the USSR is not the only or even the major reason for Russians' lingering ambivalence about charity, however. Once, Soviet authorities proclaimed that private giving was no longer necessary under socialism; now, the reappearance of philanthropy, whether home-grown or from abroad, serves as yet another painful reminder of Soviet socialism's failure and the enormity of the social problems confronting the population of the former Soviet Union.

The charitable organizations founded since 1985 also share some responsibility for the Russian public's negative attitude toward philanthropy. A recent survey, based on detailed interviews with Russian businesspeople (currently the only significant source of funds for charity after foreign donations), revealed their 'ever growing distrust of specialized charitable organizations engaged in redistributing donations'. Bloated staffs, administrative inexperience, and financial malfeasance by some charities have discredited the very concept of private philanthropy in the eyes of potential donors and the public at large.

Finally, there is the mixed legacy of the history of philanthropy in twentieth-century Russia. Many Russians are uncomfortable with words like 'charity' and 'philanthropy', which carried negative connotations for so long. Granin himself avoids using either the word 'charity' or 'philanthropy' in his otherwise sympathetic 1987 article on private giving; instead, he uses the terms 'mutual aid', 'mutual obligation', or the somewhat archaic 'mercy' (*miloserdie*). Philanthropy has long been linked to authoritarian paternalism, whether in the form of the tsarist philanthropic agency under Imperial patronage or the Soviet 'voluntary' association and *subbotnik*. As private giving has returned, so have phenomena that Soviet propaganda have long associated with it: extreme economic inequality, and a new, post-Soviet bourgeoisie engaged in conspicuous consumption.

But postcommunist Russia also inherited from the prerevolutionary past a rich tradition of compassion and private giving, a tradition that never entirely disappeared during the Soviet era. Since 1985, a thriving – though still chaotic – voluntary philanthropic sector has been constructed on a foundation created from many diverse sources: models from the pre-1917 era, the energy of religious congregations, the expertise and funds of foreign humanitarian organizations and governments, the commitment of members of the legal, medical, social work, and educational professions, and the direct involvement of the needy themselves. Even if the idea of philanthropy has not yet been fully rehabilitated in the former Soviet Union, the practice of it has already contributed significantly to alleviating misery and to building a postcommunist political and social order.

Chapter 3

Rob Paton

FUNDRAISING AS MARKETING: HALF A TRUTH IS BETTER THAN NONE

Edited and adapted from: Paton, R. (1995) 'What's different about nonprofit and voluntary sector marketing? A research agenda', *International Journal of Non-profit and Voluntary Sector Marketing*, 1: 1, pp. 23–31.

Introduction

IT IS A COMMONPLACE that the fundraising department provides the marketing function of charities and non-profits. There is enough truth in this to make it very plausible – and it is an agreeable view for those with marketing backgrounds who transfer across to work in fundraising contexts. But it is also an odd claim, and one that carries the seeds of confusion and conflict. The aim of this chapter is to clarify both the sense and the nonsense in this conception of what fundraising is and what fundraisers do. Why does this matter? Because it has implications for marketing professionals working as fundraisers, and for those who employ them. Do 'mainstream' marketing theories and techniques apply equally well? Do fundraisers and campaigners have distinctive expertise, or can one readily find these skills in the commercial sector? What sort of a professional identity is appropriate for work in fundraising?

Narrow and broad definitions of marketing

Conventional definitions of marketing – for example, 'the management process responsible for identifying, anticipating and satisfying customer demand profitably' (Mercer, 1992) – assume a profit-orientated, trading context. The implication is that fundraising and campaigning are not marketing. There is a logic to this: how could there be marketing if there is no market, if no trading is taking place? But, on the other hand, what is going on in non-profit and voluntary organisations when they employ marketing professionals, use marketing concepts and techniques, and hire advertising, direct mail and other such agencies, if it is not a form of marketing?

If one accepts such a definition, then much of what is called marketing in non-profit and voluntary organisations has to be seen as a derivative – interesting perhaps, but not the real thing. The field becomes defined in terms of a series of metaphors: donors as customers, the cause as a product, the donation as the price. Metaphors can be illuminating, but they can also be misleading. As Robin Wensley, the doyen of marketing academics and one of the most senior figures in management thinking and research in the UK, points out, where service delivery is distinct from resource acquisition (i.e. those who fund are not those who use the service), then 'simple' marketing remedies or language have little value (Wensley, 1990).

At the very least, a broader conception of marketing is needed, one that encompasses for-profit and not-for-profit contexts, social marketing as well as commercial marketing, and that provides a less restrictive vocabulary within which one can explore the differences and similarities between marketing in different contexts.

Kotler offers such a definition, one that encompasses both for-profit and not-for-profit contexts:

> marketing . . . is the analysis planning, implementation and control of programmes designed to create, build and maintain beneficial exchange relationships with target audiences for the purposes of achieving the marketer's objectives.
>
> (Kotler, 1991, p. 38)

The central ideas here are those of beneficial exchange relationships, and programmes designed to create them. How well does this work in fundraising contexts?

Fundraising as (broad) marketing

We can explore this by considering the sorts of programmes that flow from the fundraiser's objective (of securing financial resources to support the organisation's mission) and the types of exchanges that may be involved. The different ways of securing resources and support can be distinguished in terms of *who* is being asked and *how*. Are individuals being asked face to face? Or are individuals

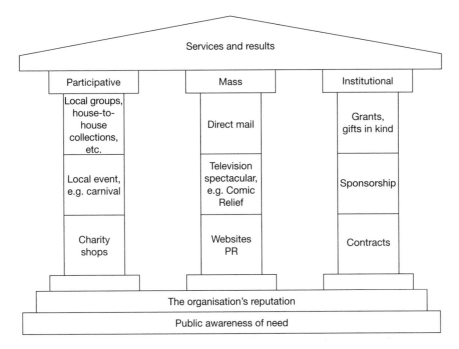

Figure 3.1 The three pillars of fundraising

being asked indirectly, through the media or by letter? Or are institutions being approached rather than individuals? These three broad possibilities are represented as pillars that support the organisation's services and achievements, and that rest upon its public reputation and the awareness of its cause (see Figure 3.1).

The first pillar covers what is called participative fundraising and campaigning. It includes many of the traditional, people-intensive methods of winning support. Hence the key skills are those of mobilising people and organising events. Usually this family of methods achieves results through large numbers of modest contributions or actions. However, participative approaches are also used to attract more substantial personal contributions from a smaller number of relatively wealthy or powerful people.

The second pillar ('mass fundraising') is much more modern; it uses the media to interest and appeal to large, remote, distributed audiences. It could be called impersonal fundraising and campaigning – but its practitioners claim this approach can and should be personal. The key skills here concern the media, communication, and information management.

The third pillar is institutional fundraising and campaigning, and again this is a time-honoured approach that has existed for as long as there have been governments, companies, trusts and other powerful organisations with resources, decisions and influence to dispense. Lobbying, networking and negotiating become particularly important in this context.

This classification should not be taken as implying that the different methods are always used separately. Arguably, a major development in modern fundraising and campaigning has been the trend towards integrated campaigns – for example, the modern advertising methods used by Christian Aid to support the classic participative technique of house-to-house collection. But the classification provides a coherent overview of the field, and highlights the underlying competences that are at a premium in the different types of fundraising and campaigning. It thus begins to clarify what different forms of fundraising and campaigning do (and do not) have in common with the many different approaches to marketing in other contexts.

For example, the approaches in the second pillar have a great deal in common with many forms of mass marketing, and it is in these approaches that large charities make the most use of commercial agencies. By contrast, the similarities between forms of participative fundraising campaigning and for-profit marketing are more limited: 'network marketing' and the use of events provide some correspondences, but this pillar depends heavily on volunteer involvement – a difference that has pervasive implications for organisations that rely on it.

But is a gift an exchange?

The other issue raised by Kotler's definition concerns the nature of the exchanges that marketers in fundraising contexts offer to those from whom they seek resources and support. Put simply, is a gift an exchange?

To explore this, the different motivational bases on which people provide support to organisations and causes can be represented in terms of a continuum stretching from the pure gift to the pure exchange, as shown in Figure 3.2. Viewed in these terms, gifts and donations can be more or less altruistic. The pure gift is altruistic in a strict sense; it is unaffected by any personal or social considerations, such as the hope that giving will mean the donor is remembered after their death, or a concern to meet the expectations of the donor's peers. Other gifts may be marked by, say, a sense of guilt or duty, but are still relatively disinterested.

Similarly, there are exchanges and exchanges. In a pure exchange the cause is completely irrelevant because the support is essentially a payment provided for what it brings in return – be it the chance to win a car, or the excitement of abseiling down a building. But if a charity Christmas card is chosen because it is sold by an organisation whose work is approved of, in preference to a commercial card, this is not a pure exchange; the purchaser wants the Christmas card, of course, but the purchase is also intended to support that organisation.

In the middle of this continuum lies a broad category of support – that which is provided from a mixture of motives. This is probably the most important category as far as many fundraisers are concerned. The benefits enjoyed from the exchange may be social contact and approval, recreational enjoyment, a sense of achievement, or an opportunity to learn or gain valuable experience – the range

Figure 3.2 The gift–exchange continuum

Table 3.1 A matrix of fundraising and campaigning methods

	Participative	*Mass*	*Institutional*
Gifts	Petitions Street collection	Direct mail Telemarketing	Grants Gifts in kind
Mixed	Local events (e.g. carnival, sponsored activities) Fundraising dinner	Television spectacular (e.g. Comic Relief, Band Aid)	Social sponsorship Parliamentary lobbying
Exchange	Charity shop Car boot sale	Catalogue sales Televised concert (e.g. Band Aid)	Contracts Commercial sponsorship and joint promotions

of possibilities is vast. So, although terms like charity, benevolence and philanthropy point to important elements of what is often going on, on their own they offer an idealised picture of what moves people to offer support. Moreover, in many cases, such as arts centres, schools, clubs and self-help groups, the aim is really to persuade people who use the service and already pay for it (in one way or another) to 'pay' voluntarily a bit extra – for their own benefit, as well as for the benefit of the organisation and its clients.

These distinctions highlight more of the variety of ways of securing resources and support. Table 3.1 combines the different reasons for support with the three pillars, to form a matrix of fundraising and campaigning options. The examples given are only indicative, not exhaustive, of each category.

Viewed in these terms gifts *are* exchanges, in the sense that the great majority have a significant, if hidden, exchange element. But it is also clear that the bases of the exchange relationships are, in some measure, different from those in for-profit contexts. For example, the ways of gaining support that fall in the middle row of the matrix have in common a considerable ambiguity: is this all for the good cause, or really for our own fun, entertainment or benefit?

Perhaps, then, the similarities and differences between fundraising and marketing can be expressed in terms of the gift–exchange continuum? The closer to pure exchange as the basis on which support is sought, the more the marketing activity will resemble conventional marketing-for-profit; and the stronger the charitable and philanthropic elements in the exchange, the more distinctive marketing-to-fundraise becomes.

In fact, such a view exaggerates the differences between exchanges in different contexts. To be sure, there was a time when the task of marketers was to identify, and provide to designated market segments, a bundle of functional attributes that best met the requirements of the customer for that product or service. But in a post-modern era when social identities are constructed not given (Lannon, 1994) and when so much marketing is conducted in terms of brands (De Chernatony and MacDonald, 1995) the attributes and the exchange relationships are increasingly symbolic, and concern meanings, images and identities. Thus the purchase of classic brands – Nike trainers, Marlboro cigarettes, Levi Jeans, Estée Lauder perfume, Marks & Spencer food – does not result from careful utilitarian calculations, but is an expression of identity, of being a certain sort of person, of belonging to a global tribe.

Here the convergences with donor motivations become obvious. Greenpeace, in these terms, is a powerful brand clearly differentiated from Friends of the Earth, the WWF and other environmental organisations; and the donations it receives are as much expressions of identity and community as they are considered judgements about the long-term cost effectiveness of its activities as a response to environmental degradation. On this basis its donors do receive something significant in return. Indeed, what could be more important than meaning and identity, even if they are intangible?

So, although there are differences between marketing-for-profit and marketing-to-fundraise, the nature and extent of those differences are easily exaggerated. Donations do involve a different sort of social exchange but this does not explain the differences between marketing in the two different contexts. Indeed, brand-related fundraising draws on the central concepts of modern marketing practice.

The other half of marketing

The real difficulty with the fundraising-as-marketing view is far more basic: the donor is not the client, the recipient of the primary service. Marketing in respect of service delivery is also fundamental for many non-profit organisations (Bruce, 1994) and will often have much in common with service marketing by for-profit organisations in the same fields – including the fundamental twin purposes of attracting appropriate clients or users to the organisation while ensuring that it has appropriate services for them. In other cases there will not be clients or service users in a conventional sense – in disaster relief, say, or regarding environmental causes. More generally, marketing in non-profit and voluntary organisations characteristically involves cultivating different sorts of exchange relationships with several distinct constituencies, often including volunteers (Blois, 1993). Yes, for-profit marketers also have more than one constituency. But the customers are paramount and the others clearly secondary – as any comparison of marketing and corporate affairs budgets will quickly reveal. The point is that the nature, variety and importance of marketing constituencies in the non-profit sector are a key difference (Drucker, 1990).

This raises some important questions and challenges for marketing professionals working as fundraisers and who may be inclined to think of their work as providing the same central contribution, both strategic and tactical, as it does in for-profit settings. But, as fundraisers, they are at most only *half* of the marketing function. The other half, provided in various ways by front-line staff, analysts and social policy specialists, is where new needs are recognised, and better ways of responding to needs are devised. In the commercial sector this is the vital, strategic contribution of marketing – spotting market trends and the emergence of a latent demand, and sometimes creating whole new markets with innovative products. In fact, this is what distinguishes it from the sales function – with whom, it could be said, fundraisers often have much in common.

The dangers and difficulties arise when fundraising activity becomes separated from the primary purpose of the organisation and is reduced to raising awareness of suffering or impending plight, in order to sell a taken-for-granted suite of programmes. The marketing creativity goes into grabbing people's attention rather than devising new programmes that will better link concerned donors with the provision of lasting solutions. At worst this leads to the shrillness and sensationalism of the donor-led organisation – over-simplifying, re-enforcing stereotypes and ignoring underlying causes. Later in this book Van der Gaag considers the intense value issues (Paton, 1995) surrounding the representation of beneficiaries in advertisements and appeals, and the delicate negotiation and enactment of guidelines on representation within large charities. That such issues are so difficult is indicative of the organisational gulf that so often exists between fundraisers and their colleagues working on programmes and policy.

Indeed, the separation between fundraising and service delivery introduces a profound tension at the heart of many charities and non-profits, a tension often overlaid by differences in professional training, personal outlook and lifestyle, as well as by departmental loyalties (Mason, 1984; Miller, 1990). Too often, fundraising staff will see the communication and other difficulties associated with this divide as obstacles to 'doing good marketing' – if it weren't for these arguments and constraints we would do so much more. But that is nonsense. It would be more accurate to say that these are arguments between *two different* marketing functions in the same organisation – and handling these issues constructively is an integral part of the job, not some unfortunate preliminary to the real work. Of course, those policy and programme colleagues rarely use marketing language – but that does not alter the realities: they too can be seen as trying 'to create, build and maintain beneficial exchange relationships with target audiences' – to use Kotler's terms. Moreover, such creative integration around the funding and promotion of innovative programmes is perfectly possible – there are many examples (I would see the creation of the Fairtrade brand in these terms, but also many of the new generation of direct funding schemes – see, for example, Peace Direct and Educate Direct).

Conclusions: a broader role and a broader conception of marketing?

The trouble with the fundraising-as-marketing view is that it can easily mistake the part for the whole. Yes, fundraising is an important part of the marketing function for charities and other non-profits. And that is why so much can be usefully adopted and adapted from the marketing profession – as when Burnett took the distinction between transaction and relationship marketing and applied it to fundraising, thereby clarifying developments in the field, and providing a new framework for thinking about fundraising strategy (Burnett, 1992). Nevertheless, it is a long way from being the whole of charity and non-profit marketing. Indeed, the integration of fundraising with other functions is where some of its most distinctive and important challenges lie.

Put another way, the fundraising-as-marketing view begs the question of what sort of marketing is being implied. A *strategic* marketing perspective raises interesting questions that, arguably, deserve more attention. What, for example, are the organisational capabilities – the complex and not-easily-reproduced bundles of skills and accumulated knowledge – that consistently successful charities have developed? (Day, 1994). Such capabilities will encompass fundraising but go far beyond it. Or perhaps one has in mind the still controversial notion of *social marketing,* defined as 'the design, implementation and control of programs calculated to influence the acceptability of social ideas and involving considerations of product planning, pricing, communication, distribution and marketing research' (Kotler and Zaltman, 1971, p. 5). Such a definition and its applications means engaging quite explicitly with questions of social change – see, for example, the Institute of Social Marketing.

So fundraising can usefully be seen in marketing terms – but this does not mean the unthinking imitation of commercial practices. Applying mainstream concepts and techniques in fundraising needs to be done with awareness of the complexities and differences that the settings of a charity or non-profit intro-duces, if significant costs and errors are to be avoided. This need not mean a marketer must abandon his or her professional identity – but it will almost certainly mean extending it.

References

Blois, K. (1993) 'Marketing and non-profit organizations', Management Research Paper 93/12, Templeton College, Oxford.

Bruce, I. (1994) *Meeting Need: Successful Charity Marketing*, ICSA Publishing, Hemel Hempstead.

Burnett, K. (1992) *Relationship Fundraising: A Donor-based Approach to the Business of Raising Money*, White Lion Press, London.

Day, G.S. (1994) 'The capabilities of market-driven organizations', *Journal of Marketing*, Vol. 58, pp. 37–52.

De Chernatony, L. and MacDonald, M. (1995) *Creating Powerful Brands*, Butterworth Heinemann, Oxford.

Drucker, P. (1990) *Managing the Non-profit Organisation*, Butterworth Heinemann, Oxford.

Kotler, P. (1991) *Marketing Management* (7th edn), Prentice Hall, Englewood Cliffs, NJ, p. 38.

Kotler, P. and Zaltman, G. (1971) 'Social marketing: an approach to planned social change', *Journal of Marketing*, Vol. 35, pp. 3–12.

Lannon, J. (1994) 'Mosaics of meaning', *The Journal of Brand Management*, Vol. 2, No. 3, reprinted in R. Paton *et al.* (eds) (1996) *The New Management Reader*, Routledge, London.

Mason, D. (1984) *Voluntary Non-profit Enterprise Management*, Plenum Press, New York.

Mercer, D. (1992) *Marketing*, Blackwell, Oxford.

Miller, E. (1990) 'Missionaries or mercenaries?', *Tavistock Institute of Human Relations Review*, Tavistock Institute of Human Relations, London.

Paton, R. (1995) 'How do voluntary agencies handle values issues?', in D. Billis and M. Harris (eds) (1996) *Voluntary Agencies: Challenges of Organizations and Management*, Macmillan, London.

Wensley, R. (1990) 'The voice of the consumer? Speculations on the limits of the marketing analogy', *European Journal of Marketing*, Vol. 24, No. 7, pp. 49–60.

PART TWO

Fundamental concepts and techniques

INTRODUCTION

THESE CHAPTERS SET OUT some of the core ideas and practices of the profession, but in ways which also point towards the issues and complications that lie behind some of the 'taken-for-granteds' of fundraising. A common theme among these authors is that careful research and the formulation of considered strategies will yield more productive and sustainable fundraising plans.

Chapter 4 (Baguley) argues for a more thoughtful approach to the understanding of donor motivation. He examines the intrinsic and extrinsic motivations for giving as well as exploring factors that militate against giving by developing a theory of neutralization – the ways in which people may assuage the guilt of not giving. He argues for the importance of understanding the factors which shape donors' propensity to give, and for a deeper analysis and greater strategic thinking about whom to approach for donations and how.

In chapter 5, Ostrower takes this analysis further in her study of the way that the values of a particular stratum of society in the USA give rise to a distinct pattern of philanthropic activity. In particular she uncovers the sense of obligation to give (and the factors that shape this) that wealthy donors feel which stems from a mixture of motives as well as sheer pleasure in being able to give. There are also strong normative peer pressures to give, in particular those that reinforce commitments to institutions that enjoy the support of the very wealthy such as those in the local community. Of course, the pattern will not be the same in other countries. In the UK, for example, the motives for gifts from wealthy donors may be seen as suspect (particularly by the media) if there is any hint of political connections and the 'purchase' of honours. Nor does UK non-profit board membership carry the same expectations of active fundraising that it does in the USA. However, the ways in which social networks can be extended and reinforced by giving, creating shared cultures and identities outside business, are aspects of her description that will have manifestations in many other societies, not just the USA.

Chapter 6 (Sargeant and Jay) provides a snapshot of some of the thinking and the statistical approaches that have been influential in 'donorbase' fundraising over the past decade. Much of this is borrowed with little adaptation from marketing practice in commercial contexts. This raises a number of questions – for example, as the authors acknowledge, the term 'lifetime value' is something of a misnomer if it is arbitrarily defined with a time scale of only a few years. More importantly, and as in direct marketing, although these are potentially powerful techniques, there is many a slip between the uplifting aspirations of 'relationship fundraising' and its often rather crude implementation. The techniques can be expensive and they are far from being foolproof. Dangers arise when statistical associations are not underpinned and driven by conceptual understanding (on this point, see also Chapter 8 by Cathy Pharoah). 'Segmentation' can mean different things to statisticians and to fundraisers with a background in qualitative approaches. Finally, will these approaches need rethinking in an era when the emerging generation of donors may prefer to be increasingly self-servicing, and to provide support more directly, through web-based and peer-to-peer technologies?

Chapter 7 (Baguley) examines the pervasive notion – again taken from marketing – of the *campaign*. Baguley usefully distinguishes between campaigns that are 'opportunistic' (e.g. responses to disasters) and those that are 'planned' (i.e. those devised by organizations to generate interest in their cause). In either case, campaigns need to be aligned with their organizations' strategies, and the author develops a 'public campaign diamond' to illustrate the aspects of the organization and its environment that require consideration and assessment if the campaigns are to be successful.

Chapter 4

John Baguley

KNOW YOUR DONORS

Introduction

DESPITE THE HUGE SUMS involved in charitable giving, estimated by the National Council of Voluntary Organisations (NCVO) at a contribution to UK Gross Domestic Product (GDP) of some £7–10 billion per annum, there has been little academic research into the motivation of donors. Yet, if fundraisers are to develop efficient and cost-effective means of raising funds for their causes, then they may be well advised to move beyond trial and error, towards a better understanding of the factors that motivate donors and the complexities of response. The latter is especially relevant to any in-depth understanding as donors are not homogenous, but respond with all the variety of the population at large; which indeed they are, as some two-thirds of the UK adult population give each year, and in 2002 made up some £7 billion of approximately £10 billion donated in the UK according to the DfES (2004).

This chapter covers the findings of some current research, and sets it against traditional views on fundraising and motivation, concentrating on the need fundraisers have to attract funds to their particular cause. It looks first at the triggers to individual giving and how to pull them, then at approaches to the large variety of differently motivated groups into which potential donors divide, and lastly at the very rich – are they really so different from the rest of us?

The triggers to giving

Knowing why people give, or do not give, allows fundraisers to choose techniques and shape those techniques to meet donors' inner needs.

Internal influences

Hibbert and Farsides (2005) divide donors into two categories: those who give out of a desire to help the cause (communal givers) and those who help out of a desire for the return they receive (exchange givers). A communal giver may donate the same amount to a charity as an exchange giver, but the exchange giver may not donate if there is another way of achieving the same objective. The latter may be thinking of giving to a charity or political party because they feel it would enhance their chances of an honour; but not carry out the gift if they receive the honour first. The communal giver, who feels part of the charities 'community', will give anyway. Potential rewards are often, however, a complex interaction of the economic, social and emotional.

For any giver there is likely to be a mixture of altruism and reward: the gift–exchange continuum. The 'thank you' letter that confirms the gift has been received, and suggests it will be well spent, acts as a reward to help the donor feel good about their gift. Indeed, Hibbert and Farsides (2005) again suggest that there are two types of donor thinking in play here. Some donors will give because they wish to alleviate the pain of the beneficiaries, but others will wish to alleviate their own feelings of guilt, helplessness or anguish in the face of the problem. The former may come from an ability to empathize with the suffering of others, putting themselves in their place. The massive increase in charitable giving in the UK in response to the Tsunami appeal in 2005 may be due on one level to its widespread publicity, allowing more people to be aware of the problem and to empathize, but on another level the strength of that unmissable publicity may also have invoked a desire to alleviate the internal pain of the viewer.

Giving may also be both a learnt behaviour: the pattern reinforced by repeated donating, and a family affair originating in culture and tradition. Panas (1984) quotes several major donors, such as Walter Annenburg (Ambassador to the Court of St James), who cite the influence of their parents in giving and encouraging them to give from an early age. 'It was expected of me' is a typical comment which encompasses family, religion and cultural expectations.

This is not the same as giving out of a sense of 'duty' which is often the motivation of the generational cohort now retired or nearing retirement. James H.R. Cromwell, son of a wealthy benefactor, quoted in Panas (1984, p. 40) states: 'No one today talks about uplifting the poor and sick, about the need to bring culture to the masses. These concerns are just not taken seriously'. He feels that the duties and responsibilities that were once held to go with money are now no longer felt to be relevant.

Theresa Lloyd (2005) discusses the influence of religion and family in UK giving, and some of those she interviewed felt the key to their family's values was religion and this heavily influenced their attitude to giving. Givers from Asian and Jewish backgrounds in particular, even if no longer actively involved in their religion, felt it as strengthening the values which resulted in their gifts. Others found the cultural influences of their country of origin formed the strong ethos behind their philanthropy.

Where inherited wealth featured, the tradition of family giving was often cited as an influence. Community involvement was also felt to be a key, especially for self-made millionaires who retained local roots. Such involvement may be linked to a wider desire to help those who are less fortunate and who lack advantages. Interestingly, she notes that where there was no pattern of family philanthropy, giving rarely started at an early age, unless it was in the context of US institutions.

External influences

The tax regime of any country obviously plays a part in motivating donors, yet every donation is a net loss of funds to the donor, whether they save some tax (as in the USA) or whether the charity can reclaim the tax already paid on that donation (as in the UK for donations from individuals). The UK has seen a relaxation of its tax regime in recent years, and charities report an associated increase in funds. This has yet to be as encouraging as in the USA, particularly in respect of deferred giving, where a US donor may claim the tax on a gift yet to be made, while enjoying the interest on that gift for the time being. This and other elements of reward are accepted as part and parcel of people's motivation for giving (Hibbert and Farsides, 2005).

Terry Axelrod (2004, p. 4) has said that 'we are emotional donors looking for a rational reason to justify our emotional need to give'. Tax concessions often seem to fit that bill as they appear to give value for money; so when fundraisers mention them it may not only encourage the additional revenue to the charity, but also touch an almost unconscious chord in the donor's psychology.

In large-scale, well-advertised emergency appeals, such as those run by the Disasters Emergency Committee (DEC) in the UK and during Telethons, it is likely that a collective spirit or common instinct helps to create a climate where giving is not only easy, it is seen to be a social good and to add status to the donor. To choose not to give, or to be unable to give, in those circumstances may cause feelings of guilt or social exclusion.

Fundraisers also talk of 'peer group giving' as a powerful force. Here 'the ask' is made by a colleague or friend of the potential donor and thus carries great psychological weight. Interestingly, Lloyd (2005) cites 'Who asks' as the second most important reason why major donors respond to direct mail appeals; the first being the nature of the cause, and fundraisers report that 'no one asked me' is a common reason given by many potential major donors as to why they did not support the charity before.

Why people do not give

It is illustrative, as Hibbert and Farsides (1995) suggest, to look at the possible reasons people may have for not giving. If we are to construct strong cases for giving it may be necessary to counter certain belief systems or thought patterns that may militate against a decision to donate. It may be thought that people who do not donate have just been through the same decision-making process as those who gave, but decided against a gift. Indeed, the frequency of opportunities to give that most people encounter through direct mail, radio, TV and street fundraising may suggest that they may have merely got into the habit of not giving.

The theory of neutralization may, however, offer a further understanding. Strutton (1994) suggests five techniques that may be used. Though his work was based on the psychology of why people misbehave in public places like retail outlets, it may be adapted to help understand how people assuage the potential guilt of not giving.

- Denial of responsibility – e.g. they did not give owing to circumstances beyond their control: 'Sorry, I cannot afford it today'.
- Denial of injury – e.g. not giving doesn't matter: 'The money is all wasted anyway'.
- Denial of victim – e.g. it's their own fault: 'Why don't they just get a job'.
- Condemning the condemners – e.g. those who complain about non-giving are just as bad: 'I bet he hasn't made a donation either'.
- Appeal to higher loyalties – e.g. I have a good reason not to give: 'I only give to local charities'.

The relatively poor response to the 2005 earthquake in Pakistan compared to the earlier Tsunami appeal may be an example of a denial of responsibility by those who had already given: 'It is someone else's turn now', 'This is Pakistan's problem' or 'It's a Muslim problem'. Who is perceived to be asking may or may not trigger a donation linked to higher loyalties.

Donors may also blame the charity for asking them in the wrong way, stating an aversion to direct mail or phone calls as intrusive, or street and face-to-face fundraising as a public nuisance, or advertising or television appeals as being in bad taste.

Hibbert also suggests that people differ in their view of who is responsible for sorting out problems, whether this is governments, charities or the individuals themselves. They are also divided on the effectiveness of the actions of each of these agents. These beliefs may lead to a decision not to donate as it inhibits the correct agent from acting. This is mirrored in a Soviet definition of charity as 'Aid hypocritically rendered by representatives of the ruling class in an exploiter society to a part of the poor population in order to deceive the workers and divert them from the class struggle' (Tretyakov, 1989, p. 7).

The variety in giving

Motivation varies therefore according to the ways in which the donor conceives of the causes such as charity sector, national context and by their wealth; these need to be taken into account by the fundraiser who wishes to outshine the competition.

Different causes

Allford (1993, p. 3) reports: 'The Wishing Well Appeal produced so much publicity because it was appealing on behalf of a cause that tugs forcefully at nearly everyone's heartstrings – sick children'.

Table 4.1 Charities that receive most donations

Top 5 most popular causes in 2005*		Top 5 most popular causes in 2003**	
International aid or humanitarian causes	62%	Children's charity	36%
Major diseases or disabilities	51%	Major diseases or disabilities	31%
Children's charity 42%		An animal charity	9%
An animal charity 24%		International aid or humanitarian causes	7%
A charity for the elderly or homeless	18%	A charity for the elderly or homeless	5%

Source: * TNS conducted this survey on behalf of BACS Payment Schemes Limited in February 2005; ** TNS conducted this survey on behalf of BACS Limited July 2003.

There is, however, no strict hierarchy in the type of charities that receive most donations, as may be seen in Table 4.1 compiled by BACS (the UK's direct debit banking group).

Different charitable purposes

The above comments have been largely based on data from the UK without discrimination between the wide variety of organizations that come under the title 'charity'; indeed, the common name in the UK for the sector in which charities operate is the voluntary sector. This encompasses public schools, sports centres, art galleries and a host of other organizations. The law on charitable status in England and Wales is based on the 1601 Statute of Elizabeth and decided cases. Charitable purposes are characterized as relief of poverty, advancement of education, advancement of religion and other purposes beneficial to the community.

The motivation for a gift to, say, a fee-paying school (under 'education') may be very different from that of a gift to a disaster appeal. Indeed, it is possible that donations like this are seen as part of education or lifestyle costs rather than a gift to charity. The BACS (2005) survey quoted above also asked about motivation and stated, 'The main motivation for donating to charity appears to be helping other people (68 per cent), followed by wanting to make a difference to society (28 per cent) and wanting to share money with those less fortunate (27 per cent)'.

The nature of a donation to certain institutions may be rather removed from the feeling conveyed by the survey finding. For example, arts fundraising is often based on buying privilege such as access to special events, access to star performers or networking opportunities.

As the very nature of the institution affects donors' motivation, an understanding of their separate motivations will give perceptive fundraisers an edge over their organization's rivals.

Different countries

In other countries motivation may vary according to tradition, culture and the political and economic circumstances of that country. In India, for example, requests for donations must be culturally appropriate with due deference to religion. In Ukraine charities are new, trust in them is hard to establish and personal responsibility for 'national problems' is in its infancy.

If 'charity' can be obscure in any one country it is an even more difficult target across countries. Salamon and Anheier (1996, p. 3) state that there is little agreement worldwide on the definition of the third sector outside the realms of the market and the state:

> The German concept of *Verein*, the French *économie sociale*, the British *public charities*, the Japanese *koeki hojim*, the American *non-profit sector*, the Central European *foundation*, and the Latin American and African *NGO or nongovernmental organization* are not simply linguistically different. They reflect wholly different concepts and refer to distinctly different groupings of institutions.

It is likely therefore that donors' motivations in interacting with these varied institutions will also vary; again more research is needed to engage with the degree of that variance and possible common factors across countries or institutions.

Very rich donors

Jerold Panas (1984) insists that giving is not done to challenge, motivate or inspire others; it is done for the joy of giving. He goes on to quote over a dozen US millionaire donors who all state that they give for the joy and deep satisfaction that this brings them. He concludes, however, by observing that he found 'a sense that life has been better to these major donors than they perhaps really deserve. And philanthropy is their most direct way of repaying the debt'. This desire to give back to the community from where their wealth has come is often observed in US donors.

In the UK recent research by Theresa Lloyd (2005) provides a fuller picture of what is often presumed in the UK to be a private and personal business. Lloyd found five key influences on the millionaire donors she surveyed. These were:

* 'Belief in the cause' which came from an alignment of views with the charity and a desire to see change in society. This was also the most powerful motivator.
* 'Being a catalyst for change' which meant that they felt their contribution 'made a real difference' and this difference was cost effective.
* 'Self-actualization' which is the highest of Maslow's hierarchy of needs, and most important for those affluent enough to have satisfied the lower needs for personal and family security. As Maslow reported, 'They attempt to grow to perfection and to develop more and more fully in their own style.

For them motivation is just character growth, character expression, maturation, and development'. For Lloyd's rich donors this involved the personal change in being effective in a new arena, acquiring new talents, and using their funds judiciously, perhaps to help to acquire 'a place in history'.

- 'Duty and responsibility' which, in a similar way to US donors, indicates a desire to pay back the community, helping the disadvantaged and satisfying one's conscience.
- 'Relationships' by which they indicated the personal contact they had with the charity, the networks they became part of and the joy of those associations.

Lloyd aligned these motivational factors with a question about the strongest factors in increasing giving. The factor that was held to have the most effect was simply an increase in available funds. Locating a new cause which excited their passion was the next most important and cited by over half of the respondents. Third came better tax incentives, though this could be equated to having more money to give.

The relationship that grew out of a gift was very important to responders, who wanted to be appreciated and valued for their gift; but more important was recognition of their passion for the organization so that the relationship was based on more than the money. Public recognition was appreciated, but so too was the quiet word of thanks, and occasionally a donor might also value anonymity. This may contrast to the donor of small sums who, though pleased to be appreciated, might find such overt attention embarrassing and would not necessarily wish the organization to spend its time, and therefore money, on them.

A few donors wanted to use their skills, where relevant, to help the charity or at least to be consulted. They were keen to give more than money, and expertise was one area they often felt could be appropriate. Naturally, many donors took care to look into the management and work of an organization before giving. When very large donations were made, particularly during capital campaigns, donors were most likely to require a stronger role in the development of the project.

The way philanthropy itself is viewed in the UK may be depressing the level of donation and demotivating donors. Lloyd reports that the very rich regret the lack of status and respect accorded to philanthropy; which links to the lack of UK role models for charitable giving at a high level.

Though no single quotation could sum up the complex motivations of all donors, one from Lloyd's research (2005, p. 102) may be useful:

> Supporting the arts is a bit of a luxury, as is giving a bursary to my children's old school. That's not what it's all about. There is a spectrum. It's not completely altruistic if you get looked after. I should be tackling hard, social problems. Giving a scholarship to a violinist is very important, but it doesn't feel the same as supporting the disadvantaged. I tend to ration that kind of giving. If I get pleasure out of it, it is not quite right, it's about the importance of the success and wellbeing of the city in the round. It leads to the success, and wellbeing of the company.
>
> (Male, sixties, self-made/entrepreneur)

What this means for fundraising

The sheer variety in the well-springs of donor motivation indicates a reassessment of any view that there is a typical 'charity donor', not least the view that this is a 'little old lady'. Indeed, the very disregard for such variety may be why many charities are now left with donor bases of very elderly ladies and have failed to attract, cultivate and retain profitable sectors of diverse donors.

Joint platforms and combined fundraising campaigns have never been the hallmark of UK fundraising, yet the motivation behind the huge success of the DEC appeals should give fundraisers pause for thought – perhaps they too could tap into donors who are motivated by 'communal giving'. To take advantage of this, fundraisers may need to sacrifice the individual pull of their organizations to join with others in maximizing their pull on some donors' herd instinct. Similarly, the oft-frowned-upon 'recognition' strategies may meet more basic needs than they are given credit for, and fundraisers may therefore be advised to consider making available a variety of public 'honours'; for example, in the form of wall plaques and naming opportunities, as well as feedback on the good work achieved through their donors' gifts.

The adage that certain charities will always do better than others is one we can at least undermine. This does not necessarily contradict the traditional view that people in the UK are motivated to donate in descending order to animal charities, children's charities, health charities and then a variety of other causes; but indicates that this hierarchy can be upset by forceful publicity, indicating that the motivation for giving is not entirely generated by pre-existing internal preference but, for many people, can be influenced by external actions such as publicity and promotion. This may be particularly true if others are visibly responding to such appeals. For fundraisers this indicates that, though their organization may be placed at an inherent disadvantage over other charities, this can be overcome by the judicious use of enterprising communications.

Many people, however, expect to give to certain institutions, perhaps following a family or religious pattern. This discourse brings us back to the dictum 'know your donors' and reminds fundraisers that the wider context in which their organization operates also influences giving, and should not be forgotten in setting out their fundraising shop. For example, Community Links in East London, in the UK, makes a convincing case that they operate in the community of Canary Wharf which houses some of the UK's largest financial companies. Faith-based organizations should not, however, take it for granted that donors will pick up this context if it is not present in their literature; and a balance must be struck with those donors who may prefer to donate to a secular institution.

Although donors may be willing to give emotionally, their need for an intellectual justification suggests that fundraisers should illustrate the pragmatic along with the moving examples. The logistics of help, why a certain amount is needed, the tax advantages and so on all help to move some donors towards the act of giving, and may meet a subconscious need.

In approaching certain groups with differing motivations, different techniques are required. For example, in approaching the rich where 'who asks' matters and the potential rewards allow additional resources to be deployed, fundraisers would be advised to build powerful networks of those connected to potential major donors, as well as using the pulling power of their most influential supporters. Indeed, this process is often at the heart of successful capital appeals where large donations are essential.

The concept of neutralization is a useful tool that may help fundraisers thinking to move beyond that which is currently taken for granted. Strutton suggests neutralization may be countered by developing a closer bond between the retailer and consumer. In a similar way relationship marketing may be used by charities as a 'blocking' strategy against such neutralization on the part of donors. This indicates that those techniques which fundraisers use to help potential donors understand the charity, and the environment it operates in, may be well founded in meeting the objections of non-donors to giving. This is exemplified by charities that use a 'cradle-to-grave' approach in developing donor commitment. Deconstructing and reassembling these techniques so that they counter the various denials should strengthen their effectiveness. Indeed, a reassessment of technique in the light of our current knowledge of donor motivation may be the next big thing.

The competition

Fundraisers seeking to raise funds for their charity ahead of the competition may be wise to consider this rich motivational tapestry of potential donors. That a donation may be more than an impulsive gift has always been known, but the studies cited above begin to give solid ground to an analysis of the warp and weft of that tapestry, allowing those seeking funds to communicate far more effectively with both existing and potential supporters. This lends weight to the importance of solid research on your donor base. Knowing who your donors are will help you to understand their likely motivations for giving to your particular cause.

References

Allford, M. (1993) *Charity Appeals: the Complete Guide to Success*, London: Dent.

Axelrod, T. (2004) *The Ask Event Handbook*, Seattle: Raising More Money Publications.

BACS (2005) Survey http://www.bacs.co.uk/BPSL/presscentre/pressreleases/2005.

DfES Task Force Report (2004) *Increasing Voluntary Giving to Higher Education*, Nottingham: DfES Publications.

Hibbert, S. and Farsides, T. (2005) *Charitable Giving and Donor Motivation*, ESRC Seminar Series Report.

Lloyd, T. (2005) *Why Rich People Give*, London: Association of Charitable Foundations.

Panas, J. (1984) *Mega Gifts: Who Gives Them, Who Gets Them*, Chicago, Ill.: Pluribus Press.

Salamon, L. M. and Anheier, H. K. (1996) *The Emerging Sector (Johns Hopkins Nonprofit Sector S.)*, Manchester: Manchester University Press.

Shaw, C.S. and Taylor, M.A. (1995) *Reinventing Fundraising: Realizing the Potential of Women's Philanthropy*, San Francisco, Calif.: Jossey-Bass.

Strutton, D., Vitell, S. J. and Pelton, L. E. (1994) 'How consumers may justify inappropriate behaviour in market settings: an application on the techniques of neutralization', *Journal of Business Research* 30, 253–260.

Tretyakov, V. (1989) *Philanthropy in Soviet Society*, Moscow: Novosti Press Agency.

Chapter 5

Francie Ostrower

THE CULTURE OF ELITE PHILANTHROPY

Edited from: Ostrower, F. (1995) 'Why the wealthy give: the culture of elite philanthropy', in *Trustees of Culture*, The University of Chicago Press.

Introduction

SIGNS OF THE PHILANTHROPIC involvements of the wealthy are not hard to find. Buildings, programmes, and even entire institutions are named for wealthy benefactors. The playbills of many performing arts organizations offer long lists of their donors. In museums, place cards next to works of art identify the men and women by whom they were donated. Hospital wings and endowed university chairs carry the names of large contributors. The sources of elite philanthropy, however, are less visible than its results. The purpose of this chapter is to explore those sources and to examine the place of philanthropy within elite groups. The result is an account of an institution that, I found, plays a central and defining role in upper-class American culture. It is also an account of how this institution has been adapted, and has thus endured, in the face of changing circumstances.

The significance of elite philanthropy

When they participate in philanthropy, elites share in a set of activities and values that are widespread in American society. Elites take philanthropy, however, and adapt it into an entire way of life that serves as a vehicle for the cultural and social life of their class, overlaying it with additional values and norms. In the process, philanthropy becomes a mark of class status that contributes to defining and maintaining the cultural and organizational boundaries of elite life. As donors themselves put it, philanthropy becomes a 'way of being part of Society' and 'one of the avenues by which Society makes its connections'. In this respect, philanthropy is also one of the activities that contributes to facilitating cohesion among elite groups.

At the same time, the values, interests, commonalities, and divisions that characterize elite groups come to shape attitudes and behaviour in the philanthropic arena. One of the major themes of this chapter is that philanthropy grows out of the donor's sense of identity. Class affiliation is one basis of identity available to members of the elite, but there are others as well, rooted, for instance, in ethnicity, religion, and gender.

Secondly the organizational character of elite philanthropy has a profound effect on how and why individuals give. Involvements and identifications with organizations become a central focus of donor loyalties and concern, which in turn foster and perpetuate their donations.

The entire world of elite philanthropy is built around a series of organizations. The character of elite philanthropy is shaped not only by the values and priorities of the elite, but also by the needs and evolution of the non-profit organizations they support. The two, moreover, do not always coincide. As Paul DiMaggio and Michael Useem point out in the case of cultural institutions, elite concerns with status exclusivity can come into conflict with organizational requirements for funds. Traditional upper-class board members, for instance, have resisted including trustees capable of contributing large sums but who are perceived as 'outsiders'. Historically, elites have also endeavoured to monopolize organizational services, resisting their extension even to the upper middle class. On the other hand, if elites are totally unwilling to adapt, the organizations that they value will die. One reason the organizational nature of contemporary philanthropy is so important is that financial needs of recipient organizations influence the thinking and behaviour of the elites who serve as their donors and trustees.

Within the sphere of philanthropy, elites carve out a distinctive niche for themselves and maintain a separate set of relationships with prestigious recipient organizations. This permits them, in turn, to retain a special sense of identification between these institutions and their class, even as the organizations themselves have changed.

The normative basis of elite philanthropy

This chapter focuses on men and women who live in a milieu in which giving is a norm, and characterize philanthropy as an obligation that is part of their privileged position. They want to give, and believe they have a right to give, and to give as they choose. In some cases, they even have etiquettes concerning how to give. These donors defend, moreover, an ideological position according to which it is legitimate (and desirable) to maintain, through philanthropy, a set of institutions whose mission is 'public' but that remain under private, rather than governmental control. Although there are differences in the kinds of giving found among subgroups of these donors, members of all these subgroups share a fundamental orientation toward, and emphasis on, philanthropy.

The vast majority of donors agreed that 'for wealthier members of our society, philanthropy is not only a matter of personal choice, but is an obligation'. Specific interpretations of 'obligation' may vary among individuals and particular charitable traditions. One donor emphasized that 'obligation' be viewed positively, saying, 'There's a certain reasonability that goes with success, let's put it that way'. A Jewish donor explained that 'the Hebrew term for charity is a word called tzedaka – and that means justice, not charity. So it's considered as an obligation'.

Some donors talked of 'giving back'. Thus one man explained, 'The principal reason that I give money is, having started with very little, and having been the recipient of aid and scholarships, and having a sense of how people that are disadvantaged can be helped by philanthropy . . . I've always felt it was the right thing to give back something of the largesse that you make in this country'.

Some tied their giving to personal lifestyle, explaining that they did not choose, or even felt uncomfortable with, higher levels of spending on luxuries. As one donor said, 'What I should tell you is that I'm driving [an old, less expensive model car], not a BMW. This is a decision we've made about the way we want to live. We're not ascetics. We live very well and eat at good restaurants. We're just not into things like fur coats. It's just not us'. In one unusual case, a donor who truly did appear to live in middle-class surroundings explained, 'We have more money than we can sensibly use. Neither one of us is interested in large Cadillacs and diamond rings. We weren't brought up that way. They're simply unimportant to us'.

Others pointed to guilt as a motivating factor. One man readily acknowledged that he enjoys the material advantages of wealth, but feels he must put some money aside, explaining, 'I think I'd feel very guilty if I didn't give any money away'. Such comments suggest the role of philanthropy in legitimating wealth. Philanthropy has also been postulated as a method of legitimating the upper class to the rest of society. I found, however, that wealthy donors are generally more focused on their peers, rather than those outside their class, as the audience for their philanthropy. At the same time, philanthropy may well help to legitimate their own position to donors themselves, allowing them to feel more comfortable with their wealth. As Weber observed, the well-off are not content to merely enjoy their good fortune; they want to feel that it is deserved: 'Good fortune thus wants to be "legitimate" fortune'.

While characterizing philanthropy as an obligation, donors readily acknow-ledged that it is also enjoyable. It is something they want to do. One donor, for instance, noted that even if you receive no explicit reward for making donations, 'there's a return in my own head that I've been a person who is generous, and have helped some person or some cause. So I think all philanthropy does have a payback, if not in kind then in sort'. Yet another explained, 'It's something I feel everyone has to do. It's just simply a sense of obligation, which is then tied into a sense of pleasure, by choosing a philanthropy in which one can get emotionally and intellectually involved'. As this comment highlights, donations of money are bound up with donors' broader interests and priorities. One reason that philanthropy is a source of satisfaction to donors is precisely because of the connection they feel to specific organizations and causes. Indeed, some were frustrated when they felt forced to make gifts in response to external pressures (such as business considerations), without having a personal interest in the recipient.

The picture of philanthropy conveyed by these affluent men and women did encompass an investing blend of both constraint and voluntarism. Donors feel it is important to support causes of their own choosing, but readily acknowledge that a considerable amount of giving is done in response to requests from friends and associates. Their readiness to characterize philanthropy as an obligation was of particular interest, because many also strongly defended the idea that people are free to use their wealth as they choose. In fact, this very freedom is one of the rationales they offer in support of philanthropy. Some comments expressed the tension between these views. For instance, one man said: 'I dislike as a [New England] Yankee, people telling me what my obligations are, but I do feel if you are fortunate enough to have something, that you should share it'. Donors generally regarded the actual selection of particular causes as a matter of personal choice. Yet a number felt people have an obligation to support causes in their local community and, in practice, felt personally obligated to support certain organizations.

Furthermore, many were highly critical of affluent people who they feel do not make adequate contributions, and said they thought less of people they know who fall into that category. Some expressed bewilderment over the failure of some wealthy individuals to give, and speculated that something must have 'gone wrong' for this to happen. Thus one person accounted for an acquaintance's lack of generosity as 'perfectly understandable if you know him. He's just a warped person, unhappy, insecure, damaged by his past'.

Individuals from wealthy backgrounds expressed the view that training in philanthropy is part of a proper upbringing. When one such man sees people who contribute little,

> It gives me a real clue about them as people, especially if they have the same background as I do. In other words, if they've been brought up with money and choose not to give when their parents were givers. I wonder about them. And I wonder what went wrong. . . . You see, I was brought up with that idea of stewardship and obligation. And I'm sure that's very capitalist and very old world. But nevertheless, that's a large component in a lot of our lives. And I simply do not understand people who don't give to anything. You know, they will give money to the small animal league because they have a poodle. Forget nuclear disarmament!

Disapproval of non-donors was by no means confined to those who grew up wealthy. One woman who was not from a wealthy family finds it 'revolting' when affluent people do not give. Another, who described his family and childhood as 'very poor', commented,

There are many very, very wealthy people who give hardly anything, and who give only under extreme pressure when they can get some powerful advantage in our New York society. And I think they're looked upon with disdain, disfavour, and are highly criticized. There's such an enormous amount of need. It doesn't matter where you give – as long as you give to something.

A number of factors lend strength to attitudes concerning non-donors, in addition to any feelings concerning the obligations of those with so much money to contribute. The majority of these donors also raise money for causes they support, and attitudes toward those unwilling to contribute can reflect their role as fundraisers. In speaking of such people, one woman who raises money said, 'It annoys me when I see them going off on expensive trips, and yet if they're asked to subscribe to some contribution . . . they'll say they can't afford it, or they'll make a very modest contribution'.

An additional factor that may contribute to donors' views is that they interpret philanthropy as involving support for organizations in the community. One donor expressed this view as follows: 'Every city has certain institutions which make it the city that it is. They give it the colour, substance of a civilized aggregation of people. There are a number of such [places] in New York, and I think that people in New York owe it to the city to preserve those institutions'.

Accordingly, wealthy people who do not contribute risk being perceived as not 'doing their share', while benefiting from organizations supported by other people. One donor emphasized that people should give to several institutions in a community, and referred to those who do not as 'free riders'. Thus, when wealthy people do not give, they are failing to conform to expectations of their peers and to support institutions that other members of the elite believe it is important to maintain.

It should be emphasized that few background characteristics distinguished donors who regard philanthropy as an obligation from those who regard it as a matter of individual choice. These differing views are unrelated to variations in donor occupation, age, religious affiliation, religiosity, gender, ethnic background, educational attainment, asset level, income, or to whether donors inherited or made their wealth. The ideology of 'noblesse oblige' associated with the social elite might suggest a greater willingness among its members to characterize philanthropy as an obligation, but this was not the case. Similarly, according to another view, held by some donors, growing up in a philanthropic family inculcates a sense of obligation. While this may be one way it can develop, it is clearly not the exclusive one. Donors raised in families with a philanthropic background were no more likely than others to regard giving as an obligation.

The sole factor that had a clear association with donors' willingness to characterize philanthropy as an obligation was membership in a religious congregation. Those who belonged to a church or temple were more likely than non-members to view philanthropy as an obligation. This may stem from the fact that religious teachings present giving as an obligation. Accordingly, people who are involved enough with organized religion to join a congregation might be more likely to support that view. Additional findings suggest a further explanation.

Higher percentages of donors who identified themselves as either Republican or Democrat viewed giving as obligatory than did Independents who split their vote. Taken together, the findings concerning congregation membership and party affiliation suggest that donors who view philanthropy as obligatory may generally be more likely to identify with and become involved in organized social groups. While noting the interest of these differences, however, we must also keep in mind that the majority of donors from all subgroups viewed philanthropy as an obligation.

Paths to philanthropic involvement

Although individual experiences vary, there are certain typical routes through which wealthy donors become involved in philanthropy. As we shall see, the very pervasiveness of philanthropy in donors' social milieux contributes to drawing individuals into giving and volunteering. It is not surprising, therefore, that one donor said he had not planned to spend this part of his life involved in philanthropic activities, but 'just slipped into it'.

Some people are introduced to philanthropy by their family. Inheritors told of how exposure to giving began for them as children. The example of one donor, whose parents expected her to set aside a portion of her allowance each week for charitable purposes, illustrates this process. Another woman's family taught her that 'no matter what, no matter how busy your life is, this is something you must be involved in, and it isn't something that simply involves giving money . . . it's something that involves time'. Some described various ways that they encourage their own children to be philanthropic, and 'teach' them how to give. One donor, for instance, said that she and her husband view this as part of preparing their children for the fortune they will inherit. Typical mechanisms for encouraging children's philanthropy included involving them in a family foundation and providing them with a set sum each year to give away. Sometimes, parents leave funds in a foundation after their death, which ensures that children will engage in philanthropy. Sometimes, where relationships have developed between particular non-profits and particular families, donors may also become involved with those specific institutions.

Another route into philanthropic activity is through marriage to someone who is involved. One woman thus described how, after her marriage to a wealthy man, numerous organizations began to approach her for donations. Initially, she was very uncomfortable and at a loss about how to handle such requests. She discussed this with her husband, who told her, 'It's your duty as a woman with money to hear everyone, and then you can decide whether you want to support them'. Over time, she said, she learned from her husband's family, and has become quite active as a donor and volunteer.

Exposure to philanthropy may also occur through business associates. Some donors described people who served as their 'philanthropic mentors'. One man was cautioned at a young age by a senior person in his field whom he greatly admired that, as he accumulated wealth, he should remember that someday he would 'have to give it back to society'. Another man became involved after going to work for a firm where he 'was surrounded with a tradition of giving'. As his interest developed in this setting, his associates arranged for him to go on the board of a non-profit organization.

Religion provides yet another setting in which exposure to giving may occur. One donor remarked that 'like everybody who has gone to Sunday school or church' he was 'indoctrinated early in putting something into the plate every Sunday'. This brings up the more general fact that philanthropic involvement may begin because someone is a member of, or uses the services of, a non-profit organization. Throughout their lives, members of elite groups are likely to be involved with organizations that ask for donations. Indeed, the donor cited above, whose exposure began in church, added that he attended a private prep school, college, and professional school. When you graduate, he said 'you're badgered incessantly by the alumni fund', so that 'my obligation to be philanthropic was not something that I was allowed to forget'. These comments further testify to the importance of the organizational character of contemporary philanthropy.

There are certain characteristic times in the lives of the wealthy when they are predisposed toward greater philanthropic involvement. For men, retirement from business is such a time. Having generally led active professional lives, philanthropy provides an arena into which energy and expertise can be directed after retirement. One business executive, who became involved and started devoting time to non-profit boards after retiring, said, I'm retired and I have nothing other than these activities to take up [my time]. They take it up and it's very interesting'. Similarly, another donor became involved with a particular cause 'when I stepped back from the day-to-day operations' (of his business).

Wealthy women, who are frequently not employed, may seek greater involvement as their children age. One woman said earning money was not important or necessary for her, but that she did need to do something where she could make an impact. Therefore, when her children began school and she had free time during the day, she turned to volunteering on a full-time basis, becoming deeply involved with one particular organization for many years. The relationship between philanthropic involvement and stages in the life cycle reinforces the point that philanthropy is an activity that many donors find fulfilling and enjoyable, allowing them to pursue their own interests and goals, while feeling that they are helping others as well. Indeed, the woman just described explained that 'doing good' did not even initially enter into her volunteer activities.

Personal tragedy, such as an illness or death of a family member, also proved to be a catalyst for philanthropic involvement. For some, an initial involvement that occurred for this reason later led to a greater commitment. One man told me that prior to a relative's accident, he had never been a major contributor and was 'oblivious to charitable causes'. Another did make donations before a close relative developed a serious illness, but said it had 'been unemotional, with no distinct feeling of accomplishment or pleasure. I've given because I should give and was supposed to give. Now I want to give, and there's a helluva difference'. First motivated by a desire to find a cure, he emphasized that 'that feeling will carry over' to supporting other causes, because the type of experience his family has undergone 'unblocks your thinking'.

The examples concerning family illness highlight the individual and even emotional aspects of philanthropy. Indeed, philanthropy as a social institution derives strength from the fact that it becomes a channel through which individuals can express various personal experiences, attachments, and relationships with other people.

Criticisms of elite philanthropy

Elites are sometimes perceived more as corrupters than practitioners of philanthropy by those outside their class. Volunteers outside the elite and popular stereotypes often depict elite philanthropy as superficial and frivolous. From this perspective, the willingness of the wealthy to become involved does not extend much beyond going to fashionable fundraisers. Such attitudes were expressed, for instance, by volunteers studied by Robert Wuthnow. He found that those who 'dirty their hands daily in the trenches' recognized the importance of wealthy patrons to organizations but were irritated by their 'casual and seemingly superficial assistance'. For example, one woman spoke of volunteering for a programme where the wealthy were willing to serve as trustees, but not to 'really get involved'.

Such perceptions contrast radically with the way in which wealthy donors themselves experience their philanthropy. For so many of these donors, a deep sense of involvement with particular organizations is the very motivation, and even precondition, for their larger donations. From their perspective, moreover, board membership represents the height of involvement and identification with an organization. As board members, they do not see themselves as detached, but as functioning at the very 'core' of an organization, dealing with major decisions and policies. Similarly, the affluent attorneys and business people who donate their professional services to organizations would surely object that they are indeed giving of themselves. Donors are well aware of the social aspects of philanthropy, which some also criticized. Yet those (generally women) who invest considerable time and energy in organizing benefits would see all their logistical work and planning as 'working in the trenches' to produce events that raise so much money for organizations.

The characterizations of volunteers outside the elite and popular stereotypes do, however, correspond to certain truths about elite philanthropy. In particular, they reflect the separate and exclusive nature of elite philanthropy that we have discussed. It is not that the wealthy are unconcerned with the organizations they support, or unwilling to give of their time. Clearly, many were deeply committed to the causes they supported, and maintained their commitments over very long periods. What is true, however, is that the elite do keep their distance, and remain apart, in their philanthropy. In essence, their philanthropy is an extension of, not a departure from, their general existence as elites. Their participation in non-profit organizations parallels their participation in the business world – they are at the top.

Although there were exceptions, the volunteer work of these wealthy donors typically focused on serving organizational entities rather than directly and personally assisting people. Thus, serving on a hospital board was a typical volunteer activity, but this was not true of working with patients. Affluent volunteers serve in capacities that involve them in issues of policy, planning, and decision making at the highest organizational levels. As board members, for instance, they participate in hiring and firing the institution's director. Fundraising, organizing benefits, and serving on advisory committees, as well as board membership, were also characteristic activities. The people with whom the wealthy deal in such volunteer roles tend to be their social and business peers, and the organization's top professional personnel. In short, many wealthy donors care about the organizations that they support, but in the ways in which they involve themselves and demonstrate their support they function in a separate and privileged arena – as elites. The boundaries separating the elite from others are not ones that the wealthy are generally any more interested in crossing or blurring in philanthropy than they are elsewhere.

Critics of the nature of the recipients of elite donations also suggest that the wealthy corrupt, rather than practise, philanthropy. The wealthy have been criticized for failing to give more to the poor, and for favouring causes such as cultural and educational organizations. Such criticism assumes that redistribution is a basic aim of philanthropy and the criterion by which it should be measured. These are assumptions that others have recently questioned. The study on which this chapter draws shows that, although wealthy donors believe philanthropic gifts should have a public benefit, they do not equate it with redistribution for the poor. Indeed, they view gifts to hospitals, museums, and the broader range of philanthropic institutions as equally legitimate. Some wealthy individuals, such as Carnegie, have even rejected the notion that the role of philanthropy was to provide aid for the destitute. In general, affluent donors often argued that philanthropy was best suited for handling smaller-scale issues than large-scale social problems. In this respect, we have seen that affluent donors define the boundaries of philanthropy (and, by contrast, the responsibilities of government) in a way that validates them in following their own preferences when making donations. Many donors ardently defended the social value of philanthropy. Yet the way in which they interpret philanthropy allows them to enjoy the sense that they are making a contribution to society while defining social benefit on their own terms.

Conclusion

Elite philanthropy has evolved and changed, but this change has occurred within the context of a larger continuity. Elite philanthropy has, however, remained *elite* philanthropy. It continues to be exclusive with respect to those outside the elite, and its character and role within the elite has endured. There has been a fundamental continuity of values among the participants, even as there has been a shift in their composition and prominence. The newly wealthy and the formerly excluded shared the priorities of previously established elites and valued similar organizations. The philanthropic values of the social elite function as a reference point for the broader elite. This provides an important and basic source of continuity to elite philanthropy. Although the relative dominance of the members of the social elite may have declined in philanthropy, their values have not been rejected, but have been universalized and institutionalized within the larger elite.

Philanthropy has also continued to maintain its basic role as the elite has undergone change. The basis of elite status has increasingly shifted from family and community to organization. In philanthropy, managers chosen on the basis of their corporate position, rather than families or social status, have increasingly been joining the ranks of trustees. Yet the use that elites make of philanthropy within their group has endured. Indeed, to the extent that the elite is becoming a more atomized collection of corporate managers, philanthropy's role may become even more important. In an elite whose members are less likely to be drawn from a closely integrated group, philanthropy may assume particular importance in providing a shared culture, identity, and setting for interaction outside of business. Furthermore, because the boundaries in philanthropy are more fluid than those within the elite itself, philanthropy may further facilitate elite integration by providing a common meeting ground for more separate segments of the elite.

Continuity in the nature of philanthropy's function within the elite has also been fostered by the ways in which exclusivity has been maintained under changed organizational circumstances. Even as non-profits' services are utilized by growing numbers of people, and they move into commercial ventures at odds with more clublike, former ways of operating, elites carve out a separate world for themselves by the way they organize their philanthropy. Through charity benefits, board memberships, private events open only to large donors, and related mechanisms, elites maintain a separate relationship and sense of identification with the non-profits they value.

Dynamics of continuity and change in elite philanthropy are also shaped by the organizational character of contemporary elite philanthropy itself. Tensions between the financial needs of non-profit institutions and class-based status concerns are virtually inherent to contemporary elite philanthropy. A central conclusion of this study is that, ultimately, more entrenched members of the elite were willing to open up the doors to 'outsiders' in order to preserve the organizations they value. This conclusion need not presuppose any inordinate degree of rationality, omniscience, or coordination among the elite. The concern and behaviour of donors, fundraisers, and board members toward the organizations with which they are involved is sufficient. I refer here particularly to the willingness of members of a board to admit new trustees able to make large donations, whom they might otherwise prefer to exclude. We can thus see that board membership does represent more than just a status game to participants, who have feelings of loyalty and responsibility to the organizations they oversee. It further shows that organizations are not merely conduits for philanthropy or intermediaries between individual donors and beneficiaries, but are themselves the focal point of donors' interests and concerns. Elite philanthropy does not exist in a vacuum.

Chapter 6

Adrian Sargeant and Elaine Jay

MEASURING AND MANAGING DONOR VALUE

Edited from: Sargeant, A. and Jay, E. (2004) 'Donor development', in *Fundraising Management*, Chapter 7, Routledge.

Introduction

THE BULK OF THE INCOME generated from donors comes through retention and development activity rather than at the point of recruitment. Non-profits have to invest in the acquisition of new supporters. That initial investment is repaid and additional income is generated over time if the donor continues to give. The identification of different types of donor, of their actual and potential value to the non-profit, and of the optimum levels of investment that should be made in them is vital to successful donor development. The database, and the effective and efficient use of the information that the database can provide, is the key to this process.

In this chapter we will look at some of the tools currently used in donor segmentation and measurement, such as lifetime value, recency/frequency/value analyses and relationship fundraising techniques. We will also look at what drives donor loyalty and what non-profits can do to encourage retention.

Relationship fundraising

At the core of relationship fundraising is the development and maintenance of long-term relationships with donors, rather than simply a series of discrete transactions.

While the move from a transaction to a relationship approach to donors may seem little more than a play on words, the differences in terms of the impact on strategy and performance are profound. In a transaction-based approach, development activity is driven by the need to maximize the returns generated by each individual campaign (except perhaps where a campaign has been jointly designed to achieve other goals such as awareness, participation or education). Strategy is based on achieving the highest possible return on investment (ROI) when the costs and revenues of a campaign are calculated.

Fundraisers following such a strategy tend to offer donors little choice – to do so would merely add to the cost. Little segmentation takes place and donors typically receive a standard pack. The emphasis of the content is usually on the immediacy of each appeal and donors are exhorted to give 'now' because of the urgency of a specific situation. They may then be approached in a few weeks' or months' time with a further seemingly urgent issue the charity feels they should support. The donor thus receives a series of very similar communications, each designed with an eye to achieving the maximum possible ROI.

A relationship approach, by contrast, recognizes that it is not essential to break even on every communication with a donor. It recognizes that if treated with respect donors will want to give again, and fundraisers are therefore content to live with somewhat lower rates of return in the early stages.

They recognize that they will achieve respectable ROI over the full duration of the relationship. At the heart of this approach is the concept of 'lifetime value' (LTV). Once fundraisers understand how much a given donor might be worth to the organization over time, they can tailor the offering to that donor according to the individual's needs/requirements, and yet still ensure an adequate lifetime ROI. These differences between the transaction and relational approaches to fundraising are summarized in Table 6.1.

Burnett (1992: 48) was the first to recognize the need for what he termed 'relationship fundraising', which he defined as:

> an approach to the marketing of a cause which centres not around raising money but on developing to its full potential the unique and special relationship that exists between a charity and its supporter.

Burnett championed a move towards dealing with donors individually, recognizing each donor as unique in terms of their giving history, their motivation

Table 6.1 Comparison of transaction and relational approaches

Differences	Transaction-based	Relationship fundraising
Focus	Soliciting single donations	Donor retention
Key measures	Immediate ROI, amount	Lifetime value
Orientation	Urgency of cause	Donor relationship
Time scale	Short	Long
Customer	Little emphasis	Major emphasis

for giving and the overall standard of care that they expect to receive from the charities they support. The entire relationship with a donor, he argued, should be viewed holistically and fundraising decisions taken in the light of the perceived value of the overall relationship.

Fundraising departments operating relationship fundraising make every effort to segment their donor base and to develop a uniquely tailored service and, importantly, 'quality of service' for each of the segments they identify. At the core of this approach is the concept of lifetime value.

Lifetime value (LTV)

Bitran and Mondschein (1997: 109) define lifetime value as 'the total net contribution that a customer generates during his/her lifetime on a house-list'. It is therefore a measure of the total net worth to a fundraising organization of its relationship with a particular donor. To calculate it one has to estimate the costs and revenues associated with managing the communication with that donor during each year of his or her relationship. If, for example, the relationship extends over a period of four years, one can subtract the costs of servicing the relationship with that donor from the revenue so generated. In essence the contribution each year to the organization's overheads and charitable appeals can be calculated. Of course there is a certain amount of crystal-ball-gazing involved since it becomes increasingly more difficult to predict costs and revenues the further one looks into the future. To take account of this uncertainty and to reflect the fact that a €20 donation in four years' time will be worth in real terms much less than it would today, it is also important to discount the value of the future revenue streams that will be generated. After all, instead of investing the money in donor acquisition activity the charity could simply elect to place the money concerned in an interest-bearing account. Unless the return from the fundraising activity can be expected to match, or hopefully exceed, what could be generated by an interest-bearing account, it will clearly not be worthwhile. If this analysis is conducted right across the database a key advantage accrues. Charities can employ an LTV analysis to increase their overall profitability by abandoning donors who will never be profitable and concentrating resources on recruiting and retaining those who will (see also Lindahl and Winship 1992).

There are two key decisions to be taken in this examination of donor value. First, non-profits must choose between the uses of historic or projected future value. Second, they must elect to calculate value on either an individual basis or, more usually, on a segment-by-segment basis, examining specific groups of donors on the database.

The majority of voluntary organizations continue to equate lifetime value with 'total historic value' and thus to calculate lifetime value by conducting a simple historic analysis of their database. The question fundraisers are asking, by conducting their analysis in this way, is simply 'How much has this particular individual, or segment, been worth to my organization in the past?' However, lifetime value can and should be used as a projective measure, offering information in respect of how much a given donor or segment may be worth in the future.

Of course the lifetime value of donors should take into consideration more than just the revenue from their direct donations and the costs of the communications they receive. Donors are worth much more than this to an organization, because, for example, they often purchase goods from trading catalogues, sell raffle tickets, donate their time to fundraising events and so on. Each of these contributions needs to be accounted for in the equation. As an example, the net contribution figure for each year could therefore take account of the following costs and revenues.

Costs
- newsletters;
- appeal letters;
- acknowledgement/thank you letters;
- cost of promotional merchandise/donor gifts;
- cost of telemarketing activity, if any.

Revenues
- cash donations;
- tax reclaimed (in the case of tax-effective giving);
- cash value of donations in kind;
- cash value of any volunteering undertaken;
- cash value of referrals (i.e. introductions of other donors);
- revenue from sale of promotional merchandise.

Calculating the LTV of discrete donor segments

Usually, charities want to understand whether specific segments of their database exhibit higher lifetime values than others. This calls for a more sophisticated degree of analysis. In attempting to measure lifetime value the following process is recommended.

1   The first stage is to decide what the purpose of the analysis will be. Although this sounds rather obvious, many organizations are not clear from the outset exactly what they are hoping to gain from it. The technique typically employed is to determine whether specific segments of the database have a higher or lower value than others. Thus if female donors appear to be worth more than male donors or donors recruited by direct mail have a higher lifetime value than those recruited by press advertising, fundraising resources may be allocated accordingly. Lifetime value analysis is therefore more commonly employed to determine the LTV of donors who have specific characteristics. The nature of these characteristics needs to be determined from the outset. Clarity in respect of the purpose of the analysis can also guide the organization in assigning appropriate categories of cost for inclusion in the calculations.

2   The next stage is to decide the period of the analysis to use. It is not essential here that the chosen time period is based on the longest-standing donors (Carpenter 1995). Since predicting behaviour becomes progressively more difficult the further one looks into the future, it is only important that the

time period captures the majority of the contribution for a given segment of donors. Previous research in the commercial sector with similar value products suggests that a time frame of five years might be most appropriate for application in the fundraising context (see Jackson 1992). In a sense therefore, the term 'lifetime' value is something of a misnomer. It is entirely up to the organization concerned to set a suitable time frame for the analysis and to look at the lifetime value of its donors over a very specific horizon.

3   The next step should be to segment the database into a manageable but distinct group of cells on the basis of the primary variable to be explored. One might therefore allocate donors to cells on the basis that their donation was between:

- €1 and €5
- €6 and €10
- €11 and €15

And so on.

4   It is then necessary to establish the giving behaviour of each of the cells identified at (3) above. A historical analysis of donor behaviour should yield valuable information in respect of attrition rate and giving history.

5   The final stage is to outline the intended development strategy, including, for example, the number of mailings and the projected costs thereof. This should include the costs of maintenance communications that a donor would typically receive (e.g. newsletters), even though they are not specifically aimed at raising funds.

6   The preceding information may then be employed to predict future value. Armed with information about likely attrition rates, the future costs of servicing donors, the predicted revenue streams and an appropriate discount rate, one may then proceed to make predictions about the projected lifetime value of each cell, or category of giver.

The benefits of LTV analysis

Lifetime value may be used to drive four management decisions:

1   assigning acquisition allowances
2   choosing media for initial donor acquisition
3   setting criteria for donor marketing
4   investing in the reactivation of lapsed donors.

1 Assigning acquisition allowances

An understanding of the lifetime value of a charity's donors can guide the determination of how much should be spent to recruit each new donor. Many charities conscientiously strive to achieve as close as possible a break-even position at the end of each of their recruitment campaigns. While commendable this is not necessary, so long as the future income stream from the donors being recruited is a healthy one. Charities employing the lifetime value concept would therefore tend to assign somewhat higher acquisition allowances than those which do not.

In financial terms this is simply because a fundraiser employing a transaction-based approach will calculate campaign ROI thus:

$$ROI = \frac{\text{immediate revenue generated}}{\text{cost of acquisition campaign}}$$

A fundraiser adopting a relational approach based on lifetime value (LTV) would by contrast calculate ROI as:

$$ROI = \frac{\text{initial revenue} + (\text{sum of all future contributions less discount})}{\text{cost of acquisition campaign}}$$

where
ROI = return on donor acquisition investment
Future contribution = estimated annual contribution to profit
Discount = reduction in value of future dollars to today's rate (discounted cashflow).

2 Choosing media for initial donor acquisition

Fundraisers engaged in the perennial problem of donor recruitment are well versed in the necessity of asking questions such as:

- 'Which media should I be using for my recruitment activity?'
- 'What balance should I adopt between the media options that are available?'

The traditional approach to answering these questions would have been to calculate the immediate ROI for each medium and consider the response rates typically received from each medium in the past. Such analyses suggest sub-optimal allocations of fundraising resource, because they ignore certain known donor behaviours. Donors recruited by one medium may never give again, while donors recruited by another medium exhibit much greater degrees of loyalty to the cause. The overall profitability from one relationship can therefore vary considerably from that of another.

3 Setting selection criteria for donor marketing

Lifetime value calculations can prove instructive for more than just recruitment planning. The information may be used to guide contact strategies for ongoing donor development. If a charity calculates a projected lifetime value for each donor on the database, donors can be assigned to specific segments, and contact strategies customized to build value. Initially, this may involve simply recognizing the difference in contribution, so as to offer particularly high-value donors a differentiated pattern of care that reflects their status. This might involve more detailed, higher-quality mailings. As charities become more experienced in the use of LTV analysis, it would also be possible to associate the impact of differentiated standards of care, or forms of contact, upon the LTV for a given donor. In a sense, one then begins to model the optimal lifetime value. A simple example will illustrate this point.

Suppose a Third World charity has conducted a LTV analysis. The charity has divided donors into segments on the basis of projected LTV and decided to mail the highest-value segments with an expensive mailshot designed to solicit funds to support Third World families. On the basis of the projected LTV the charity has calculated that sufficient funds exist to include a detailed case history of one family that warrants support, Polaroid photographs of each of the family members and a promotional video highlighting the work the organization could do with that family. While the LTV calculations suggest this is a very viable form of contact which will generate an acceptable rate of return, the charity has no way of knowing whether this is optimal. Through experience a charity can monitor the impact of different contact strategies on lifetime value (e.g. a standard mailshot, including/not including the Polaroid shots, including/not including the video). Contact strategies may then be selected which maximize the overall lifetime value of a given segment of donors. In our example, it may be that the inclusion of a video is perceived as wasteful and therefore lowers the value of subsequent donations, or it could have such an emotive and tangible feel that donors feel a greater sense of commitment and the longevity of their relationship is extended. As Peppers and Rogers (1995: 49) note:

> Instead of measuring the effectiveness of a marketing programme by how many sales transactions occur across an entire market during a particular period, the new marketer will gauge success by the projected increase or decrease in a customer's expected future value to the company.

4 Investing in the reactivation of lapsed donors

Few fundraisers would disagree with the notion that reactivating lapsed donors can be profitable. Having been sufficiently motivated to give at least once in the past, with proper encouragement it is eminently possible that donors will do so again. The problem, however, for many organizations lies in deciding which lapsed donors should be selected for contact. While one could do this easily on the basis of the total amount donated, the level of the last gift or the length of time since the last donation, it can be instructive to use projected lifetime value to inform the decision. With the right persuasion to respond, targeting those with a higher forecast LTV is likely to prove a most efficient use of resources. A 'reactivation allowance' may be built into the budget. How much an organization is prepared to commit to reactivating one donor would inform the nature and quality of the contact strategy employed.

Recency/frequency/value analysis (RFV) and segmenting for growth

An alternative to lifetime value analysis that is often available on database systems is recency, frequency and value (sometimes referred to as RFM – recency, frequency and monetary amount). Data on recency (i.e. the time since the last gift was given), frequency (i.e. the number of gifts that have been given) and value (i.e. the value of the gifts given) is calculated and used in segmentation or in the selection of data for a particular campaign. RFV data are often used in the generation of scores against each donor assuming that:

- higher-value donors are more attractive than lower-value donors;
- donors who give frequently are statistically more likely to respond to a communication than those who do not;
- donors who have given in the last six months are more likely to give than those who have not given for the past two years.

RFV scoring can reflect the differences in individual donor behaviour and give the fundraiser considerable insight into who to target in a particular campaign.

Many charities use RFV scoring in conjunction with other forms of targeting in the selection of donors for development communications. Other targeting criteria might include donor communication preferences and ratings based on the sort of campaign approaches the donor has responded to, or rejected, in the past.

RFV may be used effectively in identifying those donors likely to lapse, and in patterns of lapsing. 'Pre-lapse' campaigns can be generated for those donors who have not given recently or where frequency and value patterns have been interrupted.

> You need to keep in mind that there are really many kinds of donors inside your donor base. This diversity is important to remember because in each case there are logical things to ask for and logical ways to make the request.
>
> (Squires 1994: 37)

As discussed above, effective segmentation is an essential part of successful donor development activity. Using the tools of LTV or RFV analysis, donors can be streamed into groups according to current or predicted value levels and communication programmes designed and implemented accordingly. In database selections for particular campaigns data may also be used on past response to similar appeal themes, or past patterns of communication preference. (Donors may be segmented in the following categories: *major givers . . . legacy/bequest prospects . . . high-value donors . . . committed giving . . . low-value donors . . . lapsed donors. . . .*)

Keeping donors loyal

Loyal donors are those who give support time after time. While data analysis and segmentation exercises may indicate that certain types or groups of donors are not likely to be very profitable over time, and that little should therefore be invested in retaining and growing their support, there are very few instances where the loss of a supporter would be an optimum result. Legacies or bequests are highly unpredictable sources of charity income. There is much anecdotal evidence that even the lowest-*value* giver in life can become a major benefactor after death. While segmentation based on profitability is essential, studies have shown that a small increase in customer retention can produce a significant impact on profitability (Reichheld and Sasser 1990).

As is the case in consumer marketing, it appears that there are several different levels of loyalty. Non-profits in the field of disaster relief, for instance, commonly find it extremely difficult to elicit repeat gifts from donors who give for the first time in response to an emergency appeal. In this instance, the giving of the gift has been motivated by the urgency of the cause or event and the perceived needs of the beneficiaries, while the identity of the facilitating non-profit agency has barely registered. The donor therefore feels no loyalty to the non-profit and he or she is unlikely to consider themselves to have any sort of relationship with the charity.

The donation of a second gift is always seen as a key point in the donor–non-profit relationship. As we have seen, most non-profits report that over half of new cash donors never give again. First gifts may be seen as a 'test', with donors (consciously or unconsciously) waiting to see what feedback they receive before going further. In the 'middle' levels of loyalty a donor may give repeat gifts, but may also support other, similar causes and may not feel any great involvement with or preference for a particular organization. At the 'top' level donors feel that they have a strong relationship with a particular non-profit organization and will continue to support that organization even though competitors exist in the same field of work. At this level of loyalty the donor would be likely to be receptive to major gift or planned giving approaches, and would act as a strong advocate for non-profit.

How can loyalty be increased?

The results of research undertaken by Sargeant in 2001 into reasons for quitting suggest a number of ways in which non-profits seek to retain their donors. While there may be little that can be done to facilitate the retention of those donors who experience a change in their financial circumstances, there is much that can be done to deal with many of the other common causes of lapse.

The research indicated that only 22 per cent of donors appear to lapse because they can no longer afford to offer their support to the organization in question. Given that some of these donors may still be supporting other non-profits this result is encouraging, since it suggests that while a number of donors will be lost to a particular non-profit they may not be lost to the sector as a whole.

Indeed, the study suggested that over 26 per cent of lapsed donors typically quit because they perceive that other causes are more or perhaps equally deserving. If charities are to succeed in retaining this category of donor, the literature suggests that they need to find ways of improving satisfaction and deepening the bonds that exist between them and their supporters. Given that this study also highlighted the importance of feedback and perceived effectiveness, it seems that one way in which non-profits might achieve this goal lies in ensuring that they provide ongoing and specific feedback to donors in respect of the use to which their funds have been put and in particular the benefit that has resulted for the beneficiary group. If this feeling of impact on the cause is strengthened it seems less likely that donors will view other causes as being more deserving than those they already support.

Indeed, the feeling of identity or association with a given cause would seem to be a major cause for concern. One in ten of the lapsed supporters in the study reported that they had no memory of ever having supported the organization concerned.

Service quality was also identified as a key issue and would seem to be as much a prerequisite to non-profit customer retention as the literature suggests it is in the for-profit sector. Lapsed donors reported significantly poorer views of the quality of service they received than did active supporters, and in particular tended not to regard the organization as providing them with adequate feedback in respect of how their donation had been used. Donors viewing the communications they receive as informative, courteous, timely, appealing and convenient would appear to remain loyal for greater periods of time.

The issue then becomes one of how best to achieve this perception. The results of the study suggested that in order to engender loyalty, charities need to improve both the quality of their communications and the choice that they offer. The relationship fundraising approach, described earlier, would allow donors once recruited to select the pattern of communication they would wish to receive. A few charities, for example, currently offer donors the opportunity to specify how frequently they would like to hear from the organization, whether they would like news about how their gift has been employed, whether they would like such news but not additional letters asking for money and so on. The results of the research suggested that such practices would be likely to improve perceptions of the quality of communication received and thereby enhance loyalty. It is also worth noting that by taking the step of asking donors to specify how they would like to be treated, one is in effect engaging those donors with the organization and requiring them to think through the desired nature of the relationship. The donor thereby requests the communications he or she will subsequently receive, moving the organization's approach to marketing away from 'intrusion' towards 'invitation'. As the options for communication continue to increase, with e-mail likely to become a preferred route for many donors, offering choice will probably be all the more important in the future.

Given recent developments in database technology, there is no reason why even smaller charities cannot manage the requirements of their individual donors and ensure that each receives a pattern of communication identical to that specified. The results of this study suggest that this would enhance overall levels of satisfaction and ultimately, as a consequence, donor loyalty.

A further aspect of the study concerned donor expectations in respect of both the frequency of communication and the sums of money demanded. There was evidence that donor expectations in respect of these issues were currently not being met. It thus seems clear that charities could also offer donors some choice over whether or not they wish to be asked for specific sums. Some donors may well welcome guidance about the appropriateness of certain gift levels. Others may prefer to take such decisions themselves and not be prompted by the charity. Again, there is no reason why charities should not capture this information and use it to inform the communication strategy employed. Moreover, a consideration of relational issues, such as donor lifetime value, would ensure that, where specific sums are requested, these are appropriate to the financial ability of the donor.

Asking donors to specify what relationship (if any) they would prefer to have with an organization would therefore appear to offer considerable utility. Indeed, if donors are offered an additional opportunity to interact with their chosen charity, it would seem ultimately rather unlikely that they will lapse simply because they have no memory of ever having supported the organization.

The consequences of failing to embrace these relationship marketing techniques appear all too evident. Donors will be likely to increasingly complain that they are over-mailed and inundated with requests for inappropriate sums of money.

References

Bitran, G. and Mondschein, S. (1997) 'A Comparative Analysis of Decision Making Procedures in the Catalog Sales Industry', *European Management Journal*, 15(2): 105–116.

Burnett, K. (1992) *Relationship Fundraising*, White Lion Press, London.

Carpenter, P. (1995) 'Customer Lifetime Value: Do the Math', *Marketing Computers*, January: 18–19.

Harvey, J. W. and McCrohan, K. F. (1988) 'Fund-raising Costs – Societal Implications for Philanthropies and Their Supporters', *Business and Society*, 27 (spring): 15–22.

Jackson, D. R. (1992) 'In Quest of the Grail: Breaking the Barriers to Customer Valuation', *Direct Marketing*, March: 44–47.

Lindahl, W. E. and Winship, C. (1992) 'Predictive Models for Annual Fundraising and Major Gift Fundraising', *Nonprofit Management and Leadership*, 3(1): 43–64.

McKinnon, H. (1999) *Hidden Gold*, Bonus Books Inc., Chicago, IL.

Peppers, D. and Rogers, M. (1995) 'A New Marketing Paradigm: Share of Customer Not Market Share', *Managing Service Quality*, 5(3): 48–51.

Raphel, M. and Considine, R. (1981) *The Great Brain Robbery*, Business Tips Publications, New York.

Reichheld, F. F. and Sasser, W. E. (1990) 'Zero Defections: Quality Comes to Services', *Harvard Business Review*, September/October: 105–111.

Sargeant, A. (1998) 'Donor Lifetime Value: An Empirical Analysis', *Journal of Nonprofit and Voluntary Sector Marketing*, 3(4): 283–297.

Sargeant, A. and MacKenzie, J. (1999) *A Lifetime of Giving*, Charities Aid Foundation, West Malling, Kent.

Squires, C. (1994) 'Picking the Right Gift to Ask For: Donor Renewal and Upgrading', *Fund Raising Management*, 25(5): 37.

Stone, M., Woodcock, N. and Wilson, M. (1996) 'Managing the Change from Marketing Planning to Customer Relationship Management', *Long Range Planning*, 29(5): 675–683.

Chapter 7

John Baguley

FUNDRAISING CAMPAIGNS

Introduction

T HE WORD 'CAMPAIGN' is used indiscriminately in fundraising to describe the application of almost any fundraising technique, from the huge media appeals run by the Disasters Emergency Committee (DEC) to the introduction of a small organization's legacy campaign. This chapter uses it to describe large or small fundraising drives that are designed to be highlighted in the media to generate a public response beyond that of the organization's existing supporters.

This chapter divides the organizations that run public campaigns into two types. The first are the emergency appeals featuring natural or man-made disasters that are already appearing in the news, such as the DEC appeals in the UK or the Red Cross appeal in the US for victims of hurricane Katrina. These are characterized as 'opportunistic' campaigns.

The second type are self-generated fundraising campaigns where organizations themselves purchase space in the media such as the NSPCC's Full Stop campaign in the UK or Amnesty International's human rights campaigns. These may hope to become news items in themselves, but do not start with the advantage that their subject is already featured in the news media. They are labelled 'planned' campaigns.

Similarly, at the local level, a fire at the village hall may be given strong coverage in the local press and lead to an opportunistic campaign, perhaps backed by a local paper; but a church development project, say, to provide an after-school club for local children, may need to raise some funds from the congregation to fuel a fundraising campaign, which can then reach out to the whole community in a planned campaign.

Why do organizations run campaigns?

The simple answer is that they need, or choose to, raise funds from the public for tasks they could not accomplish by appealing only to their own supporters. For efficient organizations this will be part of an agreed fundraising and communications strategy, in which provision is made for both taking advantage of media opportunities when they occur (e.g. well-publicized disasters) and for budgeted advertising or other public fundraising drives. For these organizations campaigns are likely to be only one of a range of fundraising techniques employed. For others, campaigns may occur in default of strategy, perhaps because funds are urgently needed and other techniques demand too much time to implement or long-term financial input. They are, however, unlikely to succeed unless they can effectively occupy the theoretical framework set out below.

Successful public campaigns bring huge rewards in terms of public awareness and this often generates a knock-on effect on other forms of fundraising. The Greenpeace campaign in the 1970s and early 1980s to save whales caught the public imagination and ensured that its direct mail, loose-leaf inserts and local groups all grew with rapidity; though as they moved beyond this to cover other environmental issues the same level of response became harder to maintain. Similarly, Friends of the Earth's front-page advertisements in the *Guardian* in the 1980s fuelled its membership development and when these advertisements were no longer viable the response to other forms of direct marketing showed a downturn.

Local campaigns too help to build organizations. More recently the Medical Foundation for Care of Victims of Torture's successful capital appeal for a new centre in the late 1990s helped develop its relationships with many existing and new major donors. Conversely failed appeals can depress response and capital appeals are advisedly preceded by a feasibility study to ensure the appeal, and in particular any public launch, will generate the right response.

The scheduling, resource requirement analysis and target setting common to capital appeal feasibility studies is also an essential part of the build-up to a public campaign. However rapidly the organization needs to move, these elements are advisedly part of its essential framework to ensure the appeal does not dissolve into a very public failure.

The campaign diamond

Whether it is on a national or local level a successful campaign inhabits a certain framework in a positive manner. The 'diamond', developed by Rob Paton (Figure 7.1), draws on Moore's (1995) work on strategy in public organizations, defining the critical features and 'space' of a campaign.

The first facet of the diamond is a clear *problem or need* that requires solution: either local (the village hall has burnt down) or national (an earthquake has levelled several villages). Though 'facts never speak for themselves; it is how they are interpreted', organizations can find themselves wrong-footed by the media

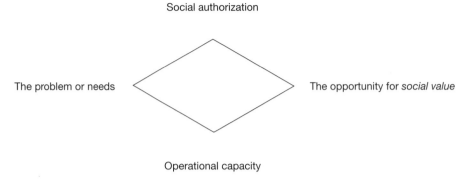

Figure 7.1 The public campaign diamond

as coverage of a situation progresses. For example, 'needy victims' of a disaster can become 'scroungers' from one day to the next.

The second facet is the requirement for *social authorization* – the *visibility* and *endorsement* that these are indeed important (awful) problems or needs. Social authorization is about *who* says, *how many* say, and *where* it is said. For any campaign, media exposure is vital, and key elements of the media such as television news give visibility and legitimacy. Organizations may influence this by using their celebrities and ambassadors to back the campaign (though this too can misfire). Mere reporting of need may not carry adequate authorization for a campaign, unless it has an implicit call to action. This is implicit in the macabre joke that a newspaper's reputedly most boring headline was 'small earthquake in Chile not many killed'.

The third facet is *operational capacity* – the logistics of converting sympathetic awareness into some form of support/donation. This is where DEC-type campaigns excel because they can mobilize call centres, banks and other parts of the donation process. Other opportunistic campaigns may not find this crucial step so easy. For planned campaigns securing operational capacity should be inherent and relatively easy to achieve given they have time to organize this programme.

The last facet is *the opportunity for social value*. That is the goal or creative definition of 'a solution' to the problem or need, but one that 'resonates with' (induces and draws on) the social authorization; and that is at the same time feasible, in terms of the practical logistics of prompting and handling enough donations.

The problems or needs

For opportunistic campaigns the occurrence of need is largely outside any organization's control, though the decision to follow any particular event requires sensitive analysis. When a major disaster strikes such as the series of natural disasters in 2005 – the tsunami in Asia, the hurricanes in the Caribbean or the earthquakes in various parts of the world – the public's generosity can be touched by the magnitude of the obvious need displayed by images and accounts of people's suffering. Donors who have never given before can be reached and brought into the pool of fundraising prospects.

Similarly, on a local level, the event must be of such significance that it has adequate coverage which triggers the 'social authorization'.

Wright (2002) states, however, that there are three required components before such coverage is likely to be effective. First, that the crisis is so large it will not fail to be reported. Second, that it must produce emotionally moving images, and lastly that the coverage itself must be so different or new that it causes the viewer to respond. Therefore one needs to be aware of what else is being reported in the news so that a campaign is not overshadowed by another, more prominent event.

For the planned campaign, especially at a local level, the need is known well beforehand but the same criteria apply. The organization must be sure it can effectively present its campaign as being designed to meet an appropriate need which will resonate with the public.

Social authorization

Opportunistic campaigns are hoping to buy into the existing social authorization, but planned campaigns have the more difficult task of seeking to generate such legitimacy.

The risks for these organizations, particularly if they go it alone, are huge because they are investing so much of their scarce resources in a fickle medium. Judging the right time to launch such an appeal requires estimates of the state of the public's current concern with an issue, the likelihood of the media maintaining their interest and the immanence of other similar media subjects. Launched too soon the public will not be sufficiently aware of the problem. Launched too late the media will move on to illustrate other problems in the world. For example, the starvation in Mali and Niger was hardly mentioned during the weeks surrounding hurricane Katrina's entry to the US in 2005.

Two other key risks that need addressing in the pursuit of social authorization are those associated with the use of celebrities and those associated with the message(s) conveyed. We live in a culture whose media appears devoted to featuring celebrities; and organizations take advantage of this by inviting celebrities to become patrons (or ambassadors) who will help carry their message to the public and their supporters.

Joseph Harker of the *Guardian*, in 'Imaging Famine' (2005), follows this trend seeing celebrities using their fame for good, but then goes on to reiterate some of the criticism this brings; such as the ability of those celebrities to return to their own security when a publicized visit to a disaster area is over. Though this smacks heavily of the politics of envy, he argues that the use of celebrity means we have only a shallow engagement with the real subject. Yet Lawrence Ways of Action Aid (2005) argues that, on the contrary, using celebrities gives agencies the chance to address serious issues in the media, and organizations are increasingly using celebrity patrons to effect entry to narrowly focused news agendas.

When celebrities like Bob Geldof and Bono become seriously involved with issues their conclusions are not, however, always the same as the agencies or campaigns they may be seen to represent. The fall-out between Geldof and Live8 in 2005 showed a different set of expectations and evaluation of outcomes from the Gleneagles G8 Summit Meeting, with Geldof feeling the Summit had delivered satisfactory results and the Live8 coalition believing it had fallen far short.

The role of television in particular has a strong role in commanding and shaping social authorization. Benthall (1993) argued that television tended to go further than reporting and actually defined some disasters. He cites the coverage of the 1985 Ethiopia relief efforts followed by the coverage of the Live Aid concert as giving both concern and televised relief. This is, perhaps, an example of the theory of social constructivism; which shows how our understanding of society (and events in society) is a social construct of our culture and the event's context (Derry, 1999; McMahon, 1997).

This shows one clear advantage of the opportunistic campaign as it can ride on existing television coverage (once that coverage has materialized), while the planned campaign has to buy such coverage which is often prohibitively expensive.

Operational capacity

This is not usually a problem for planned appeals unless they greatly underestimate the response they are likely to receive, but it is sometimes problematical for opportunistic campaigns and organizations may be overwhelmed by the response. How excess funds will be treated needs to be stated at the start of any campaign, as is usual in capital campaigns, otherwise an organization may need to offer to return excess funds. Médécins Sans Frontières was reported to have offered to return funds they could not spend on Tsunami relief as early as January 2005, though donors were apparently happy that their donations could be used on other relief work.

The ability to process thousands of offers of funds in a very short time can also fall short of donor expectations, as very large numbers of people are likely to phone or post donations, jamming lines and burning out volunteer teams. Getting the resourcing of the campaign wrong can lead to donor cynicism about the effectiveness of agencies. Telethons are particularly prone to such risk because they tend to be one-off phenomena and the scale of the public's reaction is hard to judge beforehand.

For planned campaigns by organizations dealing with problems no less important, but perhaps too slow-rolling to impact on the news in the same way, launching successful campaigns is much harder and success may depend on their ability to buy or acquire media space through which to reach the public. This, then, is the first risk: how confident can organizations be that their spending will have the effect they require? It is at this point that organizations may begin to hedge their bets. Yes, they would like the fundraised income to cover costs and produce a healthy profit with a defensible cost-to-income ratio; but if that is to be the sole judge of success then the organization will be open to accusations of wasting existing donors' money if the campaign fails to bring in sufficient income. It is safer to claim that the idea is also to change hearts and minds or merely to inform the public. The former is to some extent measurable, the latter less so, and may be said to be successfully accomplished by the act of placing the advertisements. Of course, some campaigns are purely information and lack a fundraising component, but we are not concerned with those at this time.

How organizations use the space they buy is the next dilemma. Given a limited space, and a public apparently gripped with severe attention deficit syndrome, there is a strong temptation to strip messages to their emotional core and use shocking images to create impact. A typical case may be the series of advertisements run by Barnardo's in the UK national press in 1999. These featured children with adult problems such as babies about to inject themselves with a syringe. 'In January 2000 the Advertising Standards Authority (ASA) rejected 28 complaints attacking these advertisements' (Baguley, 2000, p. 168). The ASA said that Barnardo's had tried to convey a 'serious and important message' in using this stark image. Their ruling in favour of Barnardo's was based on the difference between shocking people, by exposing the shocking problems with which many charities are dealing, and causing offence or undue distress.

Cohen (1995) looked at a series of shocking full-page advertisements taken by the fundraising department of Amnesty International UK with headlines such as 'Brazil has solved the problem of how to keep kids off the streets. Kill them' and 'When our children were dying you did nothing to help. Now God help your children'. Successful at the time in raising funds, recruiting new members and raising awareness of human rights abuses, they attracted criticism for their shock tactics – not least from the governments concerned. Cohen looked at the range of responses from denial that the acts had taken place, to interpreting them differently, to justifying them, to attacking the messenger by denying their right to comment.

He also considered Amnesty's claims that one could go too far in the use of images. Though there was no hard evidence, the organization felt that at a certain point people would be so nauseated they would turn away. This he calls the 'severed head rule' (Cohen, 1995, p. 137). Counter-intuitively, what evidence there was came from a few of the organization's own supporters who, as already convinced supporters, felt they didn't need to look at any gruesome information again.

Cohen goes on to compare debate about negative imagery (e.g. the use of pictures of starving children) in aid and development organizations' campaigns with the debate about shock in human rights campaigns. He sees that empower-ment and positive imagery are now the conservative beliefs of aid organizations; yet they retain the problem that development education, while worthwhile in its own right, does not effectively and efficiently raise the funds necessary to carry out their work.

He also points out that organizations rarely do more than a simplistic monitoring of either their own coverage in the media or that of their news releases or campaigns. This fails to provide them with the criteria they would require to run effective campaigns in a media often indifferent to their concerns. Neither do they tend to survey public reactions and grasp of the information given, which leaves them unable to adapt their campaigns in these respects, nor counter criticism based on perceived public reactions. Fundraisers may be advised to heed these latter points.

To minimize risks, strategy setting is essential, whether this is in the form of a feasibility study or a briefer action plan. Inherent in the strategy-setting process should be a risk analysis and the acceptance that if certain conditions are not met the campaign will not be launched. The diamond (Figure 7.1) indicates that the operational resources are a prerequisite as well as a clear knowledge that the social authorization exists or can be created (sometimes the latter is simply that the organization has pledges from enough key celebrities to ensure media coverage). Any strategy should contain:

- The financial and personnel resources required throughout the campaign.
- The campaign's financial targets and potential sources for that income.
- A schedule of specific campaign actions with a clear commitment stage(s).
- A complete budget with contingency.
- A risk assessment.
- An 'acceptance of funds' policy and fundraising guidelines.
- An exit strategy.

Once the organization has agreed the above, its operational capacity should be in place.

The opportunity for social value

Planned campaigns can establish this from the start; and indeed they are often merely building on existing work the organization is undertaking giving a solid foundation for the campaign, which can demonstrate capability with monitoring and evaluation of the results. It is not sufficient to pay lip-service to the latter as major funders are increasingly looking at the indices used to measure project evaluation, and even small campaigns should be clear they can prove their work is creating real social value.

The NSPCC's Full Stop campaign is one prominent example of a large-scale planned campaign, though criticism has been levelled at the campaign by critics who claimed it gave the impression that donations would stop child abuse. Furedi (2004) argues that the NSPCC does a disservice to children by suggesting their ordinary fears need to be brought to a professional; and that in stressing first 'stranger-danger' and now 'parent-danger' they are overstating the problem, and spending too much of their overall budget on campaigns that in themselves 'have no effect on the serious cases of violent abuse'. Were this criticism to be widespread it might weaken the considerable social authorization for this campaign.

Opportunistic campaigns may be in a similar position, and react when media interest touches an area within which they are capable of operating; but, unlike planned campaigns, when marginal opportunities arise they may need to critically, but rapidly, assess their ability to create the expected social value or risk their future public support.

Small organizations too are not immune from this dilemma. Can the organization really rebuild the village hall successfully? It may have lost its venue but is it up to the job of seeing through a rebuilding project? Is a new hall really needed? A local benefactor may have paid for some press advertising, but has the local church the capacity to organize the after-school club and will it really give the suggested social value?

Fundraising campaigns in perspective

The campaign diamond gives fundraisers a tool for assessing whether they have the necessary building blocks in place for a public campaign, but each facet of the diamond involves some risks; and, while some opportunities look too good to miss, a critical look at the four elements is essential to minimize the potential downside.

Organizations of all sizes can use the diamond as a framework, but opportunistic and planned campaigns will need to pay different levels of attention to each facet.

References

Baguley, J. (2000) *Successful Fundraising*, Bibliotek Books, Warwick.

Benthall, J. (1993) *Disasters, Relief and the Media*, I. B. Tauris, London.

Burman, E. (1994) 'Innocents abroad: Western fantasies of childhood and the iconography of emergencies', *Disasters* 18(3) 238–53.

Cohen, S. (1995) *Denial and Acknowledgement: The Impact of Information about Human Rights Violations*, University of Jerusalem.

Coulter, P. (1989) 'Pretty as a picture', *New Internationalist*, 194 (April).

Derry, S. J. (1999) A fish called peer learning: searching for common themes. In A. M. O'Donnell and A. King (eds).

Furedi, F. (2004) A danger to the nation's children, Spiked Life. www.spiked-online.com.

Gidley, R. (2005) Aid Workers Lament Rise of Development Pornography, Reuters. www.alertnet.org, 4 September.

Hagos, A. (2001) *Hardened Images: The Western Media and the Marginalisation of Africa*, Africa World Press.

Harker, J. (2005) Imaging Famine, www.imaging-famine.org.

McMahon, M. (1997) 'Social Constructivism and the World Wide Web – A Paradigm for Learning'. Paper presented at the ASCILITE conference. Perth, Australia, December.

Moeller, S. (1999) *Compassion Fatigue*, Routledge, London.

Moore, M. (1995) *Creating Public Value: Strategic Management in Government*, Harvard University Press, Cambridge, MA.

Trocaire (1986) 'Draft document on Images of Africa', Trocaire.

Van der Gaag, N. and Nash, C.(1987) *Images of Africa: UK Report*, FAO/FFHC, Mimeo.

Ways, L. (2005) Imaging Famine, www.imaging-famine.org.

Wright, T. (2002) *Collateral Coverage: Media Images of Afghan Refugees during the 2001 Crisis*, Oxford University Press, Oxford.

PART THREE

Environments for fundraising

INTRODUCTION

THE CHAPTERS IN THIS SECTION explore the four main contexts in which fundraising takes place – from individual donors, from companies, from foundations and from governments.

In Chapter 8, Pharoah focuses on the demographics of giving and examines what is and what is not known about current giving patterns. Significant changes are taking place in the age distribution of the population, in household patterns, in the ethnic and religious composition of society, and in the distribution of wealth. Together these undermine many of the assumptions fundraisers often make about who their donors are. Pharoah deftly exposes the limitations of the current datasets on giving, particularly their narrow scope which fails to explore motives and values behind giving behaviour, the lack of consistency between different survey techniques and the scant information they offer about donor profiles. She throws down a challenge to fundraisers to be more alert to social changes and to question their assumptions about the nature and meaning of giving – because tomorrow's donors are going to be more sophisticated and discerning about the causes to which they give.

Corporate sponsorship and partnerships are the focus of Chapter 9. Schaefer teases out the different forms these relationships may take to help fundraisers assess which approach will work for their organization. What distinguishes these relationships is that the corporate sponsor usually expects some form of tangible benefit for their involvement. Schaefer suggests that fundraisers need to consider very carefully both their own motives and those of potential sponsors for seeking such a relationship and the potential impact of this on other relationships that their organizations might be seeking to build. This is a difficult balance to strike, and there is as much danger of being overly delicate about which relationships to enter as of becoming sucked into being the pawn of rapacious corporations!

In Chapter 10, Leat explores the often secret world of independently endowed grant-making foundations. Taking control as her theme, she explores why foundations were established, their relationships with government, and how they protect their independence and privacy. When foundations are established they face a choice about how to achieve their mission. Leat argues that this cannot be achieved without their grantees. The foundations then face a classic trust-versus-control dilemma over the funds they disburse and how they will be used. Moreover, although foundations are less constrained than other funders – essentially being accountable only to the terms of their Trust deed – their Trustees and officers do not exist in a vacuum. They tend to move together in shoals, copying what is done in other leading or progressive foundations, and adopting practices that are 'in good currency' in the wider society. Leat explores the impact of these 'isomorphic tendencies' on foundations, how they cope with uncertainty, and how all this impacts on the demands they make of their grantees.

In Chapter 11, Wallace and Mordaunt examine the hard choices faced by organizations seeking funding from governmental and quasi-governmental funders. They base their discussion on a case study of international NGO funding, but directly comparable issues arise in all complex policy fields. If you want government money, especially sizeable amounts and not just a one-off, then you need to be in the thick of things; you need to be known, and to be able to read the codes and understand the agendas. Even more than other funders, interested parties swarm around governments – they always have and they always will – and the attention span of those disbursing money, however upright and capable, is inevitably quite short. Overloaded officials cannot afford to treat everyone the same – so reputations and relationships are used as filtering devices. There are more or less bound to be 'insiders' and 'outsiders'. If you want to be an insider, or close to the insiders, you will have to invest time, or hire people, in order to possess the expertise to join in the discussions and to build up relationships and credibility. There is usually a second price to pay – in the form of baroque bidding procedures and reporting requirements. In these circum-stances, disconnects and miscommunication can easily arise between those who negotiate the resources, the expectations of the beneficiaries, those who have to deliver the programme requirements, and the mission and values of the organization. The dilemma for organizations that have chosen to engage with government funders is how to find a path between two attractive pitfalls. In one case, the organization may seem to prosper but it does so by progressively diluting its mission and funda-mental values. In the other case, the organization can take comfort from upholding its principles, but its inflexibility in doing so means it steadily loses influence and becomes marginalized.

Chapter 8

Cathy Pharoah

GETTING TO GRIPS WITH THE DEMOGRAPHICS OF GIVING

Introduction

MANY PEOPLE COULD easily afford to give more to charity, and the better-off could double their giving, according to research carried out in the UK by CAF in 2004. So why don't they? Now worth £8.2 billion per annum, individual giving to charity has not increased its share of the national cake for at least fifteen years, hovering at around 1 per cent of Gross Domestic Product. While fundraisers can certainly be congratulated on maintaining the level of individual giving within a changing social context, why has giving to charity not been accorded greater priority among new consumer groups whose spending on luxury goods over the past couple of decades has seen enormous growth? It seems that charities may not be getting to grips with the new demographics of giving.

This chapter will explore some of the current issues in the demography of giving. It will review strengths and weaknesses in current approaches to the measurement of giving, and highlight some key gaps in current understanding of donors and giving behaviour. Finally, it will try to identify some of the most important demographic trends which will shape the fundraising context of the future, and how some fresh strategic thinking will be needed to get the most out of the opportunities and constraints in the new donor environment.

The changing demographic environment

Major changes have been taking place in the demographic environment for fundraising. Some of the most important features include:

- Changes in wealth distribution – until the mid-1990s the gap between rich and poor widened fairly sharply, and since then has seen little change. It is not only that the rich have got richer. The past couple of decades have also seen the rise of a class of 'super-rich' (*Sunday Times* Rich List, April 2004), and the new wealthy have a significantly different profile from previous generations of landed gentry. Philip Beresford reports that successful entrepreneurs now constitute three-quarters of the UK's 1000 wealthiest people.
- In contrast, the number of low-income small and single-person households has been increasing due to family fragmentation and increasing longevity. Eighty per cent of the growth in the number of households over the next decade or so will be due to the increasing numbers of single-person households.
- Equally importantly, the UK population is ageing. Since 1991 the proportion of the population aged between 16 and 24 declined by 3 per cent and the over-65s increased by almost the same amount.
- Many more young people are entering higher education, and the activity rate of working-age women grew from 56 per cent in 1971 to 72 per cent from 1998 onwards.

How much attention are charities paying to the implications of these changing demographic structures for the shape and character of the donor market?

Heads in the sand

It is certainly not difficult to find evidence of some fundraising heads in the sand, and of the continuing use of old stereotypes about who gives what to whom and why. For example, the Christmas 2005 edition of *The Lady*, a magazine which targets a niche market of genteel, relatively affluent middle-class women/carers, carries a batch of fundraising advertisements reflecting a range of stereotypes about what such a market might support. There are appeals for Second World War veterans, elderly people in difficulties, the blind, children with cancer, religious causes, and – representing more than half of all the charity advertisements – eight animal rescue charities. This set of advertisements does justice to the popular 'Dorothy donor' stereotype (elderly, sentimental, traditional), but ignores the evidence from the magazine itself of an appeal to a much more sophisticated market group, covering issues such as women at work, international travel, the arts, the media, literature, financial issues and fashion.

It is arguable that such simple – not to mention patronizing – stereotypes are unlikely to take giving very far in the future. The population may be ageing, but it will not be ageing in the same way. Different life careers and experiences are shaping a different cohort of elderly. But the use of stereotypes is not the only problem in fundraising strategies for middle-aged/elderly women donors. Many charities focus generic fundraising on older middle-class women: they get much less comparative market advantage from this than they would from identifying and targeting the distinct types of older middle-class women who constitute their own particular supporters. Much fundraising strategy does not genuinely constitute market 'targeting' but simply repeats what has worked more or less well in the past, suggesting fairly low expectations. This is likely to be one explanation for why fundraising has been unable to raise the bar over the past couple of decades.

One of the problems is that the data currently available on giving behaviour have some serious limitations, and this is explored in the next part of this chapter.

Measuring giving in the UK – a critique

Apart from charities' own donor databases, the main source of information on giving in the UK today is a number of quantitative surveys of giving, mainly carried out on relatively small budgets by the voluntary sector infrastructure bodies. This means that information on giving in the UK is inevitably fragile when compared with some of the very large datasets collected by government on other aspects of our economy and welfare systems. Estimates of giving are based on relatively small samples of the general population, except where claims for personal charitable tax reliefs are made to HM Revenue and Customs. So, for example, while tax data are available for around 30 million people, giving information is only available for samples of around 5000.

A second major issue is that the information is based purely on individual self-reporting and recall of giving – no records have to be maintained or are available to check the validity of personal recall. And, as is discussed below, recall of charitable giving is particularly subjective.

Third, it is important to understand that the main giving surveys are fairly narrow in their scope, aimed principally at measuring the amount of money given by individuals to specific charitable causes over a certain period. The surveys do not attempt to explore giving behaviour more broadly, to get to grips with changing demographics and donor characteristics, or elicit donors' attitudes, values, lifestyles and giving patterns. This is discussed further later in the chapter.

Fourth, asking people about their giving to charity is very popular, but the many surveys which are undertaken by the large research companies often yield conflicting results. None the less, the findings are routinely and uncritically quoted by journalists, fundraisers and policy-makers alike. The knowledge base for fundraising would take a significant step forward if results of surveys were used in a more questioning way. Good starting points for getting a better understanding of why giving surveys produce such varied results are an article on definitions and meanings of giving by Peter Halfpenny in 2004 and the brief review of giving surveys in the new CAF/NCVO report, *UK Giving* (Pharoah *et al.*, 2004/05).

Sources of variation in survey results

Most of the variation in the results of different giving surveys is due to differences in the methodologies used. While most surveys are conducted through face-to-face or telephone interviews, or postal questionnaires, with a nationally representative sample of individuals, there are huge differences in the way that questions are asked, leading to very different assessments by individuals of their giving behaviour. (Note that the Expenditure and Food Survey [EFS] carried out by the Office of National Statistics [ONS] is exceptional in using two-week diary information.) Problem areas are briefly outlined below:

- *Definitions of what is a charity* – surveys vary as to whether respondents should include gifts to registered charities only, or those to, for example, school fetes, scouts and guides, local scanner appeals, church collections, giving to beggars.
- *Time periods of giving* – different surveys ask respondents to report their giving over the past week, the past fortnight, the past few months, the past year, or the past year or two, producing hugely different results: for example, surveys which ask about giving over the previous year or two have found 94 per cent population participation rates in giving, compared with the new CAF/NCVO survey which found 57 per cent giving over the previous month.
- *Timing of survey* – surveys of giving at Christmas or towards the end of the financial year or after a major disaster appeal tend to produce higher reported levels of giving than those carried out in January or August (when people are on holiday).
- *Methods of giving* – surveys prompt for different methods of giving and vary in the amount of detail on methods (e.g. do they include face-to-face fundraising as a separate method or simply include it within street collections; do they include giving to charity shops or to beggars?): these approaches result in different levels of recall: some surveys, notably the EFS, do not include any charitable purchases in their estimates of giving, while the CAF/NCVO surveys include all purchase giving which represents x per cent of their final estimate of giving.
- *Causes to which people give* – there is very little standardization in the way in which surveys present causes to which people could give: for example, disaster appeals may or may not be included in 'international giving', hospitals and hospices may or may not be included in a broad 'health' topic, giving to homeless people on the streets may or may not be included as giving to charity: if causes are grouped or classified differently, they will get different results.
- *Concepts of the donor* – most surveys ask about level of giving by individuals, but some surveys such as the EFS ask about giving by the household: the age bands included may also vary by survey.

Many other factors influence the responses people give to surveys about their giving, of which one of the most important is 'social desirability bias' – the tendency to want to appear charitable and overstate the amount or frequency of giving: a good example of this, which CAF/NCVO detect in their new survey of giving in February 2005 and then adjust for, was the tendency of people, when asked about their giving to the Tsunami appeal, to state what they gave overall and not simply what they had given in the previous month.

Many surveys leave respondents to make subjective decisions on what to include. This is likely to have particular effects on the results derived for different demographic groups. For example, much of the charitable giving of young mothers is likely to be done at local schools, hospitals, playgroups and youth groups. Unless directed to include such giving in their answers, they may well leave it out, unaware that such organizations may be charities, and this would result in their reported charitable giving looking very low. It should be clear from the above why it is difficult to get a simple agreed set of figures on giving.

Tracking trends in giving

One of the most important purposes of repeated annual giving surveys is to enable the tracking of trends in giving over time. The great value of using data from the CAF/NCVO annual surveys until 2003 and the ONS EFS is that they have been carried out in consistent ways over time: it is therefore possible to compare results from one year with those of another, because any change in results cannot arise simply from changes of approach. These longitudinal surveys represent the best source of information on trends, and, because they have relatively large sample sizes, the data are reliable. The new CAF/NCVO survey for 2004/05 represents a new departure and the beginning of a new series whose results are not continuous with previous surveys.

A final health warning about the validity of estimates derived from surveys – because of small samples, the true results generally lie within a range, allowing for sample error and variation. What might seem like a big difference between the results of one year and the next may not be statistically significant, and too much importance should not be attached to an apparently new trend until a series of results has been obtained.

Sources of information on the demography of giving

As noted above, surveys of giving in the UK are primarily economic. While this means that there is a reasonably detailed picture of the amounts given, the methods used and the causes supported, demographic information captured on donors is generally broad-brush and is limited to demographic variables including age, gender, socio-economic status and geographical location of donors.

Results on the demographic profile of donors are much more consistent between the various surveys than the assessments of participation in giving and amounts donated. This is undoubtedly because reporting of basic demographic information is much less subject to error than other topics. Any variations in results are mainly likely to be due to differences in the nature of the survey samples and response rates.

However, with the exception of the EFS, these surveys usually provide little information on relevant areas, such as household and family arrangements, education or general patterns of consumption. None of the regular surveys include nature of employment, attitudes and values, lifestyle (e.g. memberships) or brand preferences. Charities generally derive information on donor lifestyle choices from matching their own donor databases against some of the large professional consumer databases compiled by companies such as Experian. Where a donor appears on one of these consumer databases a rich data profile can be yielded. The limitation is the proportion of matches out of the total donor database which can be made: sometimes, as a proxy, matches are made on the basis of people who 'look like' each other on a range of basic characteristics. Such donor profiling may be used to guide targeting, but it does not provide a fully comprehensive or accurate picture of a charity's donors. There are likely to be important gaps, particularly where donors' consumption patterns are low, for example, with younger and older donors.

Donor profiles

Donor profiles and typologies provide a creative way of thinking about donor characteristics and are often used to help develop strategy. Because of the relatively sketchy nature of the data available they rarely go beyond the level of the stereotype. In spite of this, donor types seem rapidly to acquire a life of their own. For example, the concept of the 'high net worth' donor has been around for at least five years or so. It is variously defined, but one of the popular images is of the young boho City worker who makes a vast fortune early in life, tires of materialism and turns to charity to find meaning and transfer his or her entrepreneurial skills to others who are less fortunate. This donor is reputedly demanding in terms of information, desire to get engaged in charity projects, and mainly interested in promising social enterprise. Yet it would be difficult to name more than a tiny handful of major donors such as Jeff Skoll, who established eBay and founded the Skoll Foundation, who fit this profile. Do they really exist? Are they an important or targetable group?

Such donor profiles can quickly become a substitute for well-founded donor understanding and should only be used as a starting point. When MORI presented an interesting survey-research-based typology compiled from how much people give, the way they give and their motivation ('Mr and Mrs Mainstream', 'committed carers', 'TV watchers', 'feel-good Freddies') their assumption was that fundraisers would go out and find which of these features characterized their own donors.

Demographics of giving

In spite of the limitations to the available demographic data on donors, however, all the evidence suggests that giving has a very marked demographic pattern, and that the success of any fundraising strategy is likely to depend on taking demographics into account. It also means that fundraising is highly vulnerable to demographic change, and needs to anticipate both declining and growing market segments. In the following sections some of the main findings of the surveys related to the demographics are highlighted.

Gender

Almost all surveys show that gender is an extremely important demographic indicator for giving.

- Across the population as a whole, women are somewhat more likely to give than men. *UK Giving* (Pharoah *et al.*, 2004/05) showed 62 per cent of the female population giving to charity per month, compared with 52 per cent of the male population.
- Survey evidence also suggests, however, that male donors give more than female donors. *UK Giving* (Pharoah *et al.*, 2004/05) showed average giving of £28 per month for men, compared with £23 for women.
- CAF's internal donor surveys also showed that, related to the fact that they make bigger gifts, men were more likely to use tax-efficient methods for giving.
- Women are twice as likely as men to support charity through purchasing charitable goods (Pharoah *et al.*, 2004/05).
- Women dominate giving to almost all causes with the exception of the arts, and are much more likely to give goods to a charity shop or jumble sale; both men and women give equally to homeless people on the street (Pharoah *et al.*, 2004/05).
- The presence of children is significant: using EFS data in 1997 the IFS noted that households with children were 3 per cent more likely to give to charity.

Age

Age is also a very important demographic indicator for giving. Most surveys have found highest proportions of givers among the middle-aged and older age groups, with highest participation and level of giving when people are aged between 55 and 64, at their earning peak but pre-retirement.

- Donors in the 55 to 64 age group give £32 per month, compared with a donor average of £25.
- Causes supported vary by age; for example, 25–34-year-olds are the most likely to give to homeless charities, and 65–74-year-olds the most likely to give to hospitals, hospices and religious causes. Higher proportions of young people give money to homeless people on the streets than in other age groups.

Socio-economic status

Of all the factors influencing the amounts given to charity, income has the strongest effect. The IFS found that a 1 per cent increase in total expenditure caused a 1.1 per cent rise in the level of donations.

Socio-economic status is a proxy for level of education, income and type of home ownership. The CAF/NCVO *UK Giving* 2004/05 report found that:

- Seventy-one per cent of the highest donors are drawn from managerial and professional occupations.
- Those in managerial and professional occupations are the most likely to give, with two-thirds of the people in this group giving to charity in a month. They were more likely to give to all causes than other economic groups except animal welfare. Two-thirds of the Tsunami donors came from these groups.
- The highest-level donors are more likely to be male, older and of a higher socio-economic group than other donors.

CAF's internal analysis of the EFS also shows that the top 10 per cent of households are much more likely to give to charity than the bottom 10 per cent, although as a proportion of their income the amount given by the top 10 per cent is considerably less than that of the bottom 10 per cent (Banks and Tanner, 1997). This finding is interesting in the light of CAF's research showing that the higher social groups can afford to give more, and reasons why richer people are less generous need to be explored.

Registering the demographic shifts

One of the biggest demographic shifts is the changing age structure of the population. Table 8.1 shows the amount of money currently given each month by each age group, taking into account the population, proportion of donors and average gift within each age group.

The table shows that the highest yield overall is the 35–44 age group, followed by the 55–64 age group. The pre-eminence of the 35–44 age group is not typical of giving surveys, and is probably a one-off result, generated by the higher giving of younger age groups to the Tsunami appeal.

These results show that broadly between the ages of 35 and 64 there are the highest average gifts and the highest pools of donors: of these three groups, the lower average gift size among the 35–44-year-olds is compensated for by the larger donor pool.

What do these patterns mean for giving in relation to demographic trends over the next few decades? As is well known, the population is ageing with numbers in the older age groups growing faster than those in the younger age groups. This will continue for at least the next half of the century, since the proportion of the population aged 65 and over will increase as the large numbers of people born after the Second World War and during the 1960s baby boom become older. Since it is these older age groups which constitute the most valuable donor pool, the changing demographics could offer charities enormous fundraising opportunities.

But charities must gear up to the values, attitudes and outlook of this generation. They will not be the same as the older people who lived through the war, were frugal and valued jobs and marriages for life. They will not accept charities as a given good, having grown up in an all-providing welfare state.

Table 8.1 Amount given each month by each age group

Age	Persons 000s	Males	Females	% Donors	Number 000s	Aver-age gift	£ Amount/ month 000s	%
16–24	6,941	3,533	3,408	50	3,470	11	39,285	6
25–34	7,937	3,954	3,983	58	4,604	23	104,868	16
35–44	9,192	4,553	4,640	63	5,791	25	141,999	21
45–54	7,639	3,780	3,859	58	4,431	27	117,856	18
55–64	6,899	3,391	3,509	59	4,071	32	128,956	19
65–74	5,033	2,374	2,659	58	2,919	31	89,623	13
75+	4,138	1,618	2,520	48	1,986	23	46,098	7
Total	47,780	23,203	24,577	57	27,272	171	668,686	100

Sources: UK Giving 2004/05, CAF/NCVO, 2005: www.statistics.gov.uk

Focusing on the middle classes will mean looking at a generation where high proportions of women have had jobs and a significant degree of equality, where people are well travelled and well educated, have high expectations of quality of life, are computer-literate and take access to information for granted. This is a demanding consumer group who will not hesitate to throw 'junk mail' in the litter bin. They will not turn into 'Dorothy donors'. Charities must do more research to find out exactly what will appeal to this cohort, who will constitute a 'generational bonus' that will not last for ever.

The working-age population, meanwhile, will fall in size as the baby boomers move into retirement and are replaced by the relatively smaller generations of people who have been born since the mid-1970s. It is this factor which partly underlies the pensions crisis, the financial time bomb lying ahead of the post-baby-boom generation. Baby boomers are already sweating their assets to help their children buy education and houses. There will be competition for their resources.

But charities will also need to be prepared for the post-baby boomers, the current 25–34-year-olds and potentially the next major generation of donors. The 35–44-year-olds will straddle the two groups of baby boomers and post-baby boomers. Characteristics of this generation are high Internet and mobile phone access and literacy, active social life, high demand for entertainment through electronic media, customized products, interest in global issues, increasing levels of ethical consumption, and possibly less consumer power and less interest in material goods than their parents. This generation will also be highly demanding, and with less money to spend will choose where it goes very carefully, giving generously where they believe it is important, as, for example, with the Tsunami.

There are many other general changes in demography and patterns of consumption, work, leisure and communications which could be factored into any fundraising strategy. This chapter does not have the space to deal in detail with all of them, but has tried to indicate some of the most significant and long-term demographic trends in relation to thinking about donor pools. A final trend which it is very important to mention is the changing structure of the ethnic composition of the population. Eight per cent of the UK population is from a minority ethnic group: 4.6 million people. More than half of these people are Indian or Pakistani. This proportion will grow partly because the age structure of the minority ethnic population is younger than that of the indigenous population, and partly through the new economic migrants from Central and Eastern Europe. Because of the tremendous traditions of the value of voluntarism in all of the world's great faiths, the minority ethnic populations are a hugely important pool of donors. Yet we are a long way from having an ethnic minority component to all of our fundraising strategies, and this needs to be addressed. It will be vital to respect the different cultural contexts for giving in new strategies for fundraising.

Beyond cash – the cultures and meanings of giving

The gap in our knowledge about the lifestyle choices and consumption patterns of the various donor groups has been noted above, but there is another equally important gap in our understanding of donor behaviour. As Peter Halfpenny has explored in detail, there is little understanding of the contexts of meaning within which people give, or of what individual charitable acts and giving decisions mean to people. The importance of the donor's personal perceptions is interestingly captured by Douglas White (1995):

> [This] inexplicable willingness on the part of people to be charitable is essential to the process of raising money. The subjective, internal and highly personal feelings donors have for their preferred causes, untraceable to any tangible activity or effort, are important elements in the decision-making processes.

There are many precedents for interpreting what giving might mean to people. Apart from the long history and traditions of voluntarism within faith-based contexts, many of the major academic disciplines have offered contrasting perspectives. Economists, for example, tend to see altruism as aberrant economic behaviour which can only be explained by a self-regarding element such as that giving to homeless people on the street removes the personal discomfort experienced when coming across such need, or giving to cancer research may benefit oneself or family one day as cancer is one of our major killers. Sociologists emphasize the role of giving in gaining an individual a place in social networks, and social anthropologists have emphasized the politics of power and reciprocity in giving. Within spiritual contexts the ethical and altruistic dimensions of giving are emphasized.

These differing explanations are likely to vary in their relevance to different demographic groups. For example, a wealthy retired businessman is more likely to look to gain access to a desired social network through a large gift to a major national institution than a young student who may look towards activism in a particular cause as a way of meeting like-minded peers. While it is not within the remit of this chapter to explore these models in detail, it is important to note that very little fundraising research and strategy has tended to address the importance of context. Such understanding, for example, could facilitate innovative experiential fundraising, which aims to reach out to people in a range of life situations. Face-to-face fundraising on the street has shown enough success to encourage charities to experiment with more sensitive and possibly more effective personal approaches in other settings: some charities are already beginning to experiment with this, inviting donors to participate in much more interactive ways in experiencing their work.

International context

Even the briefest of glances at giving within different international contexts reveals just how much cultural variation exists in understandings of what giving means. One of the biggest differences to note is that in many countries, including in Central and Eastern Europe, much charitable giving consists of gifts to extended families. If such gifts are excluded from the measurement of charitable donations, levels seem to compare very poorly with giving in the US and Western Europe. In developing countries, with a more informal charitable infrastructure, charitable giving often consists of direct gifts of money, food and clothing to the less well-off. A good example of this occurred in the recent Pakistani earthquake where communities and individuals outside the disaster zone packed their cars with goods and drove them personally to those in need. Such giving is generally excluded from mainstream charitable giving surveys in the US and Western Europe. The Johns Hopkins Comparative International Non-profit formally excluded giving to religious causes from its mainstream definition of giving, which led to significant undercounting of charitable giving in countries such as Italy. Gifts in kind, such as to charity shops, constitute a major feature of giving in the UK, but are barely significant in countries such as France.

One indicator of varying perspectives on what is charitable is the different tax treatments of gifts in different countries. Few countries in the world have as liberal a system of tax reliefs on charitable donations as the UK: in other regimes restrictions are placed on either the amounts which may be given tax-free, or the types of organization and causes which can legitimately attract tax reliefs. These contrasts of fiscal regime reflect beliefs about the true nature of charity, which arise specifically from different historical and cultural backgrounds. For example, many countries exclude overseas gifts from tax reliefs, and indeed payroll-giving tax breaks in the UK are not available on gifts to overseas charities.

The above examples are intended to illustrate that a narrow focus on measuring the monetary value of a gift excludes enormously important information on perceptions of and commitment to charitable giving. This means that fundraisers often have little information on the most fruitful approaches to further engagement from donors. One of the most powerful criticisms of recent appeals for disaster relief is that the opportunity to educate and engage donors in the underlying causes of global problems has been consistently missed. Long-term sustained support for issues is not achieved.

Bringing the meaning and the value of giving together

Understanding how to bring the symbolic value, or meaning, of gifts and their monetary value together is often seen as the 'Holy Grail' of the 'fundraising quest for knowledge'. There has been very little exploration of how 'internal' values about the gift relate to its external value, if at all. A gift may bear little financial value but have immense value in relation to an individual's beliefs, or alternatively high monetary value but distributed without the donor's involvement. In other words, the actual financial value of a gift may reveal little about a donor. Often, however, this is all the donor information available to a fundraising strategy. CAF's study of the charitable involvement of business leaders revealed some complex and contrasting relationships between belief and amounts donated, as the following quotations illustrate:

> 'I don't mix time and money [in giving]. It muddies the waters. It's a purist view, but, if I'm getting seriously involved in something, I don't give money – conversely, I do give money to things that I really approve of but am not going to take so seriously in terms of my time. No, I don't feel guilty about not giving money to those I give time to. I think, by being chairman of the charity, I'm giving them a huge amount, which has a monetary value and which my money won't necessarily give them.'

> 'I have the puritan ethic deep in my soul. I was brought up in middle-class, semi-impoverished gentility and taught to believe in public service, and in giving a substantial amount of one's income to others. As a result, ever since I was knee-high to a grasshopper I have always done a lot of pro bono work and given a substantial part of what I earn away.'

Historically we have not always been coy about the relationship between internal and external commitment. A good example is the practice of mandatory tithing within certain faiths: spiritual health and the giving of 10 per cent of one's income are intimately linked. Only a small proportion of today's givers are tithers, although some think it is a practice that is overdue for revival! And there are some modern and secular equivalents which involve fixed amounts of giving. For example, membership of certain charitable organizations has a set fee, and access to fundraising events often involves fixed entry fees or ticket prices. Desirable donation amounts are often suggested to donors. The call of the Per Cent club for companies to donate a minimum standard 1 per cent of their income to charitable causes is another example. Generally, however, donors are rarely formally asked to prove their commitment to a cause – either to themselves or to others – by donating a certain amount.

In conclusion, this chapter has outlined the many ways in which our understanding of the demographics of giving has some serious gaps which are limiting the development of more effective forward-looking fundraising strategy. Fundraisers need to:

- look more critically at how giving is measured
- take much more detailed account of the changing demographic and lifestyle characteristics of donors
- develop a more holistic understanding of what giving, and giving to particular causes, means to donors
- create contexts for giving within which they can legitimately ask for higher and more regular gifts.

Tomorrow's fundraising environment is likely to consist of donors who are more demanding, discriminating, informed and ethical consumers, and of charities seeking committed and sustained support. Potentially it is an excellent match, but it will only be realized if fundraisers begin to pay serious attention to the new demography of giving.

References

Banks, J. and Tanner, S. (1997) *The State of Donation: Household Gifts to Charity, 1974–96*, The Institute for Fiscal Studies, London.

Halfpenny, P. (2004) 'All things to all men', *Professional Fundraising*, March.

Pharoah, C., Walker, C., Wilding, K. and Wainwright, S. (2005) *UK Giving 2004/05*, CAF/NCVO, London.

White, D. E. (1995) *The Art of Planned Giving: Understanding Donors and the Culture of Giving*, John Wiley & Sons, USA.

Chapter 9

Anja Schaefer

CORPORATE SPONSORSHIP AND PARTNERSHIPS

Introduction

CORPORATE SPONSORSHIP and partnerships are becoming an increasingly important source of funding for charities, as they receive fewer funds from traditional individual and corporate giving and from government sources. Charities also often feel that they can better influence corporate behaviour if they work in partnership with industry, rather than in opposition to it.

While these are good and important reasons for charities to pursue corporate sponsorship and partnership arrangements there are also dangers associated with such a course of action. If arrangements do not work, either because inappropriate partners have been chosen or because the partnership has not been well managed on either or both sides, considerable damage to a charity's reputation may be sustained. In order to choose the right partners, use sponsorship and partnership arrangements to best advantage and avoid the pitfalls associated with them, fundraisers need a good understanding of the reasons why corporations enter such arrangements.

This chapter addresses the following questions:

- What are corporate sponsorships and partnerships?
- Why do charities seek corporate sponsors and partners?
- Why do corporations sponsor and partner charitable organizations and activities?
- What are the potential pitfalls of such arrangements?
- How should sponsorship or partnership arrangements be designed to avoid pitfalls?

What are corporate sponsorships and partnerships?

There are a number of different forms of corporate sponsorship and partnerships. Understanding their characteristics and the distinctions between them is a key aspect of deciding what type of arrangement with what kind of partner is likely to prove successful for a charity, and what kind of arrangements harbour most dangers and are best avoided.

Corporate involvement with charitable organisations and activities has developed considerably from the charitable donations which were once its mainstay. Various types of corporate sponsorship and partnership arrangements differ from traditional charitable donations mainly in that the company expects some kind of concrete and often tangible benefit in return. The nature of this expected benefit is often a crucial element in a charity's decision whether an arrangement with a particular corporate partner is advantageous or not. The various types of arrangements include:

- direct sponsorship of particular charitable events or activities;
- cause-related marketing (Varadarajan and Menon 1988);
- advocacy advertising (Haley 1996);
- longer-ranging alliances or partnerships with charitable organizations (Andreasen 1996).

Direct sponsorship of a charitable activity or event is perhaps the most traditional and familiar of these. Typical causes and institutions that benefit from this kind of direct sponsorship include sports, the arts and, increasingly, schools, but they may include any type of charitable concern. The corporation funds or partly funds a particular event, activity or aspect of the charity. In return the donor will get benefits such as increased recognition of their company name or product, the chance to distribute their product at the event or the placement of their corporate logos on various collateral materials (Talisman 2000).

Cause-related marketing campaigns link contribution to charity to product sales (Andreasen 1996; Varadarajan and Menon 1988). High-profile examples in the UK include Tesco's Computers for Schools and Walkers' Books for Schools but there are many more examples, including online versions such as Microsoft's link to the NSPCC (Staples 2004). In these kinds of arrangements consumers' purchases come first and then, as a result, the company makes a donation to the cause. For example, an individual buys a particular brand of coffee and a small percentage of the amount paid goes to a fund that will help save the rainforests of the world (Cornwell and Coote 2005). Cause-related marketing communications typically feature the product prominently and are aimed at encouraging purchase of the brand, just as regular advertisements do (Menon and Kahn 2003). On the one hand, cause-related marketing has been criticised for actually giving only a very small percentage of the extra revenue raised to the charitable cause. On the other hand, it can raise quite significant sums in total, without anybody making any direct donations.

Advocacy advertising or corporate societal marketing is defined as a marketing initiative with at least one non-economic social objective (Drumwright and Murphy

2001). Here the corporation promotes a social cause, such as responsible drinking or healthy eating, through its own marketing communications (Skyman *et al.* 2004). To illustrate the difference with cause-related marketing, a cause-related marketing message sponsored by Johnson & Johnson's baby shampoo might feature the product and promise a small donation to the World Wildlife Fund for every purchase. In contrast, an advocacy advertisement message might focus on the dangers of extinction of certain wildlife species and try to persuade consumers to support the World Wildlife Fund's efforts to save endangered species. Advocacy advertising focuses chiefly on the philanthropic message and is generally independent from direct purchasing of the sponsor's product (Menon and Kahn 2003). On the positive side, corporations generally have much larger advertising budgets than charities and advocacy advertising therefore offers the possibility of reaching a much wider audience. On the negative side, however, the audience may mistrust the motives of the corporation in promoting a philanthropic message and seek a hidden agenda behind advocacy advertising, which may significantly reduce its effectiveness.

Longer-term alliances or partnerships between corporations and charities reflect the trend of increasing business interest in integrated, complex, in-depth relationships embracing wider social issues rather than just pure fundraising relationships. Again, this kind of arrangement is different from traditional corporate giving and normally implies some form of tangible return for the corporate partner. For instance, a retailer locating a business in a regeneration neighbourhood may have a vested interest in contributing to local education initiatives to improve the availability of employable labour. A financial services company may identify with organizations developing financial literacy and debt management. A utility company may work with key charities to reduce fuel poverty (Staples 2004). A partnership between corporate- and charitable-sector organizations can take all the various forms that have been discussed for sponsorship and may be looked at as essentially a long-term version of such sponsorship activities. In addition to the corporate receiving some kind of public relations or marketing benefit from its involvement with the charity, the charity may sometimes also perform a particular service for the corporation. For example, some water companies in the UK have made partnership arrangements with local wildlife trusts to help manage the often extensive landholdings of these companies in the interest of biodiversity and conservation.

Partnership arrangements may include multiple corporate and NGO members. For example, the Energy and Biodiversity Initiative, convened by the Centre for Environmental Leadership in Business (CELB), has four corporate and five NGO members and 'brings together leading energy companies and conservation organizations to develop and promote a framework of best practices for integrating biodiversity conservation into upstream oil and gas development' (CELB 2005).

Tri-sector partnerships include government as well as corporate and NGO partners. Hamann (2003) describes a tri-sector partnership linking a mining company, the government, local communities, external NGOs and aid organizations in a development programme for self-employed, small-scale miners and a community health partnership. An existing building was donated by the government and upgraded with the company's support and voluntary labour from the communities, while an international NGO was involved to supply medical equipment and training. The outcomes include a community health centre, as well as improved communication channels between local communities and government departments, and enhanced conflict resolution and organization skills among local community representatives.

Partnership arrangements have a number of advantages. They can harness complementary capabilities and resources of different partners (such as the financial and management capacities of corporate partners and the social credibility as well as particular types of knowledge and skills possessed by NGO partners). As they are longer-term they allow dealing with larger issues rather than one-off agreements and can provide greater security of funding for the NGO. They also offer opportunities for the charity to advise and influence the business policy of the corporate partner. Disadvantages include the greater extent to which the charitable partner's reputation may be at stake, greater difficulty of managing a complex, long-term partnership, particularly with multiple partners involved, and the danger that policy and staff may change in either partner's organization, thus jeopardizing a long-term arrangement.

Why do charities seek corporate sponsors and partners?

In order to choose the right kind of corporate partners and manage the relationship well, fundraisers should be aware of their own motivations for seeking sponsorship or corporate partnerships. Motivations may fall into two broad categories: they may be broadly financial, focusing on the income to be gained, or they may be broadly ideational, focusing more on potential influence over corporate policy and behaviour. Depending on the motivation, different partners may be chosen, and the agreement may be managed in different ways.

In recent years many charities have seen their income from government and private donations fall. They therefore often find that they must redouble their efforts to gain funding from the corporate sector and are increasingly encouraged to do so by government. This applies to all kinds of charitable organizations, including sporting organizations (Berett and Slack 2001), arts organizations (Reiss 2000), and charities concerned with a variety of other social issues.

The main reason for charities to seek corporate sponsorship and partnerships is often to gain much-needed funds. However, charities may also receive other benefits from corporate sponsors or partners, such as support in kind, managerial or secretarial time, use of premises, commercial expertise or help with publicity.

Partnerships with business offer the additional benefit that NGOs may be able to influence the behaviour of the corporate partner(s) in a way which is compatible with their own objectives. This chance to influence corporate behaviour may be as important to the NGO partner as any financial benefit or even more so. It is argued that NGOs in partnership with business (and sometimes government) can achieve more social change than either can achieve on their own. In these cases, corporate 'logistical and engineering capacities and financial and human resources can . . . be complemented by the local knowledge and social capital of . . . NGOs, as well as the broader development framework provided by the government' (Hamann and Acutt 2003: 261).

Why do corporations sponsor and partner charitable organizations and activities?

By sponsoring or partnering charitable organizations, corporations generally expect some form of benefit for themselves. Often such activities are best regarded as part of a company's marketing activities. By aligning itself with a 'good cause' in an open and tangible way, the company expects to achieve greater awareness of itself and its products, an improved corporate image and ultimately increased sales. In this respect a distinction may be made between sponsorship in particular, and traditional corporate philanthropic donations. Where the former is often best regarded as a form of marketing, the latter are perhaps more appropriately seen as a form of corporate social responsibility not immediately expected to relate to sales figures. Rather, companies are more likely to see them as investments in the long-term prosperity of the company by fostering a healthy, supportive environment in which they can prosper and maintaining stakeholder support and their 'licence to operate', i.e. the basic goodwill of society which allows corporations to continue to conduct their business. Thus, traditional charitable giving typically comes out of a company public relations or corporate social responsibility budget, whereas sponsorship activities are more commonly funded from the marketing budget and controlled by the marketing department.

In any kind of engagement of corporations with charitable causes, there is likely to be a balance between self-interest and philanthropic motivations involved. Cannon (1994) distinguishes between four types of corporate engagement with social issues, depending on how high or low self-interest and motivation are. This is shown in Figure 9.1.

It may be possible for charities to work with companies espousing any of the stances in the matrix, so long as both sides are clear about their level of commitment and what they expect from the partnership. A company espousing social responsibility may be able to offer an NGO much in terms of both funding and influence, but it will expect a significant return for this. A company espousing enlightened self-interest may still be a worthwhile sponsor so long as its interests and the interests of the charity are closely aligned. A company espousing pure philanthropy may be a source of useful funding with few strings attached, but may also offer little opportunity for influencing company policy. Finally, cause-related marketing is perhaps best seen as strictly a business arrangement, which may, again, provide valuable funding but little opportunity for influence.

Looking in more detail at the motivations of companies in different types of sponsorship and partnership arrangement, there are a number of reasons why companies may want to rely on sponsorship as an important aspect of their marketing communication efforts (Meenaghan 1983):

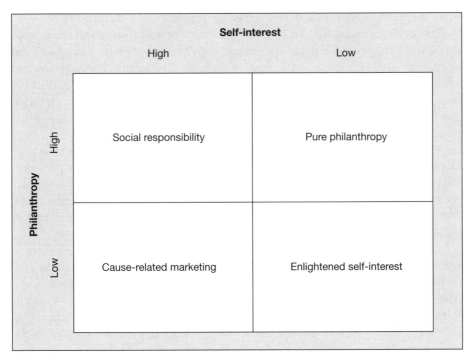

Figure 9.1 The Enlightenment Matrix

Source: Cannon (1994: 40).

1   Government policy: banning of cigarette advertising in the UK in 1965 has led the tobacco industry to pursue a number of different sponsoring arrangements. On the one hand, its sponsorship of FOREST, the campaign group for smokers' rights, may be seen as an attempt to influence public debate in a way that is more positive for the industry. On the other hand, its sponsoring of sporting events, such as Formula 1 racing, is more straight-forwardly a substitute for other forms of advertising.

2   Rising costs of commercial advertising: sponsorship can sometimes achieve the same or better media exposure than advertising at less cost to the company.

3   Sponsorship is a more suitable medium for developing a good corporate image than other forms of advertising.

4   Increased media coverage of large-scale sporting events makes sponsorship more interesting to companies.

5   There may be taxation benefits to sponsorship, which make it a more cost-effective marketing communications medium.

Partnerships may be essentially just some form of sponsorship on a longer-term basis, and be subject to the same marketing considerations as many sponsorship agreements. Sometimes, however, companies engage in partnerships not so much as a marketing strategy (i.e. in order to gain and retain customers), but as a means to engage with wider stakeholder concerns. For example, in the case of so-called 'partnerships for sustainability', pressures frequently build up on corporations to address more numerous and complex environmental impacts of their operations. In these cases, alliances with NGOs can be a source of information and knowledge about creative ways to rethink operational activities, identify new products and marketing opportunities, and address stakeholder concerns. Partnerships and alliances are often a preferred, sometimes even the only realistic option for companies interested in accessing the knowledge held by NGOs, since internal development of such expertise may be too costly, inefficient and time-consuming for most companies (Rondinelli and London 2003).

Hamann and Acutt (2003) argue that the motivations of companies to engage in such partnerships may be twofold: (1) accommodation to external pressure, often by making small contributions to social causes or minimal changes to their own behaviour in order to stave off more criticism; and (2) legitimization of the company's point of view on particular social and regulatory issues, aimed at influencing public discourse in favour of the company's way of thinking.

In short, it is important to remember that corporations engage in any of these activities because they see this as benefiting their own business. This benefit may be more directly linked to sales figures or more indirectly to generally improve corporate image, and it may be seen as accruing in the shorter or longer term, but without seeing some benefit for themselves, corporations will rarely engage in charitable giving, sponsorship or partnerships. Understanding what benefits the corporate partner is seeking and whether these are compatible with the charity's own philosophy and policies is important in order to avoid the pitfalls of such arrangements.

What are the potential pitfalls of such arrangements?

While corporate sponsorship and partnership can often provide a crucial source of financial or other support for a charity or an opportunity to influence corporate behaviour, they do not come without their problems and difficulties. There are considerable differences of opinion in the charitable sector about whether or not closer agreements with the corporate sector are desirable and to be encouraged or not.

Corporate sponsorship of schools and educational activities has been strongly criticised for putting educational institutions into a situation of dependency on the corporate sector and therefore potentially compromising independent and critical thinking. There are concerns that corporations may be able to influence the content of learning materials they are funding, removing any critical discussion of their industry. In her book *No Logo*, Naomi Klein (2001: 89) deplores this trend in the United States:

> As fast-food, athletic gear and computer companies step in to fill the [funding] gap [in schools], they carry with them an educational agenda of their own. As with all branding projects, it is never enough to tag the schools with a few logos. Having gained a foothold, the brand managers are now doing what they have done in music, sports and journalism outside the schools: trying to overwhelm their host, to grab

the spotlight. They are fighting for their brands to become not the add-on but the subject of education, not an elective but the core curriculum.

Privileged marketing access as part of a sponsorship agreement is also often criticised; for instance, where traditional school meals are being replaced with branded fast food or where vending machines mostly contain sweet drinks and snacks. This is particularly problematic where cash-strapped schools become reliant on the income from vending machines or fast-food franchises, and are being pushed into allowing more and more commercial access and selling more foodstuffs and other items which may not be healthy or otherwise in the students' best interest.

Similar criticisms have been made about the corporate sponsorship of other social and charitable concerns. Longer-term partnerships between corporate and charitable sectors have also been the subject of fierce debate, particularly where this has involved endorsement of corporations by charities. In a recent debate in the UK environmental magazine *The Ecologist*, Mark Rose, chief executive of the charity Fauna & Flora International, argued that 'conservation must become fully integrated into social, political and economic processes, not isolated in a "box" [and that] working with leadership organisations that can influence their sector is strategically wise' (*The Ecologist*, July/August 2004: 31) as no pressure group can stop major infrastructure programmes around which governments have planned their national economies. On the other side of this debate, Marcus Colchester, director of the charity Forest Peoples Programme, argued that agreeing partnerships and endorsing 'less environmentally harmful' companies only served to legitimize corporate unsustainability: 'We mustn't let companies use partnerships to "greenwash" their overall operations. . . . Giving such companies positive spin and not exposing their tragic records of environmental ruin is giving "conservation" [a] bad name' (*The Ecologist*, July/August 2004: 31).

Cause-related marketing partnerships have come in for criticism as the display of a charity's logo on products, which are closely related to its cause, is generally seen by consumers as product endorsement by the charity. For instance, a charity concerned with health issues may enter a cause-related marketing partnership with a company producing food products. If the charity's logo appears on these food products many consumers will assume that the charity endorses the products as being healthy. The British Heart Foundation's cause-related marketing agreement with cereal producers and Cancer Research UK's similar agreement with a supermarket chain have come under criticism for this reason, as critics felt they were seen to be endorsing food products which were not necessarily healthy.

Partnerships may also run into trouble which stems from issues inherent in the nature of any partnership between two different organizations. The strategies of one or both of the partners may change in such a way that the partnership no longer fits. Partnerships also frequently run into problems because there are:

- culture clashes;
- differences in expectations which were not made clear at the beginning and/or prove irreconcilable;

- one or both partners may not be able or willing to devote enough time and effort to the management of the partnership;
- crucial people within one or both partner organizations may leave – and many further potential pitfalls.

Business Partners for Development (BPD) list common, practical challenges to tri-partite partnering processes as 'an inadequate understanding of what parties could offer each other, an unwillingness to modify or compromise, ineffective attempts to institutionalise the partnership within the participating organisations, and insufficient orientation of newcomers to the partnership' (BPD 2002: 16).

How should one go about designing sponsorship or partnership arrangements?

As we have seen, corporate sponsorship and partnership arrangements have significant potential benefits for both corporations and charities but are also subject to considerable risks. It is therefore important for charities to consider carefully the corporate partners from whom they seek sponsorship or with whom they want to enter partnership agreements and how they can minimize the risks involved.

In order to maximize the chances of success in finding corporate sponsors and partners, Staples (2004) suggests that charities need to be clear about their own brand value and worth in any relationship with a corporate, and to look for good alignment between their own objectives and the CSR programme of the corporate partner. By understanding what they have to offer and to what extent this matches the benefits sought by different potential corporate partners, charities may be better able to select good partners and avoid unsuitable ones.

Unequal power relations between the corporate and the NGO partner are often a source of conflict and problems. Banerjee (2001) argues that the idea of partnership is built on the twin assumptions that both parties are relatively equal in their power and access to resources, and that all external stakeholders are in favour of the agreements reached, but that neither of these assumptions is valid in all cases. According to Hamann (2003) some argue that partnerships cannot succeed without a level playing field created by the state, whereas others maintain that a balance of power is not necessary so long as the partnership benefits each partner more than is possible by any other means. Most commentators agree, however, that partnerships cannot succeed if companies misuse their significant advantage.

Covey and Brown (2001) argue that partnerships between business and civil society organizations can be successful even where full power parity does not occur so long as the partners seek to fulfil four conditions:

1   balancing power asymmetries;
2   acknowledging critical rights (e.g. the right to litigation for civil society groups);

3   negotiating both converging and conflicting interests;
4   managing relations with stakeholder constituencies.

Charities should seek to increase their own negotiating power in any sponsorship and partnership negotiations with corporations. According to Fisher and Ury (1981), the relative negotiating power of two parties depends primarily upon how attractive the option of not reaching an agreement is to each. If NGOs have a good alternative course of action to entering into or continuing a particular partnership arrangement they will be better able to stand up to corporate demands that they do not wish to meet or end an arrangement which proves unsatisfactory or damaging. NGOs should think carefully and develop their Best Alternative to a Negotiated Agreement, i.e. what they can and will do if an agreement with a corporation cannot be reached. If obtaining funding is the NGO's main goal, the best alternative should include alternative funding options, which would allow the NGO to discontinue its negotiations with the current partner. If, on the other hand, influencing corporate behaviour is the NGO's main goal, credible and detailed warnings of what would be the consequences of not reaching an agreement (e.g. litigation) should be drawn up. This will help civil society organizations to decide when collaboration with business is advantageous.

Charities therefore need to be careful when considering whether to accept sponsorship from or enter into a partnership with a corporation. They need to ask the following key questions:

- Is the proposed business partner compatible with the charity's own pur-pose? This relates to the company's overall business purpose and strategy as well as to its operations and products, and should take into account other divisions or parts of the corporation than the one the charity is dealing with directly.
- What benefit is the charity expected to provide to the corporate partner? Is it a mere acknowledgement of funding, an endorsement of the company's operations or products (and, if so, how far reaching is that endorsement) or the active involvement in some aspect of the partner's management?

These two questions are probably the most important in terms of deciding whether this is a partnership arrangement that would be compatible with the charity's mission or whether any aspects run counter to what the charity believes and stands for.

Charities need to strike a balance between autonomy and dependence. Complete autonomy from the corporate sector has the benefit of eliminating the danger that corporate sponsors or partners might control the charity's activities and policies but means that no income will come from the corporate sector and the charity loses potential influence over corporate behaviour and policies. On the other hand, large-scale reliance on corporate funds may ensure adequate and long-term funding of the charity's activities but can lead to unacceptably high levels of dependence if such funding comes with many strings attached, and if the charity risks its own reputation by backing up a corporation with many critics. In practice, many charities will want to steer a middle course, relying on some corporate funding and thereby accepting some dependence on the corporate sector but trying to safeguard its autonomy as far as possible. Careful choice of corporate partners is, again, key. Are the demands made by corporations of such a nature that they are compatible with the charity's reputation and ethos? If not, the decision may be to walk away from a particular corporate sponsor or partner, even if good money is on offer.

Conclusion

Corporate sponsorship and partnerships are often vital for charities. They provide much needed funds which may be difficult to obtain, and partnerships in particular may offer charities the opportunity to influence corporate behaviour. However, these types of arrangement also harbour significant risks. The charity may sustain damage to its own reputation if it is perceived to be endorsing corporations without at the same time being able to influence corporate behaviour significantly. Charities therefore need to exercise caution when accepting sponsorship or entering partnership agreements. It is particularly important to establish whether the corporation's and the charity's objectives are compatible and whether any existing power asymmetries can be mitigated. Charities will find that some corporate partners are reliable and good to deal with, whereas others may require more caution and some may be best avoided. A corporation that has clear policies regarding its social engagement and corporate social responsibility, clear auditing procedures and generally a good social reputation will often be a highly desirable and useful partner for a charity. Corporations that lack such policies, or that have policies but no clear mechanisms for enforcing and controlling them, or that have a tarnished reputation regarding some aspect of their social responsibility may need to be considered much more carefully.

References

Andreasen, A. R. (1996) 'Profits for nonprofits: find a corporate partner', *Harvard Business Review*, 74 (6), 47–59.

Banerjee, S. B. (2001) 'Corporate citizenship and indigenous stakeholders: exploring a new dynamic of organizational–stakeholder relationships', *Journal of Corporate Citizenship*, 1 (1): 39–55.

Berett, T. and Slack, T. (2001) 'A framework for the analysis of strategic approaches employed by non-profit sport organisations in seeking corporate sponsorship', *Sports Management Review*, 4, 21–45.

Brown, T. J. and Dacin, P. A. (1997) 'The company and the product: corporate associations and consumer product responses', *Journal of Marketing*, 61 (January), 68–84.

Business Partners for Development (BPD) (2002) *Putting Partnering to Work: Tri-sector Partnership Results and Recommendations (1998–2001)*, London: BPD. Available online at www.bpdweb.org.

Cannon, T. (1994) *Corporate Responsibility*, London: Pitman.

Centre for Environmental Leadership in Business (CELB) (2005) 'The Energy and Biodiversity Initiative', http://www.celb.org/xp/CELB/programs/energy-mining/ebi.xml, accessed 3 November 2005.

Cornwell, T. B. and Coote, L. V. (2005) 'Corporate sponsorship of a cause: the role of identification in purchase intent', *Journal of Business Research*, 58, 268–276.

Covey, J. and Brown, L. B. (2001) *Critical Cooperation: An Alternative Form of Civil Society – Business Engagement*, Report No. 17 (1), Boston, MA: Institute for Development Research.

Drumwright, M. E. (1996) 'Company advertising with a social dimension: the role of noneconomic criteria', *Journal of Marketing*, 60 (October), 71–87.

Drumwright, M. E. and Murphy, P. E. (2001) Corporate societal marketing. In P. N. Bloom and G. T. Gundlack (eds) *Handbook of Marketing and Society* (pp. 162–183), Thousand Oaks, CA: Sage.

Fisher, R. and Ury, W. (1981) *Getting to Yes: Negotiating Agreement Without Giving In*, Boston, MA: Houghton Mifflin.

Haley, E. (1996) 'Exploring the construct of organization as source: consumers' understandings of organizational sponsorship of advocacy advertising', *Journal of Advertising*, 25 (2), 19–36.

Hamann, R. (2003) 'Mining companies' role in sustainable development: the "why" and "how" of corporate social responsibility from a business perspective', *Development Southern Africa*, 20 (2), 237–254.

Hamann, R. and Acutt, N. (2003) 'How should civil society (and the government) respond to "corporate social responsibility"? A critique of business motivations and the potential for partnerships', *Development Southern Africa*, 20 (2), 255–270.

Juniper, C. and Moore, M. (2002) 'Synergies and best practices of corporate partnerships for sustainability', *Corporate Environmental Strategy*, 9 (3), 267–276.

Klein, N. (2001) *No Logo*, London: Flamingo.

Meenaghan, J. A. (1983) 'Commercial sponsorship', *European Journal of Marketing*, 17 (7), 1–73.

Menon, S. and Kahn, B. (2003) 'Corporate sponsorships of philanthropic activities: when do they impact perception of sponsor brand?', *Journal of Consumer Psychology*, 13 (3), 316–327.

Reiss, A. H. (2001) 'Partnerships are a Key to Future Arts Development', *Fund Raising Management*, 32 (5), 33–34.

Rondinelli, D. A. and London, T. (2003) 'How corporations and environmental groups cooperate: assessing cross-sector alliances and collaborations', *Academy of Management Executive*, 17 (1), 61–76.

Skyman, L. R., Bloom, P. M. and Blazing, J. (2004) 'Does corporate sponsorship of a socially-oriented message make a difference? An investigation of the effects of sponsorship identity on responses to an anti-drinking and driving message', *Journal of Consumer Psychology*, 14 (1 and 2), 13–20.

Staples, C. (2004) 'What does corporate social responsibility mean for charitable fundraising in the UK?', *International Journal for Non-profit and Voluntary Sector Marketing*, 9 (2), 154–158.

Talisman, B. (2000) 'Creating an integrated corporate sponsorship program', *Fund Raising Management*, 6 (August), 26–27.

Tully, S. R. (2004) 'Corporate–NGO partnerships and the regulatory impact of the Energy and Biodiversity Initiative', *Non-state Actors and International Law*, 4, 111–133.

Varadarajan, R. P. and Menon, A. (1988) 'Cause-related marketing: a co-alignment of marketing strategy and corporate philanthropy', *Journal of Marketing*, 52 (July), 58–74.

Chapter 10

Diana Leat

WHAT MAKES FOUNDATIONS TICK?

Introduction

FROM THE VIEWPOINT of fundraisers the life of the around 11,000
grant-making foundations in the UK may appear carefree. Grant-making
foundations 'merely' have to dispense funds rather than raise them, and surely
spending money has to be easier than getting it? So, with around £2 billion to spend
each year largely as they choose, what could possibly keep foundations awake
at night?

Before attempting to answer that question it is important to distinguish
between different types of grant-makers. To fundraisers grant-making foundations
may appear to be very much alike but not all foundations are grant-makers –
some operate their own programmes – and not all grant-makers are endowed
foundations.

There are four broad types of grant-makers:

- statutory;
- semi-public – for example, Big Lottery Fund;
- fundraising (including, for example, community foundations and, in a
  somewhat different way, most corporate foundations/givers);
- independent/endowed foundations.

The first three types of grant-maker are constrained in what they can and cannot
fund, and the risks they can take. Statutory grant-makers are constrained by their
usually fairly narrow terms of reference and powers, set by government to whom
they are publicly accountable. Semi-public grant-makers such as Big Lottery Fund
are similarly constrained by the priorities set for them and by their accountability

to Parliament; in addition, if, as in Big Lottery Fund's case, they depend on income from the general public, then they have to consider public sympathy for their patterns of grant-making. Similarly, fundraising foundations, such as community and corporate foundations, have to consider the wishes of donors, shareholders and customers in how they spend their money.

Independent/endowed foundations are the least constrained of all grant-makers in that they are not beholden to anyone or anything other than the original deed and the law. Nevertheless, endowed foundations vary dramatically in age, size, orientation, founder influence (even from beyond the grave) and so on, in ways that make generalizations hazardous.

This chapter focuses primarily on independent/endowed foundations. It begins with the theme of control, exploring the role of control in the creation of grant-making foundations and the tension between control and the inherent uncertainties/riskiness of making grants which foundations operate and why and how this has affected them. Finally, the chapter considers some of the strategic, operational and relational dilemmas faced by foundations and the implications these have for fundraisers.

Foundations and control

Relatively little is known about why people create foundations in the UK (Lloyd, 2004). Data from the US suggest a variety of implicit and explicit reasons including tax efficiency, avoiding company take-over, leaving a living memorial (to the founder or related others), paying back for luck in life, preventing heirs from inheriting (for a variety of reasons), religious and moral beliefs about the responsibilities of wealth and entering heaven, as well as wanting to improve society or help others (Odendahl, 1987). Running through these supposed motivations for creating a foundation is a strong theme of control – controlling how much tax is paid, how much your children inherit, how you, or others, are remembered, and so on. Even when the motivation is 'pure altruism', in many respects, the very act of creating a foundation, rather than giving directly to a charity/charities, may be seen as an exercise in control, even if, at the same time, the law somewhat constrains the power of the founder.

The theme of control also runs through foundations' relationships with government. In the US recognition of the amount of control exercised by the large foundations (in influencing public priorities and provision directly and indirectly with private grant dollars) lies behind the continuous stream of Senate Inquiries and Congressional Committees (see e.g. Brilliant, 2000). Somewhat differently, in the UK the Lottery-funded grant-makers struggle with the fine line between accountability and government control.

In the US and in the UK foundations have traditionally emphasized and carefully protected their independence and privacy as essential elements of control. But, set alongside and in many ways in tension with a desire for control, foundations have other values and demands, as well as a set of operational problems arising in large part from the distanced, and thus risky, business of grant-making. The development of grant-making foundations illustrates these tensions.

In many respects the development of grant-making foundations on any scale was an accident of history or a solution to a set of pragmatic considerations peculiar to both a particular period and to the needs of the large foundations involved. For the major early-twentieth-century US foundations, such as Carnegie and Rockefeller, grant-making was not the chosen or ideal option. Both Carnegie and Rockefeller began as operating foundations running organizations such as the Rockefeller Institute, the Carnegie Institution, the Rockefeller Sanitary Commission and the Carnegie Endowment for International Peace.

The story of Rockefeller's move from operating to grant-making is particularly interesting. The creation of the Rockefeller Institute as a fully independent institution is said to have appealed to John D. Sr. not least 'because the new entity would have no history of opposition to the homeopathic remedies that he and his personal physicians believed in' (Jonas, 1989: 13). Control and the ability to support the unorthodox, irrespective of grant applications, are two advantages of operating.

The first task of the Institute was to build a laboratory but the Board of Directors were anxious to be seen to be doing something and so decided to give small grants to promising young scientists as a stop-gap. Both Gates and Flexner, key advisers, were against the plan. Gates described the grant-making programme as an 'utterly futile' system of scattered subventions; and Flexner saw it as demeaning, keeping 'the recipients on their knees, holding out their hats from year to year' (quoted in Jonas, 1989: 37). Once the laboratory was built the grants programme was severely curtailed and then stopped. The Carnegie Institution conducted a very similar experiment with grant-making as a stop-gap and again dropped it in favour of strong, effective direction from a central office. Jonas argues that in the cases of both Rockefeller and Carnegie the problems were:

- Lack of precedent and process – there were no precedents for grants to independent researchers.
- The problem of choice/moral hazard – it was not clear how rational choices could be made among competing applications, and the attendant dangers of patronage, or perceptions of patronage.
- Control and accountability – it was not clear how it could be ensured that funds were spent on the purposes intended.

So why was grant-making eventually adopted by Rockefeller and Carnegie? In part grant-making developed because of increasing pressure to support others, exacerbated by the demands of the war in Europe, and in part because the creation of more operating centres or the expansion of existing ones could only be achieved by stripping universities of their best researchers. But there were other factors. One was that the war led to the creation of a National Research Council providing a respected, 'neutral' intermediary through which grants could be channelled. Another factor was a fear that centralized operating science organizations might come under the influence of government, reducing the control of the donor and trustees. In Rockefeller's case, in particular, there was also a public relations/image imperative. The Rockefeller Foundation Board had become embroiled in controversy over its creation of an Investigation of Industrial Relations only a year after the Ludlow massacre. The Foundation needed to find a way of distancing itself from the Rockefeller family. By moving to grant-making, 'the trustees were giving up the authority to monitor the day-to-day performance of their beneficiaries; as compensation the Foundation would be insulated from direct responsibility for the use of its funds' (Jonas, 1989: 95). Operating continued in a narrow range of (then) non-controversial subjects such as public health, medicine and agriculture.

We know very little about why subsequent UK foundations adopted grant-making rather than operating, but one factor may have been that the major US foundations created a precedent (which also existed in the form of the British government's funding of scientific research) and a notion that this is how foundations work. Grant-making in the UK seems to have come to be seen as the only or best model, rather than one that was (reluctantly) developed in the US as a largely pragmatic response to particular circumstances (on wider issues of definition and regulation relating to grant-making and operating foundations in the US see Toepler, 1999).

Grant-making and loss of control

While grantees are apt to see grant-making foundations as powerful and controlling bodies, the reality is more complex. Of course, money brings power but purely grant-making foundations are, by definition, powerless to achieve their missions without 'suppliers' or 'agents' (i.e. grantees). Comparing the characteristics of making grants versus operating programmes it is clear that grant-making typically involves dependence on independent others, loss of control and all that goes with that, but it also brings certain advantages (Table 10.1).

The aim, then, for grant-making foundations is to maintain the advantages of grant-making while minimizing the disadvantages attendant on distance and lack of control. Different foundations will attach different levels of value to different advantages of grant-making (e.g. to a democratic/responsive image); and trustees and staff will have different comfort zones regarding loss of control.

For example, the Big Lottery Fund as a semi-public grant-maker, spending 'the people's money', attaches considerable significance to ensuring a wide geographical spread of funds, support to a range of organizations, high accessibility/openness and a democratic/responsive image – but, at the same time, because of its public accountability it is necessarily sensitive to accusations of failure and controversy. By contrast, the Joseph Rowntree Charitable Trust, for example, as an endowed foundation does not attach significance to a wide geographical spread of grants or to support for a wide range of causes, and is free and willing to risk failure and controversy. However, although all fully endowed foundations are theoretically freer to take risks and to be less open in their grant-making than semi-public and fundraising grant-makers, it does not follow that they actually do so. Some endowed foundations are cautious and narrow in what they fund (in some cases due to the terms of the deed); some fund less cautiously and more widely. Some endowed foundations have very open policies and processes; some do not.

Table 10.1 Advantages and disadvantages of grant-making and operating

Grant-making	Operating
Flexible priorities/programmes But danger of lack of focus	Lack of flexibility (staff choices constrain) But focus
Scope for wide spread	Limited spread
Support to a range of organizations	No/little distribution
Hedging bets	All eggs in one basket
Problems of rational choice and moral hazard in selection	Selection of recipients and associated problems not an issue
Restricted by availability of agents/demand and supply	Free to 'create' demand, but may be restricted by supply
Democratic/responsive image	Autocratic image
High transaction costs	No transaction costs
Low apparent overheads	High overheads
Lack of control/management at a distance	High control/direct line management
Unclear ownership of project/results	Clear ownership of project/results
Lack of follow-through after grant ends	Scope for follow-through
Loss of knowledge	Knowledge retained
Distanced from failure and controversy	Direct association with failure and controversy

The implication for fundraisers is that it is necessary to explore grant-makers' status, stated policies and preferences and their practices case by case. Generalizations about foundations can seriously damage your financial health!

Foundations in a changing world

Fundraisers need to be aware of the differences between grant-makers and to understand the changing pressures grant-makers face. In recent years the foundation world has experienced a number of changes. These have included:

- Fluctuations in income due to market circumstances.
- Increasing pressures and legislation for accountability regarding public benefit and what they do.
- The assumptions and demands of the wider culture of efficiency and effectiveness.
- A more broadly risk-averse culture and regulatory frameworks.
- A changing environment and relationship with government as the role of the state changes.

In the early 1990s British foundations most often adopted the style of gift-givers and, more rarely, investors or collaborative entrepreneurs (Leat, 1992). In 2006, British foundations appear to be at a turning point. Old roles are no longer clear or viable. Successive governments have changed the old expectations and rules of the game: government has taken on the role of experimenter and innovator, government and the voluntary sector are now 'in partnership', and there is little ideological space between the two. In the new world of contracting, issues of substituting voluntary funding or provision for that of the state take on a new and troublesome dimension (Anheier and Daly, 2006; Leat, 2006; Murray, 2000).

There are new demands for demonstrable 'impact' and 'effectiveness', as well as impending changes in charity law that will require a 'public benefit' test, as well as regular audits of effectiveness. 'Accountability', 'standards' and 'quality frameworks' are the orders of the day. Doing good is no longer good enough (on the wider move in the voluntary sector, including foundations, towards performance measurement see, e.g.: Herman and Renz, 1997; Kendall and Knapp, 2000; Kramer, 2000; Light, 2002; Paton, 2003; Porter and Kramer, 1999).

Understanding change in foundations

In the wider non-profit world the move towards greater accountability and emphasis on performance measurement has largely been explained in terms of resource dependency and other institutional pressures for organizations to become more alike (see e.g. Powell and DiMaggio, 1991; Schlesinger, 1998).

Very broadly, 'neo-institutional' theories assume that resource dependency and/or environmental uncertainty result in organizations becoming more alike as they respond to the demands and expectations of those they depend on for income or as they imitate each other in order to gain legitimacy in the face of uncertainty (Powell and DiMaggio, 1991). But endowed grant-making foundations are not resource dependent and thus do not experience the resource uncertainty that drives other non-profits. Furthermore, endowed foundations are, more generally, relatively immune from external pressures. They are immune to the pressures of external funders, the public or donors (given the way in which foundations have typically been created in the past, many donors are already dead – community foundations and some new foundations are interesting exceptions), and the accountability requirements of government and the law have been minimal and, such as they are, generally focused on process matters.

What relevance, then, do theories of isomorphism (the observed tendency for organizations in disparate settings to become more alike) have in explaining endowed foundations' apparent tendency to conform to the dominant frameworks of the time? Does isomorphism still arise without resource dependency and uncertainty? This question is not just an interesting theoretical question but is also important for fundraisers in understanding the differing demands foundations make upon them, and the reasons why. Isomorphism may help to explain 'where foundations are coming from'.

One argument may be that although foundations are not subject to the resource dependency and uncertainty of other non-profits they are nevertheless part of that institutional field and thus take on the same institutional expectations and constraints (sometimes referred to as mimetic isomorphism). The difficulty with this argument is that foundations see themselves as distinct from the wider non-profit sector precisely because they are not resource dependent and do not suffer the same constraints (Leat, in Anheier and Daly, 2006). It is also worth noting that the same study revealed that UK foundations are uncertain as to whether they constitute a sector in their own right, emphasizing their independence and diversity. This is reflected in membership of the Association of Charitable Foundations which although growing is still only a very small percentage of the total population of foundations. The foundation world appears to be a case of weak institutionalization and, as such, likely to demonstrate considerable variability (DiMaggio, 2001: 83).

Although coercive isomorphism in the form of legal regulation has been weak in the past, new accounting and reporting standards have required foundations to document not only process issues but also address outputs and outcomes in narrative form.[1]

Mimetic isomorphism (imitating each other) may also accurately describe the way in which some foundations appear increasingly to borrow vocabularies and approaches derived from the US foundation sector (where foundations directly face coercive pressures and reputational and regulatory uncertainty in the form of Congressional and media investigations). Strategic planning, outcome funding and investment approaches, for example, are all derived from US foundation practices. UK foundations may not need to adopt these approaches in the way in which US foundations do, but may nevertheless adopt them as new, more modern clothes even if the climate does not require them. Electronic communications, the growth in international conferences and travel may encourage mimetic isomorphism more as fashion and the attraction of the new rather than necessity.

Perhaps the most satisfactory explanation of changes in parts of the foundation world is a variety of forms of normative isomorphism (i.e. becoming more alike via adoption of shared norms and values). Although employment of paid professional staff is by no means the norm among UK (and US) foundations, larger, and some not so large, foundations have in recent years increasingly employed professional staff. Arguably, professional staff may bring a more instrumental viewpoint (i.e. as compared with the expressive emphasis of family members), experience and cultures from other fields, and a professional pride in 'doing a good job' and being able to demonstrate that. Grant-making staff may also 'import' standards of equity and transparency from public-sector accountability frameworks from their own experience, from training or from the wider culture. Professionalization may introduce an element of competition not so much for resources as for reputation. But it could also be claimed that the normative isomorphism argument is weak because there is, as yet, no profession of grant-making with established, agreed norms and standards.

Trustees are another potential source of normative isomorphism, especially perhaps if they are not associated with the founding family and/or bring perspectives from fields in which a culture of efficiency, effectiveness, account-ability and so on is well established (e.g. business). Data from a recent study suggest that in some foundations in the US trustees may indeed be an important source of normative isomorphism (Anheier and Leat, 2006), but there is little evidence, one way or the other, in the UK.

Another source of normative isomorphism may be the entry of new donors to the foundation scene. 'These new donors are confident, aggressive venture capitalists for social change who view charitable actions as investments and who demand a demonstrable "return" on their philanthropic dollars' (Centre for Philanthropy and Public Policy, 2001: 2). Significantly, in the light of the above discussion regarding control, these donors adopt a focussed hands-on approach to giving. In addition, they are both more individualist and more global in their orientation. Bill Gates is one obvious example here.

Yet another factor in normative isomorphism may be the creation of the Association of Charitable Foundations (ACF), increasing communication and informal benchmarking among foundations, and encouraging reflection and 'best practice'.

Although all of these factors may have played some part in prompting change, perhaps the most important source of normative isomorphism may have been the entry of new, large, high-profile semi-public players such as the Big Lottery Fund, previously the Community Fund and New Opportunities Fund. These grant-makers have identified themselves with charitable grant-makers not least in order to stress their independence. In reality, however, these semi-public grant-makers are very different from endowed foundations – they are not resource independent and they are accountable to Parliament (and the tabloid press) and clearly subject to pressures for performance measurement. These semi-public grant-makers have set new standards in foundation accountability and practice that, despite their dissimilarities from independent grant-makers, have created normative isomorphic pressures on resource-independent foundations.

Dealing with uncertainty

The UK findings from a study of roles and visions of foundations in Europe depict foundations living in a world of uncertainty (Anheier and Daly, 2004; Leat, 2005). If, following Duncan (1979), we break environmental uncertainty down into complexity and dynamism, then it is arguable that in the past decade foundations have experienced a greater degree of complexity in the number of elements in their organizational task environments (e.g. in terms of what the grant-making process is now seen to require) and increased heterogeneity in terms of demands and expectations (e.g. from different types of grant-seekers), and a higher degree of dynamism in the rate and predictability of change in the elements. In other words, foundations have moved from an environment of low to medium complexity and low dynamism, creating low uncertainty, to one of medium to high complexity and high dynamism, creating high uncertainty. The list of uncertainties for foundations is long: uncertain income, uncertain legal frameworks, new and unpredictable attention from the media; constantly changing government policies;

new and unpredictable demands from a greater variety of grantees; new and not always predictable social issues (e.g. a new concern with rural issues, asylum seekers and refugees, Islamophobia, and so on).

This uncertainty and its effects were reflected in the UK study referred to above. In a number of interviews there was a sense of a desire to do something different but, at the same time, as one director noted, a feeling of being over-whelmed by 'so many problems and too much to do'. Lack of staff, a cultural resistance to spending time thinking, the flow of government initiatives and the growing complexity of the political and policy environment created a temptation for some to 'just hunker down and retreat into our own world'. In addition, some staff felt constrained and frustrated by the time required to get trustees to address roles, think about and then accept change.

Changing needs and the withdrawal of public funding were seen as particularly important in the light of fears regarding the future of the Community Fund (now the Big Lottery Fund): 'If the public are going to be ticking boxes about who should be funded that would leave big holes, especially for those most in need of help'. Decreasing foundation income created further dilemmas and uncertainty here.

We know something about the ways in which operating non-profits tends to cope with uncertainty:

- Goal displacement – focus on strategies for organizational survival and maintenance;
- A search for stability either in terms of new niches or in the form of copy-cat behaviour modelled on organizations perceived as successful.
- Stronger stakeholders crowd out weaker stakeholders, leading to changes in the balance of organizational power.
- Dropping controversial programmes in the hope of attracting donors and fitting in with government priorities.
- Increased pressure for professionalization and technocratic control (Anheier, 2005: 189).

Again foundations' lack of resource dependence complicates matters. En-dowed foundations do not, for example, need to drop controversial programmes in order to attract donors – but some may do so in order to maintain a low profile keeping the tabloids and the government regulators at bay. All of these strategies may have some relevance in understanding foundation behaviour in a time of uncertainty and would certainly be a useful starting point for further study.

Foundations' resource independence is certainly an interesting challenge in explaining what moves foundations. Instead of looking at external drivers of change, suppose we look at internal forces – are there any useful frameworks for understanding foundations' current situation?

Understanding from within

Anheier provides a useful set of tables summarizing theories of organizational life cycles and developmental stages (Table 10.2).

Table 10.2 Theories of organizational life cycles and developmental stages

	Birth stage	Youth stage	Midlife stage	Maturity stage
Organizational life cycle				
Bureaucracy	Non-bureaucratic	Pre-bureaucratic	Bureaucratic	Post-bureaucratic
Emphasis	Creativity, survival	Growth	Control, efficiency	Renewal
Structure	Informal, overlapping tasks	Formalization, specialization	Formal procedural control systems; centralization	Extensive financial controls; push towards centralization
Management style	Entrepreneurial	Mission driven	Accountability	Enabling, team approach
Transition requirements	Leadership crisis	Control crisis	Red tape crisis	Turn-around crisis

	Entrepreneurial stage	Collectivity stage	Control stage	Elaboration stage
Organizational development and stages				
Structure	Little	Informal	Centralization	Decentralization
Focus	Survival	Growth	Efficiency	Restructuring
Innovation	Invention	Enhancement	Implementation	Renewal
Planning	Little	Short term	Long range	Strategic
Commitment	Individual	Group	Complacency	Recommitment
Managers	Entrepreneurs	Entrepreneurs as managers	Managers as consolidators	Managers as strategists

Source: Anheier (2005, 151).

Again these cycles and stages have been developed largely on the basis of for-profit firms. Nevertheless they are of recognizable relevance to fundraising/operating non-profits. For example, the changes involved in the move from the entrepreneurial or founder stage to the collectivity and then control stages are observable in non-profits; and it is not difficult to think of examples of larger non-profits that display signs of moving from the control to the elaboration stage. But, while these stages may have considerable value in understanding fundraising non-profits operating in supply-and-demand markets, they require some adaptation for resource-independent foundations. Nevertheless, arguably at least some of the changes in some foundations' structures and processes could be explained in terms of a transition from youth to mid-life and from the collectivity stage to the control stage rather than solely by changes in their external environment outlined above.

So what are the implications of these two sets of approaches – external and internal – to explaining change in foundations? If we adopt the external isomorphic approach, then we would expect all foundations to become more and more alike (subject only to differences in terms of resource dependency and uncertainty related to the distinctions between different types of foundations outlined above). If we adopt the life cycle and organizational development approach then we would expect differences between foundations; while some foundations may be at the birth and entrepreneurial stages – with all of the associated characteristics – others may be at the mid-life and control stages with very different characteristics. The reality may be a mix of the two approaches – more established/older (and often but not always larger) foundations do appear to be becoming more alike in some respects (e.g. their concern with effectiveness, value for money, sustainability, accountability) while some of the newer foundations are different – or perhaps not changing at the same rate. Again the moral for fundraisers is that there is no such thing as the average foundation.

Considerations and dilemmas

However, all foundations, of whatever type and at whatever stage, face a range of strategic, operational and relational dilemmas and pressures.

Given limited resources, foundations have to decide whether to focus on the alleviation of symptoms or on understanding causes (for a minority this choice is already made by the terms of their deed). Given limited resources they also have to decide whether it is better to spend money on the foundation's infrastructure and organizational capacity for good grant-making or to keep infrastructure costs low in order to maximize income for grant-making.

Limited resources and avoidance of overhead costs also create dilemmas around publicizing the existence of the foundation and its work, running the risk of application overload and raised expectations versus keeping a low profile and being accused of lack of accessibility and transparency. Another dilemma around profile relates to the value of privacy in allowing grant-makers the freedom to fund unpopular causes – at the cost of maximizing transparency and accountability.

Limited resources underlie dilemmas around whether to give a large number of small grants or a smaller number of larger grants, short-term or longer-term grants and core or project funding. Giving smaller, short-term project grants raises issues of 'funding for failure'. A reputation for giving large numbers of grants is also administratively costly in so far as it attracts larger numbers of applicants. Giving longer-term, larger and core grants raises issues to do with exit and 'silting up' (i.e. the inability to give any new grants because all of the foundation's money is already committed).

Closely related, trustees' legal responsibilities for responsible stewardship of funds in line with the donor's intentions create dilemmas around following the founder's formal and informal intentions to the letter versus interpreting these in the light of changing needs and circumstances. Responsible stewardship of funds also sits uneasily with real risk-taking and innovation – activities which foundations have traditionally used to provide their *raison d'être* and to distinguish themselves from government.

In addition, responsible stewardship of funds, coupled with the desire for effectiveness with limited resources, creates operational dilemmas including funding only those with a reputation and proven track record versus funding the new and the untried, funding only those known to the foundation versus equal chances for all applicants, regular monitoring of grant recipients versus allowing grant recipients flexibility to respond to changing circumstances.

The desire for effectiveness, coupled with limited resources, creates dilemmas around whether to proactively choose a limited number of priorities or to respond to a much wider range of applications, and whether to fund only those with the capacity for sustainability versus taking chances on change and innovation.

Traditionally, and still to a very large extent today, foundations have em-phasized their independence of each other and, crucially, of government. But if foundations want to be effective in achieving sustainable change and innovation, despite their limited resources and powers, to what extent should they work with other foundations and with government to achieve lasting change and greater leverage? Working with government, by design or de facto, obviously raises very difficult issues to do with subsidizing state activities. On the other hand, how is sustainable change and/or longer-term funding to be secured without government involvement? This then raises issues to do with the extent to which foundations should attempt directly or indirectly to influence public policy. (For a more detailed list of strategic, operational and relational dilemmas faced by foundations, see Anheier and Leat, 2002: 50–52.)

In certain foundations some of these dilemmas will not require either/or choices. For example, larger foundations can probably do a bit of alleviating immediate symptoms and a bit of trying to understand causes, some smaller, shorter-term project grants and some longer-term, larger core grants. But, even if the choice is not either/or, it is still a matter of balance, and those balances are under pressure from factors in the changing environment outlined above.

Implications for fundraisers

In important ways, new expectations of foundation accountability and demonstrable effectiveness change the balances which foundations can strike as well as creating new dilemmas of control for foundations. If they are required to demonstrate their effectiveness and be more accountable, then, arguably, they will tend to play for safety, take fewer risks in who and what they fund and demand greater effectiveness and accountability in terms of monitoring, evaluation and 'deliverables' from grantees. This in turn requires recalibrating control mechanisms, as well as reconsidering and managing the inherent risks of grant-making. What implications is this likely to have for applicants and grantees?

One way in which foundations may attempt to increase control over the effectiveness of their support is likely to be a continuing emphasis on pre-grant assessment of the capacity of potential grantees and the feasibility, viability and sustainability of proposed activities. There is likely to be a growing emphasis on funding to achieve specified, agreed outcomes and on post-grant performance monitoring and measurement.

Although there is undoubtedly a trend towards increased emphasis on outcome measurement, it remains to be seen exactly how this will play out. Some foundations (perhaps especially those with greater public accountability) are actively pursuing outcome measurement; others are talking about it but, as yet, doing relatively little; yet others maintain a healthy scepticism about the value, and dangers, of some of the crasser (and easier) forms of outcome measures, and may even resist the trend. One implication for fundraisers is that they need to become experts in the benefits and risks of different interpretations of outcome measurement. Grant recipients may have an important role to play in helping funders think through the implications of different demands for outcome measurement, and what it can and cannot do and at what cost. Among other things, this will require grant applicants and recipients to stop pretending that it is possible to do the impossible in next to no time on next to nothing. It will involve being honest and modest about the uncertainties of achieving change (getting to outcomes), being realistic about change as having many causes, drivers and facilitating factors (as well as obstacles), and being open about the fact that genuine innovation involves trial *with* error. Paradoxically outcome measurement may be most valuable before, not after, the event, helping grant applicants and funders to think about exactly what would count as success at the end and along the way, and how likely the proposed strategy is to get to that goal (on the dangers of different approaches to outcome measurement, see e.g. Anheier and Leat, 2004; Leat, 2005; Paton, 2003).

But there are other, perhaps more subtle, implications of the above discussion for fundraisers.

Emphasis on making the greatest possible difference and getting value for money, combined with the global orientation of some new donors, and recent political events, could lead some foundations to look at the relative costs and value of spending more money overseas rather than in the (professionalized) UK sector. Fluctuating income, new donors and concerns with ensuring value for money may lead to an increase in investment/venture capital approaches at least in the short term. More generally, there is likely to be more experimentation with funding tools (e.g. more loans).

Desire for greater demonstrable effectiveness may lead to a growing recognition of the need for sustainability, fewer one-year grants, and fewer partial grants; but larger and longer-term grants will reduce the number of grantees and could lead to tricky issues for foundations around 'silting up' (i.e. getting stuck with funding the same things year on year) and exit. Desire for sustainability and effectiveness may lead some foundations to question the value of 'charity' versus 'change' approaches, with greater interest in trying to address structural and policy issues. On the other hand, the longer-term and less certain job of achieving structural and policy change will sit uneasily with the pressure to produce demonstrations of effectiveness in the short term (Anheier and Leat, 2006).

Concern with funding for effectiveness and outcomes may lead to greater acceptance of the need for full cost funding, but this will run alongside increasing anxiety about subsidizing contracts. The desire to avoid colonization by government into supporting/subsidizing provision of public services could fuel anxieties regarding funding of large voluntary organizations working on contract to government, providing opportunities for smaller groups. However, anxieties regarding risks in grant-making look set to grow, at least in the short term. This could mean greater hurdles for smaller, new groups, perhaps especially those from ethnic minorities.

Finally, as foundations seek to gain greater control over the benefits they fund, and the demonstration of those, matters of branding will arise. Branding will in turn raise issues about ownership of projects and results, and more generally about the nature of the relationship between funder and funded.

Conclusion

So what does keep foundation trustees and staff awake at night? The answer will be somewhat different for foundations at different stages in the life cycle, operating in different 'industries' and with different peculiar and particular problems and crises. More generally, the answer may be that money per se is not a worry – although investing it wisely to achieve maximum, sustainable return may be.

But, although foundations may not worry about money per se, they do worry about ways in which it can be spent most efficiently and effectively; they worry about ways in which they can best manage grant-making while keeping administrative costs within bounds; they worry about ways in which demonstrable, sustainable effectiveness can be measured meaningfully and combined with other goals and values which many foundations hold dear. These other goals and values include independence of government, openness and fairness for grant-seekers, and remaining true to the donor's intentions.

Combining efficiency and demonstrable effectiveness with these other values is a tall order. This is especially true in an environment of risk aversion, a voluntary sector aligned increasingly with government, a government that likes to 'innovate', and pressures for potentially costly and short-term, tangible measures demonstrating contribution to public benefit. It may look easy being a grant-making foundation – but appearances can be deceptive.

Note

1   Furthermore, some degree of change may be explained in terms of anticipatory coercion in the form of the new Charities Act, the introduction of assessment for public benefit and a standard information return.

References

Anheier, H. (2005) *Non-profit Organizations: Theory, Management, Policy*, Routledge, London.

Anheier, H. and Daly, S. (eds) (2006) *Roles and Visions of Foundations in Europe* (forthcoming).

Anheier, H. and Leat, D. (2002) *From Charity to Creativity: Philanthropic Foundations in the 21st Century*, COMEDIA in association with the Joseph Rowntree Reform Trust, London.

Anheier, H. and Leat, D. (2004) *Creative Philanthropy*, Routledge, London.

Brilliant, E. (2000) *Private Charity and Public Inquiry: A History of the Filer and Peterson Commissions*, Indiana University Press, Bloomington, IN.

Center on Philanthropy and Public Policy, University of Southern California (2001) *What Is 'New' about New Philanthropy?*, The Center on Philanthropy and Public Policy, University of Southern California, Los Angeles.

DiMaggio, P. (2001) 'Measuring the impact of the non-profit sector on society is probably impossible but possibly useful', in P. Flynn and V. A. Hodgkinson (eds) *Measuring the Impact of the Non-profit Sector*, Kluwer Academic/Plenum Publishers, New York, pp. 247–272.

Duncan, R. (1979) 'What is the right organizational structure?', *Organizational Dynamics* (winter): 59–80.

Herman, R. and Renz, D. (1997) 'Multiple constituencies and the social construction of non-profit effectiveness', *Non-profit and Voluntary Sector Quarterly*, 26: 185–206.

Jonas, G. (1989) *The Circuit Riders: Rockefeller Money and the Rise of Modern Science*, W. W. Norton & Company, New York.

Kendall, J. and Knapp, M. (2000) 'Measuring the performance of voluntary organisations', *Public Management*, 2(1): 105–132.

Kramer, M. R. (2000) 'Strategic confusion', *Foundation News and Commentary* (May–June): 40–44.

Leat, D. (1992) *Trusts in Transition: The Policy and Practice of Grant-giving Trusts*, Joseph Rowntree Foundation, York.

Leat, D. (2005) 'Foundations in Britain', in H. Anheier and S. Daly (eds) *Roles and Visions of Foundations in Europe* (forthcoming).

Light, P. C. (2002) *Pathways to Non-profit Excellence*, The Brookings Institution, Washington, DC.

Lloyd, T. (2004) *Why Rich People Give*, Association of Charitable Foundations, London.

Mcilnay, D. P. (1998) *How Foundations Work*, Jossey-Bass, San Francisco, CA.

Murray, V. (2000) 'Evaluating the impact of private–public partnerships: a Canadian experience', in S. P. Osborne (ed.) *Public–Private Partnerships: Theory and Practice in International Perspective*, Routledge, London.

Odendahl, T. (1987) 'Independent foundations and the wealthy donors: an overview', in T. Odendahl (ed.) *America's Wealthy and the Future of Foundations*, Foundation Center, New York.

Paton, R. C. (2003) *Managing and Measuring Social Enterprise*, Sage, London.

Porter, M. E. and Kramer, M. R. (1999) 'Philanthropy's new agenda: creating value', *Harvard Business Review* (Nov/Dec): 121–130.

Powell, W. W. and DiMaggio, P. (eds) (1991) *The New Institutionalism in Organizational Analysis*, University of Chicago Press, Chicago, IL.

Schlesinger, M. (1998), 'Mismeasuring the consequences of ownership: external influences on the comparative performance of public, for-profit and private non-profit organizations', in W. W. Powell and E. S. Clemens (eds) *Private Action and the Public Good*, Yale University Press, New Haven, CT.

Toepler, S. (1999) 'Operating in a grantmaking world: reassessing the role of operating foundations', in H. K. Anheier and S. Toepler (eds) *Private Funds, Public Purpose: Philanthropic Foundations in International Perspective*, Kluwer Academic/Plenum, New York.

Chapter 11

Tina Wallace and Jill Mordaunt

WHEN IS THE PRICE TOO HIGH? GAINING FUNDING FROM INSTITUTIONAL SOURCES

Introduction

S EEKING FUNDING from governmental and quasi-governmental funders involves engaging with the latter's political and policy concerns. This requires building networks and relationships, assessing funders' interests and concerns, compromise and adjustment (Lindblom, 1979), and some acute ethical judgements on the part of the grant-seekers about the nature of the relationship and the degree of closeness they wish to have with the grant-makers. However, in any funding relationship there are power differentials. Working with institutional funders carries within it the dangers of being funding-led, abandoning the practice of modifying or compromising ideals and mission, and allowing these instead to be determined externally outside of the organization's control.

This chapter deals with the challenges fundraisers face in negotiating and applying for funding from public institutions. It illustrates these by using the case of international development – a field in which various government bodies hold funds for which international non-governmental organizations (INGOs) can bid. In particular it will explore the paradoxes and the multiple agendas that are masked by the apparently rational processes of big bureaucracies and the ways in which these shift as political analyses of the problems and their solutions change. We argue that this poses profound dilemmas for fundraisers operating in this context. In particular, where and how should managers and their fundraisers seek to position their organization on the autonomy–dependency continuum? Too close to the independence end can mean isolation and exclusion from key decisions that affect your organization and its beneficiaries. However, there are significant dangers in being too close to the dependence end. We suggest that much more consideration needs to be given to how charities engage with these processes both within any organization seeking institutional funding and within the wider networks of charities and government funders in a given field.

Shifting sands and the funding of INGOs

Changes in the funding environment for UK development INGOs directly affect the way they access and account for funding; in turn how funds are obtained shapes their development work on the ground. Traditionally, not-for-profit organizations raised their money locally, from the public through fundraising events, from members, from advertising and building a reputation for expertise and effectiveness in their chosen field. In the 1980s many development INGOs took no money from government at all (e.g. Christian Aid), or limited their acceptance of institutional funding from all government donors (including the European Union [EU]) to no more than 10 per cent of their total income (e.g. Oxfam). The motivation was to ensure their independence of analysis and action from government; they defined themselves as working with and for the very poorest in ways that government could not. They also wished to lobby and critique government when they felt government policy was ignoring issues around the environment, gender inequality and the wider needs of the poor.

The situation has changed dramatically over the past twenty years. More government funding has become available for INGOs as development resources were channelled through INGOs rather than governments in the global South, which were seen as corrupt. Partly as a result, many INGOs placed more importance on expansion and growth than on autonomy and independence. Many of the larger INGOs now have as a strategic aim increasing their official government funding, seeing this as a really key source of major funding that can allow them to significantly expand their activities, and also their influence over government policy and practice. Many small and medium-sized INGOs emerged in response to this new funding and are almost 100 per cent reliant on funding from the UK Government's Department for International Development (DFID), the EU and other bilateral donors in Europe, only minimally supplementing that income with funding from foundations, trusts and small amounts of individual funding through wills, fundraising appeals and special events. Others, the household names, now have no ceiling on their fundraising from government, and Oxfam, for example, funds 50 per cent of its programme work from this kind of funding. Funds from public giving are reserved for financing the work that governments do not support such as research, policy and advocacy work, administration and core costs.

Recently, new trends in official funding are discernible. The terms and conditions of all government donors in the EU are changing fast; the newest instruments are shifting funding and attention away from INGOs and focusing increasingly on the importance of the role of national governments in development. Direct budget support to national governments is becoming a key funding instrument, absorbing 20 per cent and more of DFID funds now, and this is also increasingly the funding modality for the EU and other bilateral funders in Europe. Yet the implications and realities of this shift for INGOs and the changing expectations of the roles to be played by INGOs at the international and local levels have been barely addressed.

In this fast-changing context, the issues of concern, 'the donor fashions', also change – gender and environment have given way to rights, policy work and advocacy; service delivery and scaling up are being replaced with the need to enable the poor to lobby for their own rights; creating a niche is being replaced with the need to fit into global poverty reduction plans and meet targets such as the Millennium Development Goals, which most governments around the world have endorsed.

These shifts in emphasis are set in the context of a bureaucratic process of application. In the 1990s the most common form of UK government funding was through special budget lines for INGOs – the Joint Funding Scheme, where funding was given to support individual projects submitted by INGOs that met quite loose application criteria. Block grant funding was given to five major INGOs to support their work more broadly with initially very little oversight. However, an increasing donor concern to see evaluation of the use of the money emerged over time. Today the government funding process has become tighter, more bureaucratic, less amenable to face-to-face contacts, and the funding streams are more diverse. The new avenues of funding available to INGOs include government contracts (these are a lucrative area of funding which some INGOs are increasingly learning to bid for in competition with the private sector), grants for INGO-initiated work (the funds for these are declining and subject to increased control), partnership agreements (replacing the old block grants), and significantly direct funding to national and local NGOs in-country, which many INGOs are repositioning themselves to access to avoid being bypassed by the decentralization of government funding to their country offices.

There are shifts too in the stringency of the requirements for application and the monitoring of progress and performance. The process for applying to the Joint Funding Scheme was relatively open-ended and negotiable, the main requirement being that organizations were working on sustainable development issues, the logframe[1] was encouraged but not essential and there was a degree of flexibility that allowed the programme to be responsive to the agendas of INGOs. However, the application processes for the newer programmes are accompanied by a multitude of performance requirements and other conditions attached to funding. The new Civil Society Challenge Fund (CSCF), which has replaced the Joint Funding Scheme, and allocates only between £8 million and £10 million a year, requires that all INGO work to be funded must be in DFID priority countries, in areas DFID wants to focus on and incorporating approaches that DFID wants to promote. There is a two-stage tendering process, all done through written forms, assessed by external consultancy staff according to clear and fixed multiple criteria. The accountability requirements and the conditions to be met for performance – again all delivered through written reports – are tightly defined. The Partnership Programme Agreement is a more flexible fund allocating larger resources for selected agencies; while five block grant agencies received £16 million in 1995 fifteen INGOs had received partnership agreements in 2003/04 and received

£59 million (with one agency receiving almost half of the total). Accessing a Partnership Programme Agreement (PPA) has become more complex over time. Initially block grant agencies and a few selected INGOs were invited to apply, and negotiations took place over many months to ensure an alignment of INGO and donor interests. Subsequently, the process has changed to a tendering process. INGOs apply if they can fulfil the increasing criteria set by DFID, which wants to ensure that their strategies and those of the INGO are in harmony and that DFID can see which part of the strategy and which outcomes it is agreeing to fund. Logframes and indicators of outcome success are essential for a successful bid, and there are criteria requiring a focus on innovation, advocacy, learning and dissemination as well as indications of congruence with DFID's priorities. In 2005 twenty-three INGOs were invited to tender for PPAs but only four or five were to be awarded; agencies applying found the terms and conditions difficult to meet in many cases. These shifts have impacted deeply on the ways in which INGOs work.

Why are these changes happening?

Essentially the funders have changed their priorities as the global failure to achieve a real reduction in poverty has led to new and different analyses of the causes of world poverty and the means of resolving this. In the mid-1990s the World Bank and the IMF primed the engines for development by promoting global economic growth through liberalization and privatization, moving money away from supporting governments into the private sector. Markets were seen as the key to promoting economic development, and governments were increasingly relegated to a minor role. Development was understood as economic growth, and issues such as distribution of wealth were to be left to the market.

Within this broad global agenda national and international NGOs were seen as critical players; they were both expected to provide services for the poor that governments were failing to provide, and to fill gaps left by market failures. INGOs were to experiment and provide successful models of working with the poor, and to develop new partnerships with local players that later other donors, markets, governments or local INGOs could replicate. They were seen both as critical service providers and the crucible for innovative development work, including around economic development for the poor. INGOs were recipients of aid money for basic service delivery, bypassing the government in providing the poor with essential services. A parallel approach that escalated at this time was the need for the poor to earn a better income. Many INGOs and their partners promoted access to income for the poor through expanding their work in micro-finance, especially by providing micro-credit. Many later became micro-finance institutions working alongside the formal banking systems to reach the poorest. International and local NGOs also had a clear political role and were expected to promote the political pluralism that was seen as necessary for developing new liberal democracies. Many INGOs worked on issues underlying the perpetuation of poverty during this period, especially, for example, focusing on understanding social and political hierarchies and the complex nature of communities, addressing the inequalities caused by gender and disability, and highlighting the growing threat of HIV/AIDS.

In the 1990s the concern about the 'overblown nature of the state', particularly in sub-Saharan Africa, and its related inefficiencies, meant it was defined as a stumbling-block to the economic reforms defined as necessary for development. Many donors felt that INGOs understood the local context and were better placed than donors to reach the very poorest; the trend was for 'privatizing aid'. There was a significant rise in funding for INGOs and growth in the number and size of NGOs in the North and in the South, which enabled them to gain an international voice and often a place at the table of powerful decision-makers.

The focus of the development project changed dramatically following intense lobbying that led to new analyses and understandings of the causes of poverty presented in the 2000 World Bank poverty report, where the key drivers of pro-poor change were identified as 'enabling governments' rather than only markets and INGOs, though they still have important roles to play within the new development agenda. Aid was realigned in relation to poverty reduction, and governments, INGOs and the private sector were all expected to work together to address poverty reduction. Clear targets for this were subsequently set out in the Millennium Development Goals. Governments are to create the appropriate frameworks for economic growth, collaboration, decentralization and responsive policy and planning sensitive to the needs of the poor. Those governments that have good pro-poor policies will receive more aid and debt relief to support their work; the dominant belief is that aid which is given to governments without appropriate policies and structures for delivery achieves little, though this is queried by many, including UNCTAD (the United Nations Conference on Trade and Development). Civil society – including NGOs has a key role to play in poverty reduction by promoting good pro-poor policies, ensuring the involvement of poor people in policy development, and by holding government to account for its actions and the use of its budgets. As governments give increasing amounts of aid directly to national governments to use in their budgets, their control over tracking and accounting for these funds is eroded; they now increasingly require NGOs at the local and international level to find mechanisms to hold governments to account for the use of this funding, involving local people. This context has created a very complex funding environment in which international and local NGOs have to operate – on the one hand, they are heavily dependent on government funds, which are disbursed in each country in line with national poverty plans that all NGOs must fit in with, and, on the other hand, they are to call the same national and local government agencies to account for their wider use of donor/national budget funds. Yet, currently, there seems to be little awareness of the issues raised by these contradictory roles.

Some of the key characteristics of the current funding context

- There is *intense competition for funding* between INGOs given changing government agendas, fluctuating aid flows and changing aid mechanisms with the new terror agenda absorbing aid funding, the shift of money to funding NGOs directly in the South and the rise in the number of UK development INGOs in the past ten years.

- *Increased control and tight accountabilities* – INGOs have to apply for funds for projects and programmes that are in line with the latest strategic plans and priorities of funders. These are increasingly tightly defined by DFID, where all work must contribute to the Millennium Development Goals and DFID's current agenda in a country and to fit their country strategy plans, and in the EU where tenders are tightly defined.
- There has been *a significant rise in contracting*, and more larger INGOs apply for significant funds through contracts, which are designed and tightly controlled by the donor to fit their overall agenda and timetables for change, although there is room sometimes for some limited negotiation around key approaches/issues where views diverge.
- There is *far less responsive funding available for INGOs' own agendas* and ideas – for this kind of funding they now have to rely increasingly on small foundations and the two relatively independent sources of funding: the Big Lottery Fund (BL) and Comic Relief (CR), which are also tightening their terms and conditions and are increasingly focused on results – demonstrable change.
- There is a *focus now on 'civil society'*, not just INGOs, and a concern that INGOs must work in partnership with the wider civil society organizations and the private sector, as well as with government, something that was not their role traditionally.
- *A wide range of conditions* must be met, usually including working partici-patively, in partnership, doing work on the ground as well as policy advocacy work, participating in networking, ensuring sustainability, addressing gender and women's rights, and ensuring human rights are central to the approach. These conditions are multiple, complex and fast-changing.
- *The logframe and its associated tools dominate all funding streams*, and to get access everyone must be able to use, manipulate and speak the language of rational management targets, indicators, results, planned change and so on in English.

Consequences

For some INGOs there is more funding available in this evolving context, for example, those able to secure partnership agreements along with government and EU contracts. Water Aid has doubled in four years from £9 million to £20 million a year and the largest agencies such as the Save the Children Fund (SCF), Oxfam and others grow year on year with current incomes of well over £100 million a year, especially benefiting from the rise in institutional funding, including large sums for humanitarian and emergency work. However, the picture is different for many smaller and medium-sized INGOs where the competition for funding is intense, the conditions they are expected to meet are numerous and their chances of success are less than before. Some are disappearing, talking about merger or struggling on the edge of survival. These changes are also having a limiting effect on the way in which all INGOs can pursue their missions of developing capacities in the world's poorest places, and tensions consequently arise within organizations between front-line staff and senior managers (including the fundraisers) over delivering projects that appear to be more concerned with delivering to the agenda of funders rather than to beneficiaries. They see this as having a very negative effect on their activities and relationships. The problems we have identified include:

- *Focus on results, but funding is tied more to ability to meet donor demands*: while the focus is on demonstrable results, meeting targets in fact it has never been shown that funding success is closely tied to proven success on the ground. Research shows that development practice is complex, long term and challenging yet those INGOs that acknowledge this are often overlooked for funding in favour of those agencies that claim they can deliver change, on time, to budget and in measurable ways, meeting all the latest donor conditions. Assessments are largely paper-based and the quality of the practice of partnership, participation, capacity building is rarely examined in depth. Success in funding is often more tied to the abilities to talk the current donor language, write reports and fill out complex and bureaucratic forms, and show success in meeting donor demands on paper, as well as the organizational reputation and its own PR, rather than any serious assessment of what works best in complex contexts of real poverty.

- *Donors change their demands on INGOs and redefine their roles*: their role as service providers and agencies to fund in order to bypass corrupt states, which was in the ascendant in the 1990s, is now seen as irrelevant as institutional donors revert to putting their funding back through the state. The concept of the enabling and facilitative state now exists alongside their concern with corrupt states, and the role of INGOs has changed accordingly. They are now seen as essential watchdogs and guardians of donor money and how it is spent by governments, as well as agencies to promote the voices of the poor and civil society in policy debates and budget and other monitoring. Some risk becoming, in effect, the tools of northern donors, legitimizing and monitoring the latter's agenda.

- This has the knock-on effect that *speaking the language of donors often undermines INGOs' own mission, values and aims*: as INGOs increasingly adapt their language and projects to the current demands of donors, the tensions between those fundraising in the UK and those working on the ground increase. For INGOs that espouse concepts of partnership and participation and the involvement of beneficiaries in defining their own needs, the contradictions grow as project applications rise through the organization and are moulded by those raising funds to meet the latest donor requirements. While some say this is just cosmetic and projects continue unaffected, the experience is that local people and staff have their ideas overturned, and they are asked to report against criteria that have little or nothing to do with their understanding of the work. There is a growing split between those trying to work in partnership with local NGOs and poor people on the ground and those completing the paperwork, and often the demands of the donors override those of the partners and beneficiaries.

- There is a massive rise in *planning and accountability requirements, resulting in greater reporting and tighter planning, monitoring and evaluation processes*: over time the belief that INGOs could deliver effectively to the poor and work in innovative ways to alleviate and change poverty has waned, and there are increasing numbers of questions about their effectiveness. This has resulted in the now almost universal use of the logframe as a tool for management control and accountability, the demands for clear pre-set indicators of success, increased levels of reporting at all stages and a rise in external evaluations, in spite of the well-known problems with these and their often remote relationship to development realities (Maudsley *et al.*, 2002; Wallace with Bornstein and Chapman, 2006).
- *The language of INGOs and donors has increasingly merged*: this is partly because of INGO involvement and lobbying work with donors and partly a result of donors picking up key INGO ideas and making them conditions for funding – these would include partnership, participation and gender. The language has also merged as INGOs feel they have to use the dominant language of development in order to access funding.
- *Promise inflation*: the rising claims of INGOs about what they can do appear less based on realities on the ground and more on the ever-increasing demands and conditions of donors.
- *Growing standardization of development and a reliance on paperwork over relationships*: the concern with control, financial accountability and proving effective performance on paper often now outweighs the realities of doing development work in complex contexts around the world. There is an increasingly uniform language used from Mexico to Nigeria, Calcutta to Cape Town that comes from donors and northern INGOs, not from local analysis and organizations. The diversity of language, processes, procedures are being squeezed out into an almost uniform set of procedures, language and concepts. The changing language, the dominance of English and the demands of donors are changing the understanding of what development is and how to do it. The gap between the reality of the lives of poor people and the claims and reports of development work held in files and used for fundraising grows apace. Failure is disguised or hidden owing to the need for future funding.

Not just NGOs – the implications for fundraisers

The story of government funding for INGOs presents a depressing picture of competitive and constrained organizations getting sucked into much larger political agendas and finding that they are used to legitimize these. But NGOs are not alone in facing these challenges – they simply face them in very stark terms, often in high-profile settings. But comparable issues are widespread in the charity field, giving rise to familiar tensions within organizations between field staff and headquarters staff (often divided by culture as well as by distance) and within a country between operations, senior managers and fundraisers as those on the ground strive to fulfil agendas that they have not been involved in negotiating or agreeing. For this reason it is important for those engaging with these issues within organizations to take a step back and understand the common issues that this case illustrates for all organizations that wish to engage and lever funding from government.

First, policy churn is a fact of life. Discourses change. New initiatives come and go. Pendulums swing backward and forward. Organizations that want to prosper on government money have to be or become light on their feet.

Second, the worlds of government policy-makers, funders and grass-roots organizations and beneficiaries are far, far apart. They talk completely different languages, have very different perspectives and concerns, and do not really understand each other. In the case of INGOs they are literally on the other side of the world; but in many other cases – disability organizations, homelessness, social enterprises – they might just as well be.

Third, more and tighter contracting is the order of the day, and the use of rationalistic – or should we say ritualistic? – tools such as logframes is now pervasive. 'Promise inflation' is often an unintended consequence. And what has been called a 'culture of dishonesty' in reporting relationships often develops as the only way to handle dysfunctional relationships.

Finally, accountability incontinence is now an epidemic. Or, more precisely, the proliferation of formal measurement and reporting requirements is in many contexts becoming ever more burdensome – as the need to report on diffuse and hard-to-measure 'outcomes' is introduced, not *instead of* reporting on activities and outputs but *in addition*.

How to respond to these challenges?

This case illustrates starkly trends which may be found in many non-profit contexts these days. Government funding for any work carried out by non-profit organizations has all the same constraints and strings attached and it is not just INGOs that have problems with these issues. In the UK some organizations are starting to have doubts about the wider implications for their independence of new programmes introduced by a variety of government departments that use voluntary organizations to deliver services.

The options are difficult: one is to walk away from government funding completely, a path which very few organizations have shown any inclination to follow. Another is to lobby government to change the terms and conditions of funding and to open up again more responsive and flexible forms of funding that enable organizations to follow their own missions and respond to their constituency and those they aim to support. This is something few organizations have as yet done in any serious way, although British Overseas NGOs for Development (BOND) (the umbrella organization for INGOs) does make some limited representations on behalf of its members, mainly the small and medium-sized INGOs which are very vulnerable to government fads and fashions.

There is little evidence that many organizations are deciding to cut their dependence on this kind of funding and/or greatly diversify their income sources; rather the opposite is the case at the moment, with many organizations having greatly increased their official funding as a key goal. Some support this alongside negotiations with more flexible government funders (e.g. using lottery funding or seeking other, more enlightened institutional funders).

All government funding carries political implications: governments seek to use funding to achieve their purposes. If there is a good fit between these and the objects of the organization this can work well, but if organizations are trying to fit into a scheme which they may find morally difficult to justify, then it is probably not worth pursuing. The corollary of this type of funding is that, having wider political motives, it often does not have sustained long-term strategic objectives, but is subject to sudden change as political analyses of the nature of problems to be addressed are reviewed or appear to fail to produce results quickly enough. This means that total reliance on any one source of funding is a high-risk strategy, as the tales of small INGOs reveal.

Seeking funding from government has many dimensions to it, and those involved in fundraising need to understand the benefits and dangers of such funding in a fast-moving context and to explore how to get greater leverage in negotiating with government around funding and diversifying their funding, rather than narrowly relying on government. However, the important thing is that organizations go into these relationships with consideration. There need to be strategic discussions between all internal stakeholders in organizations about the extent to which they are prepared to compromise and adapt their values and purposes to accept this kind of funding. This means careful analysis of these situations, and building contacts with donors to develop relationships on both an individual and a network basis.

Finally, it should be remembered that no organization has a 'right' to survive. Organizations and fundraisers need to recognize the dilemmas for what they are and to make informed strategic choices for their organization based on an analysis of the opportunities presented by the wider environment and a sense of how these fit with the organization's own mission and values. There needs to be debates and open agreements within the organization about what is and what is not acceptable in terms of funders' demands, and these agreements need to be kept under regular review. They need to be placed within a framework where staff can refer to them and raise issues when problems appear to be arising.

Externally, there need to be discussions and debates with funders about the implications of their demands and decisions. Although there appears to have been little success in engaging with these issues in the INGO world, there have been some signs of hope on the UK domestic front. For example, in England the National Council of Voluntary Organizations (NCVO) has been pursuing these issues with some definite glimmers of success and hope through Compact Plus.[2] Government and policy-makers *are* beginning to get the message that they themselves, or at least their own bureaucracies, are the problem. They are actively looking for solutions – and locally the 'lead funder' approach is beginning to appear. If this becomes more widespread, then a restructuring of funding relationships and arrangements may slowly take place over the next few years. The broad pattern may be seen in relation to some EU funds, and in the UK in some aspects of the funding provided by the Learning and Skills Councils and Learn Direct: that is, the emergence of contract management intermediaries who interface between the world of officialdom and the realities on the ground.

Done well, this will make things easier; done badly, it will simply lengthen the chain and reduce the funds available for real work.

All this being said, some organizations will always find these relationships with government deeply problematic. Ultimately there are no magic formulae that can be followed blindly. Each funding scheme has to be properly researched and judged on its merits.

Notes

1   Logframe stands for 'logical framework', and refers to a tool for project planning and management that sets out the assumptions, key activities, outputs and intended outcomes of a project or programme. It is used first for planning and project approval, then for monitoring progress against the schedule, and finally for evaluation against the intended outcomes. Like all such rationalistic tools its value-in-use is determined by the way it is applied. It may be used 'loosely' as a basis for dialogue around the (inevitable) unexpected developments that mean even the best-laid plans have to be rethought. Or it can be used rigidly, with any deviation from an agreed plan being seen as a cause for concern and possible sign of mismanagement, or worse. The latter is of course much more likely in situations of low trust, and where poorly trained and overloaded staff have no other sources of information, and are under pressure to produce favourable reports. Many would say rigid uses are actually the norm. The use of logframes is now compulsory in projects funded by the World Bank, the EU and the DFID, and increasingly by other European donors.

2   An agreement between government and voluntary sector about the principles and practices which underpin a healthy relationship that set benchmarks for good practice. Although these can at times appear bland and unenforceable, they do provide some ground rules that may be used to highlight and open up debate about poor practices (http://www.thecompact.org.uk/).

References

Lindblom, C. E. (1979) 'Still muddling, not yet through', *Public Administration Review*, 39 (6): 517–526.

Mawdsley, E., Townsend, J., Porter, G. and Oakley, P. (2002) 'Knowledge, power and development agendas: NGOs north and south, *Intrac Management and Policy Series*, 14, Oxford.

Wallace, T. with Bornstein, L. and Chapman, J. (2006) *The Aid Chain: Commitment and Coercion in Development NGOs*. ITDG, Rugby.

PART FOUR

Challenges for senior professionals and trustees

INTRODUCTION

THIS PART CONSIDERS ISSUES that are about fundraising, but go beyond it. These questions are never going to be left to the fundraisers. They may be raised in the press, or by senior managers in charities and their trustees. And it will not be enough to say, 'I am a fundraiser – trust me'. None of them is straightforward, but those working in this area and who aspire to senior positions cannot wish these issues away claiming that it is all just a matter of the bottom line. It is in the way such matters are handled that one sees the difference between the narrowly focused functionary and a mature professional.

The first such issue, explored in Chapter 12, concerns the difficulties in making judgements about the performance of fundraising departments and programmes. Paton describes the operation of the world's longest-running scheme for the confidential comparison of fundraising costs and returns. This piece was written several years ago – but little has changed. It still offers by far the most detailed data on which to make judgements about the performance of different types of programmes. However, Paton also explains why those judgements will often be qualified, uncertain and contestable.

Chapter 13 tackles the regulation of fundraising, one of the hottest issues facing the profession. Harrow and Douthwaite argue that one cannot grasp what is happening in this field without understanding broader trends in societal governance, and in the emergence of new, multi-level forms of regulation in industry and commerce more widely. This is not to endorse new regulations (they may arise for inappropriate reasons), nor to reject them (some issues really will need to be addressed). Rather it is about understanding regulatory systems – so as to address problems at an appropriate level and in ways that are proportionate to the risk.

If ethics is 'obedience to the unenforceable', then Chapter 14 by Fischer provides an essential companion to the discussion of regulation. She provides a refreshing alternative to the usual notion that ethics is about grey areas, arguing that generally things are clearly wrong or right, and when they are unclear we need a process to clarify the issues and bring the basic ethical commitments to the foreground. She highlights three basic value commitments – the organizational mission, our relationships with people and our own sense of personal integrity. While the ways these are enacted will vary from person to person, they may none the less be used to construct stories that reveal alternative ways of resolving ethical dilemmas. She offers a tool to do this and illustrates its use, while emphasizing that ethical problems will never become subject to formulaic resolution.

In Chapter 15 van der Gaag brings these discussions down to earth with a thoughtful but sustained critique of a central but often taken-for-granted decision in the fundraising process: the choice of images that fundraisers use or create in order to evoke sympathy with their cause. For years, many organizations have depicted their beneficiaries as helpless, even pathetic victims, often reinforcing negative stereotypes in the mass media. The author examines what this has meant in the fields of development and disability, questioning whether it is really necessary, and suggesting that, however well intentioned, such practices can actually undermine the very purposes the charity exists to serve. Moreover, earlier agreements to address this issue through codes of practice seem not to have been sustained.

Finally, in Chapter 16, Richard Brewster tackles the question of fundraising portfolios – how does one determine a mix of different sorts of funding to best secure a charity's future? This is a far more difficult question than might be thought – and some of the popular advice (e.g. about diversifying to spread risk) needs to be sharply qualified if it is not to be costly and misleading in particular contexts. He presents important insights from theory and research, highlighting the importance of interdependencies, of transaction costs, and of that very scarce resource – the time and attention of the Chief Executive and senior managers.

Chapter 12

Rob Paton

BENCHMARKING FUNDRAISING PERFORMANCE

Edited from: Paton, R. (1999) 'Performance comparisons in fundraising: the case of Fundratios', *International Journal of Non-profit and Voluntary Sector Marketing*, 4: 4, pp. 287–299.

Introduction

FUNDRAISERS NEED TO BE able to compare results if they are to judge the success of their different programmes and schemes. But any such comparisons are fraught with difficulties. This chapter reviews the experience of what is almost certainly the longest-running scheme for comparing fundraising performance anywhere in the world. It describes the way it has developed, the challenges it has faced and the ways in which its figures are used, drawing on the views of a wide range of participants. It concludes by highlighting the prospects and possibilities now open to the scheme, and its longer-term significance for non-profit managers.

In search of comparability

Once upon a time, it was easy for fundraisers to know how well they were doing: either the money was coming in and the appeal target was being approached – or not. Costs were so few and limited that they hardly entered the picture. Sometimes, that basic simplicity still holds. More often, professional fundraisers operate in highly complex and rapidly changing fundraising environments that involve long-term planning and investment and a multiplicity of income streams. In these circumstances truly excellent and truly awful results are still obvious, but anything in between will usually sustain a range of conflicting assessments. Internal comparisons, with a target or with earlier time periods, do not resolve the uncertainty. Fundraising managers, like managers of all sorts, also need external comparisons with a similar programme elsewhere, or with industry standards or trends.

Nor is this simply a management issue. The performance of fundraisers is under scrutiny as never before. In both Europe and North America, public confidence in charities is in doubt, and concern about fundraising costs and methods is prompting calls for new regulatory arrangements. Published 'league tables' and analyses using broad-brush measures gained from surveys and/or the data contained in statutory returns are becoming more common and elaborate (Kaehler and Sargeant, 1998; Pharoah, 1997). Charity managers may, privately and with good reason, decry these as still being too crude. But how can they respond to this combination of internal and external imperatives towards measuring and demonstrating the propriety and cost-effectiveness of their activities?

The benchmarking solution

One solution is to join a benchmarking club through which much more detailed comparisons of costs and returns are arranged on a confidential basis. In this way managers can, in principle, obtain the information they require both for internal management decision making, and for an understanding of where and why their performance may appear open to public or regulatory criticism, and how they may counter such a charge. But do they? How successful are such clubs in generating useful comparative data? Are fine-grain comparisons of performance really possible, and what are the difficulties and costs involved? How do managers use the information? In particular, does it facilitate performance improvement – for example, by highlighting activities offering scope for improvement, by suggesting where, among club members, best practice may be found and emulated, by informing resource allocation decisions, and so on? This chapter is based on a study of the Fundratios scheme – the largest and longest-running exercise in systematic performance comparison in UK fundraising. It also briefly compares the Fundratios experience with similar exercises elsewhere, and considers the prospects for performance measurement and comparison in fundraising in the future.

The Fundratios story

What became Fundratios was initiated in 1986 by George Medley, then head of WWF(UK) and Chair of the then Institute of Charity Fundraising Managers (ICFM). He saw it as one way of bringing a more rigorous business discipline into the world of charity fundraising, and turned to the Centre for Inter-firm Comparison (CIFC), whose services he had used when working in the private sector, to provide assistance and a confidential data-handling service. The first exercise in 1987–88 involved only ten charities and was not formally an ICFM project. But by 1991 Fundratios had been adopted by ICFM and a partnership arrangement worked out with CIFC, with the former promoting the scheme to its members and hosting meetings (and later taking a modest commission) while the latter administered the survey of fundraising costs and income, and collated, analysed and distributed the data.

The basic framework: annual cycle and report structure

The exercise has been repeated every year since then, and the basic pattern has not changed. An invitation to participate is sent out early in the year, and survey forms then follow in April or May to those who sign up. The return date of 1 June allows two months for those whose financial year ends in March, and longer for others, to gather the necessary data concerning the preceding financial year. For many, completion of the form is a significant undertaking, involving desk research, calculation and estimation covering both financial and non-financial data. Consistency is encouraged by providing guidance on how to complete the forms, and CIFC staff can be contacted for advice.

When forms are returned the data are checked and entered, and any inconsistencies or anomalies resolved by contacting the charity involved. A preliminary report based on the charity's individual return is then sent to it for checking. In September the main report is distributed to participants. This is in two main parts. First, there is a summary analysis, which displays and comments on trends in the different sources of revenue, compared with previous years, and which allows participants to compare their performance with the range of others on the key ratios of 'Percentage growth' and 'Income per £1 spent' for the main areas of fundraising. Secondly, a detailed breakdown of costs and returns for each of these major areas of activity is provided in tabular form, in which each participating charity can, once again, compare its performance with 'high', 'low' and average results. It must be stressed, however, that participants know only their own results and who had participated in the exercise; the particular results of other charities are presented anonymously, to preserve confidentiality. The coverage of the report is summarised in the box alongside, which is taken from the 1998 'Invitation to participate' (the wording of this invitation has changed very little over the years).

Finally, later in the autumn, a meeting is held in which participants review the exercise and agree changes in the survey for the following year. Characteristically, many ideas for additional information are presented and there is little agreement on what can be removed.

What Fundratios provides to participants

The report is structured into the following modules:

*   *Summary analysis* – Provides details of the relative importance of all sources of revenue; details of voluntary income, growth rates and costs.
*   *Central appeals* – The profitability of membership; funds raised from national gaming and lotteries and special events.

- *Local fundraising* – Activities of local organisations; schools/youth groups; effectiveness of house-to-house and street collections; collecting-boxes. Productivity of fundraisers and their costs.
- *Corporate and trusts* – Value and growth of corporate donations, sponsorship, joint promotions, licensing and trust donations. Productivity of fundraisers.
- *Direct marketing* – Comparison of response rates, donation value and costs per £1 spent for warm and cold mailing, coupon response, advertising and inserts and telemarketing.
- *Legacies* – Growth and average values of pecuniary, residuary and specific legacies. Cost and marketing details.
- *Trading* – Shop trading for donated and bought goods; sales per square foot; profitability. Comparison of mail order response and average order value. Cost analysis and donations.
- *Other* – Major donations, Gift Aid, payroll giving, house-to-house collections, committed giving and covenants.

Growth and elaboration

Within this annual cycle, the scheme has expanded and grown more complex over the years. In 1991 there were 14 participating charities, and each year some have left while others join, or rejoin. In the mid-1990s recruitment and retention both improved, and a slow upward trend accelerated to the 1997–98 total of 43. Since 1993, 16 of the charities have been involved continuously, providing a core membership to the 'club'. These are all among the very largest UK charities – indeed, Fundratios was initially promoted only to the top 100 charities. In more recent years efforts have been made to make the scheme more attractive to smaller and medium-sized charities, principally by inviting them to submit a reduced data set, and providing a separate set of tables based on smaller charities.

Another clear trend has been a gradual increase in the amount of data sought from charities, and in the amount of analysis and reporting provided. The 1991 survey involved up to 245 lines of data entry. By 1996 this had grown to 466, whereupon it was cut back to 388 in the following year in an effort at simplification. But in pursuit of greater consistency the form was thoroughly reviewed for 1998, and the number of lines rose again – to 477. A similar pattern appears on the 'output' side; the 1991 survey produced a 75-page report with 17 main tables and 19 charts. The 1998 survey produced a report of about 100 pages, with two different versions (for large and small charities) of 28 tables, and with more than 20 charts and 'profiles'.

These annual changes and elaborations have been driven by efforts to improve the scope, ease of completion, accuracy and usefulness of the survey. Thus, at various times, revisions have been made to accommodate new fundraising methods (such as telemarketing) and changes in the significance of other methods (e.g. corporate fundraising); to exclude information no longer seen as essential; to reduce double counting; and to clarify the requirements and improve the layout.

Concerns about the data

Most of these changes have been in response to the three main criticisms that have been levelled at Fundratios: first, that the forms are difficult and time-consuming for staff to complete; secondly, that the data it generates are insufficiently reliable; thirdly, that the figures are insufficiently comparable. The problem, of course, is that, while everyone would like simpler forms *as well as* more useful and reliable comparisons, in practice these criticisms tend to pull in opposite directions. The trade-off is stark and unavoidable. It is also inevitable that even the most worthwhile improvement carries with it the price of undermining the year-on-year comparisons, which are also valuable.

The basic philosophy of the scheme has always been pragmatic, as the following paragraph, which has appeared in every version of the General Notes, indicates:

> Figures need not be accurate to the penny, please state costs and income to the nearest £1,000. It is recognised that in many cases it will be necessary for participants to make estimates of some of the information. Similarly it is recognised that not all participants will be able to provide all of the data. Where, for instance, a particular activity is insignificant, do not waste time researching it.

However, this leads to the difficulty, as expressed by one respondent whose charity had withdrawn from the scheme, that:

> We didn't have all the figures and had to put in guesstimates. But if we were doing it, others would be as well, so how reliable were they?

Nevertheless, this respondent acknowledged that with a new accounting system completion of the forms might be easier in the future, and her charity was thinking of rejoining Fundratios. More broadly, there seemed to be two responses to the issue of data quality.

The 'good enough' view

Some accepted that the comparability and reliability of the data are suspect, but consider the scheme is good enough for most of the purposes for which it is used, and is by far the best available. It was pointed out, for example, that it becomes available relatively quickly; other sources of data tend to be at least two years out of date. And, regarding comparability, one director of fundraising argued that, although other charities calculated their costs in somewhat different ways, so long as they all went on doing so fairly consistently, comparisons of relative performance over time were still meaningful. This was also the view of CIFC who have some 40 years' experience of arranging such comparisons in a very wide range of industries. Their view was that such concerns are normal, and more or less inevitable. The collaborative effort required to achieve significantly greater precision and confidence is very considerable and is not usually available. The project manager accepted that there were some particular difficulties in the

Fundratios scheme – mainly because charities might be pursuing campaigning and public education, as well as fundraising goals, through their activities, which complicates cost allocation – but he did not think these made much difference or undermined the value of the exercise. In his view, the customers were the participating fundraisers, and they were broadly content with the service they received.

The 'improvers' view

The opposing view is represented most clearly by a senior finance officer in a large national charity who believed that the forms had 'lacked integrity' and that the comparisons were of 'no value'. His complaints were that the form totals were not tied back to the figures in charities' accounts; that some data could be entered three times, perhaps by different staff, generating inconsistencies and double counting; and that in some charities the forms were completed by fundraising rather than finance staff, who would be unlikely to recognise the pitfalls. In consequence, he had arranged for one of his staff to spend a couple of weeks thoroughly reviewing and revamping the form and its accompanying guidance. The resulting proposals included an explicit link between the charity's annual accounts and the figures entered in the 'summary of sources of income and resources expended' section. They were discussed and largely accepted by a subset of the participating charities, and were introduced in 1998. It remains to be seen, however, whether the undoubted advances, both technical and presentational, that this effort has produced will do much to reduce the concerns about data quality.

The comparability issue

Data quality was only one factor calling in question the value of the comparisons generated by Fundratios. Respondents referred to three other reasons:

- The anonymity of the data meant that one did not know which of the other charities were in a situation comparable to one's own. 'It was disillusioning; it made us look inefficient. But it is much harder to raise money for mental health, compared to children and animals' (former participant). This view was not universally shared; other participants claimed to have informal discussions in which the anonymity rule was relaxed.
- As well as different situations, charities operate different policies, and it was claimed that these affect their returns. 'Performance is a function of your own standards and self-imposed constraints', as one respondent put it. For example, a charity that chooses the constraint of using only methods that will not exceed a 20 per cent cost ratio is unlikely to achieve the same net revenue growth as a charity that sets out to maximise net revenue more or less regardless of cost. Again, in this case, the anonymity rule precludes, or at least limits and drives underground, like-with-like comparisons.
- Performance figures and comparisons can be misleading because 'when you spend the money' and 'when you get the return' often fall in different accounting periods. This is particularly true in relation to direct marketing,

which can involve substantial long-term investment and where there is all the difference in the world between 'milking' an established donor base, and trying to build up or renew such a base by recruiting donors. Although a distinction is made between 'warm' and 'cold' mailings this was not felt to be adequate by some and, according to one respondent, 'It is impossible to tell what is going on'.

How the data are used

Given these widely acknowledged limitations, why do the participants sign up for Fundratios year after year? How do they use the comparative information? Essentially four different benefits were claimed by those interviewed.

'The reassurance factor'

Often the information confirmed what was already believed to be the case or was otherwise 'nice to know', without prompting new courses of action. As one respondent explained, 'It shows that others are facing the same difficulties, it does that fine'.

Strategic review

Specific instances were offered by two informants of occasions when the information provided by Fundratios played an important part in strategic decision making: in one case concerning the implications of an emergent decline in legacy income upon which the charity had been very dependent, and in the other concerning a decision to pull out of certain sorts of local fundraising. It may be asked whether the participants are wise to make such judgements on the basis of figures from a small, self-selected sample of charities. However, this was not an issue for the participants themselves, for three reasons: although few in number, they raised approaching half of UK voluntary income; in terms of detail and recency the figures were by far the best available; and strategy decisions would never be based on information from Fundratios alone. Hence, in conjunction with other information, the data were seen as useful market intelligence: 'an incredibly valuable tool that gives weight to the whole function within the organisation', as one of the core members put it.

A political resource

In discussion, it became clear that overwhelmingly the Fundratios data were seen, used and valued by fundraisers as a resource in their discussions with colleagues and staff over resource allocation or performance expectations; 'to bash others over the head' in a respondent's blunt terms. Another said he used Fundratios data with his Trustees 'to get them off my back'. Interestingly, this director used his organisation's poor showing in a particular line of activity to support proposals to spend more on it ('we're under-performing because we have been under-investing'), while another director had used his position at the top of a cost–return table to argue the same case ('our position is unsustainable, and we can afford to spend more and still look good against industry norms'). However, this same director also said that he might pull out of the scheme because, in the context of an uncertain relationship with a new chief executive, he was concerned that the figures might be used against him.

Supporting inter-organisational learning and collaboration

While Fundratios itself aims only to provide comparative data, a subset of 22 participants from the largest fundraising charities (who meet informally as the Appeal Directors Group) have gone further to discuss it in detail, in the manner of a benchmarking club. Starting in 1996, several sessions were spent discussing how different activities were carried out, informed by the relevant subsets of Fundratios data, and with the ground rule that everyone would share their information equally and honestly. Apart from generating much greater insight into the meaning of particular figures and the reasons for variations, this had a powerful effect in building the new group, allowing it to tackle other matters of common interest. More specifically, it has led to plans for collaboration in a generic legacy campaign – a constructive alternative to 'grinding each other down in competition', as one participant put it.

Why do some leave?

Given these apparent uses and benefits, one can ask why it is that more charities have not joined the scheme, and why a few have left it, either indefinitely or for several years at a time. Respondents echoed the limitations discussed earlier, referring to the cost in staff time, the cost of subscribing (about £800 per year, which is very little for the large charities but significant for others), the doubtful quality of the information, and the lack of comparability. But most importantly – and, indeed, most reasonably – charities seemed not to re-subscribe because they found that they were not using the figures:

> We were just looking at a load of figures . . . people gave them a quick flip through but they were not really used . . . I didn't see that anyone was working any differently.

The CIFC project manager interpreted this slightly differently. His view was:

> By and large, the information required is information that they should have anyway . . . we try to sell to organisations, but it is individuals that buy, and some of them are not drawn to this sort of analysis.

The prospects of Fundratios

How is the scheme likely to develop? Participants think it needs to address two further issues. First, the pursuit of more reliable data continues, with some informants suggesting there was scope for tightening base definitions further, and perhaps for some auditing of data quality. Secondly, as the number of participating charities grows and becomes more diverse, there is likely to be demand for a more differentiated range of services, especially to address the comparability issue. This trend has begun with the introduction of the smaller charities subset into the annual Fundratios report. But one can envisage further developments, including tailored reports providing comparison with selected, but still anonymous, subsets of charities.

Another distinct possibility is the introduction of a very limited quarterly return, to act as an 'early warning system' for the sector regarding trends in giving. This has in fact been tried once before in the mid-1990s, but what had been intended to be a simple exercise 'turned complicated' as sponsorship by a bank attracted 60 charities of all shapes and sizes, many of whom had not had prior experience of Fundratios. After the initial sponsorship expired, many did not renew and the scheme was abandoned. Learning from this, the new scheme is likely to be limited to 20 of the largest charities, which have the administrative capacity for such an exercise. Between them, they are likely to account for some 40 per cent of the income of the top 500 charities, which is quite enough to provide indications of broad trends in giving behaviour.

Discussion

So what light does Fundratios throw on the issues raised at the start of this chapter? How do these compare with experience elsewhere?

Fundratios as a benchmarking club

First, it is clear that Fundratios is a benchmarking club only in a colloquial sense. It was originally promoted as an exercise in 'fundraising research', and seems to have adopted the benchmarking terminology later as it became better-known. In the management literature (Camp , 1989; Zairi and Leonard, 1994), benchmarking usually refers to a method of performance improvement in which performance comparisons are used to identify the 'best in class' whose detailed methods are then studied and adapted. Although some club-like activities have been informally associated with Fundratios (e.g. the discussions of the Appeals Directors Group), the CIFC sees its role as enabling participants to identify and measure the extent of any performance 'gap', and hence to focus attention where it matters; the follow-through into performance improvement is up to individual members and outside the scope of the scheme.

Nevertheless, there are similarities in the Fundratios experience to what is reported in the benchmarking literature, especially concerning the fact that benchmarking is overwhelmingly a large organisation's game, and concerning the difficulties and limitations of performance comparisons. The general view of practitioners and experts is that close comparability is a chimera, its pursuit is a sink for time and effort, and it distracts from the more important fundamental purpose of identifying likely sources of better practice and investigating and learning from them. However, this general view is in the context of one-off benchmarking projects and temporary clubs. Even if it strikes a cautionary note over the degree of precision and comparability it is realistic to expect, it is doubtful how relevant it is to the sort of long-term scheme that Fundratios has become.

Scope for benchmarking projects?

Could Fundratios support benchmarking groups aiming more specifically at performance improvement? It seems quite possible, for example, that Fundratios data now provide enough of a foundation for finer-grain examination of methods and working practices in order to identify both specific areas and the means for nuts-and-bolts improvement. The additional information required would probably not be very great, although on the basis of benchmarking clubs in other fields this will be much easier and more productive if it is undertaken by small subsets, which are comparable in terms of the particular activities being examined, and if it involves staff directly responsible (instead of, or as well as, those at director level). Perhaps this is unnecessary, because good practice already diffuses well between organisations informally, through professional networks and in many other ways. But the idea may be worth some consideration; little would be risked in an experiment, and the example of the Appeals Directors Group shows how it could be done within the current confidentiality rules.

Whose data for what purposes?

Perhaps the most fundamental issue for Fundratios concerns the expanding range of uses to which the data are now being put, and hence the conflicting requirements that those interested in the figures have of them. What seems to have started as a rough-and-ready exercise in market intelligence owned by the fundraising function of large charities is increasingly used for performance measurement and strategic planning, while issues of public trust and accountability lurk in the background. But, of course, the more the figures are used politically within or without the organisation, the more their validity and reliability will be examined and challenged. It is not surprising, therefore, that finance professionals are now becoming closely involved, as has happened also in the USA (Greenfield, 1994). This quickly leads to debates about the 'real' costs of fundraising.

For example, Rooney (1997) argues that the methods recommended for US universities and colleges are misleading. The two main distortions are:

*   the inclusion of funds that were attracted with very little (if any) involvement of development programme staff; for example, faculty research grants obtained as part of normal academic work.
*   the omission of various expenses that should be included in costs; most notably for space utilisation, depreciation, maintenance, utilities and a share of the salary costs of the most senior university staff who commonly spend a significant amount of time supporting development efforts (and may have been recruited partly with this in mind).

These are not trivial technicalities: Rooney suggests the former can increase the apparent yield of fundraising by a factor of four, and the latter can understate expenses by 20 per cent.

These issues may have some parallels in the Fundratios scheme. For example, some debate took place over whether and how to include income from 'captive' trusts (currently, if this income is significant it is included, but not as part of the income generated by efforts at fundraising from trusts). Likewise, the Fundratios guidance notes have always focused on direct costs, making no mention (except in shop trading income) of accommodation costs, and explicitly excluding any apportionment of general management time associated with approaches to major donors. If the purpose is to obtain useful (and confidential) market intelligence, the Fundratios guidelines cannot be faulted – anything else would introduce further complications and reduce comparability. But obviously these aspects of any charity's Fundratios figures need to be clearly understood, and perhaps some adjustment made, if they are being used in other contexts.

Underlying accounting difficulties

These points begin to illustrate the sorts of issues that are involved in constructing cost and income figures for fundraising activities. Arguably two others are at least as important.

First, there is the problem of cost allocation between fundraising and closely related activities. For example, are the costs of 'response handling' part of fundraising, or more properly allocated to the finance function and hence general administrative costs? And how should one disentangle fundraising expenditure from member and public relations or from public education, from campaigning, which may be an important part of the organisation's mission and be carried on through a range of mass fundraising activities? Thus a children's, or health, or environmental charity can reasonably claim that part of the benefit of, say, the family cycle run is increased awareness and even some lasting attitudinal and behavioural change; therefore it is quite reasonable to allocate some of the cost of organising such events to mission-related programmes. And is it not perfectly reasonable to charge part of the director of fundraising's salary costs to the general management overhead, given the vital (and time-consuming) contribution such a person makes to the senior management team?

The arbitrariness of these judgements is well illustrated by the story one director of fundraising gave of the way this issue had been handled in his charity. Originally he had devised a formula, based on separate allocations in 16 areas, under which 60 per cent of the overall costs of his area were allocated to other activities. However, in his absence one year a figure of 50 per cent across the board was used instead, which had the effect of suddenly increasing his publicly reported costs of fundraising by 25 per cent without any commensurate increase in income. This brought the matter to the attention of the Trustees of the charity, who asked for a briefing so they could decide a proper policy. The fundraising director then produced a proposal based on separate allocations in 20 areas that would have led to 57 per cent of the overall costs being allocated elsewhere. In the event, the

Trustees decided that he was being too conservative and they agreed allocations that resulted in 63 per cent of that year's costs being attributed to other activities! Their formal position was that the charity managers had to have written and defensible procedures which the Trustees could support. But, tacitly, it was well understood that the charity operated in a highly competitive environment and that it was to its advantage to allocate costs to other headings wherever and whenever the opportunity arose.

On this issue, the Charity Accounting Statement of Recommended Practice (Charity Commissioners, 1995) argues that:

> It is not possible to define precisely what should be included under each heading as each charity's circumstances will be different. (p. 35)

It therefore restricts itself to enunciating a few general principles without elaboration. Given the severe difficulties involved, one can certainly argue that such discretion was the better part of valour. Nevertheless, the clear consensus among charity accountants and fundraisers is that the new standard has done little if anything to restrain 'creative' accounting – and the researchers agree (Pharoah, 1997). Meanwhile the growing regulatory and public concern about fundraising costs and performance increases the incentive to apportion costs in ways that show the organisation in a favourable light.

Intangible assets

The second thorny issue concerns the investment costs of fundraising, and especially the treatment of donor acquisition (Reed, 1991). Currently, this is recorded as a revenue cost in annual fundraising, but everyone knows perfectly well that, for the accounting period in question, most methods for acquiring new donors are more likely to cost money than make money; it is in fact an investment, but one amply justified by the flow of future donations. The trouble is that such investments in donor acquisition and database systems are intermittent, and further undermine efforts at performance comparison. Moreover, until fundraising organisations track changes in their intangible assets and reasonable expectations of future pledges, their measures of performance are entirely backward-looking, offering no recognition of what may have been achieved in building up (or, alternatively, running down through neglect) underlying capacities and future prospects.

Arguably, this is no longer an intractable problem that simply has to be accepted. Techniques for estimating the lifetime value of donors are becoming increasingly sophisticated (Hunter and Hill, 1998; Sargeant, 1998) and one can envisage a further development of Fundratios in which the larger and most established charities, if only for certain purposes, begin to measure and compare investments and assets in fundraising using a common framework. This might be better approached as a research exercise to begin with; but, then, Fundratios was initially a research exercise.

Analysing for comparability

The final issue raised by the Fundratios experience concerns the ways in which the comparability issue can be addressed so that subscribers can have greater confidence that like is being compared, if not with like, at least with something not too dissimilar. One approach, referred to at the end of the case, is that subscribers choose their own, more or less anonymous, subset of comparators; indeed, to some extent this is what participants do already. Assuming that the number of participating charities continues to increase, this might well produce somewhat more meaningful comparisons, and it would certainly be easier for participants to interpret the figures. However, given their broadly political use and the fact that there are always many bases on which comparisons can be made, one can safely predict that this would also shift the grounds on which the figures are deemed (by some) to be questionable or misleading.

Another approach would be to make the comparisons through a statistical model that allows for a wide range of differences in inputs, outputs and circumstances. The obvious candidate here is the recently developed operations research technique of Data Envelopment Analysis (DEA) (El-Mahgary, 1995). This is beginning to be applied to questions concerning resource use (Zaleski and Zech, 1997) and fundraising cost-effectiveness (Luksetich and Hughes, 1997) in the non-profit sector. It is also being used as the basis for generic functional benchmarking services (Wood et al., 1997). However, the value of DEA or, more precisely, the appropriate conditions for its use and the extent of its contribution and limitations for managerial purpose – key issues for any sophisticated statistical tool – remain unclear and are unlikely to become clear in the immediate future. Again, this suggests that research collaboration may be an appropriate way to move Fundratios forward.

Conclusions

Fundratios has become an established feature of UK fundraising. For all its difficulties, it holds by far the most accurate and detailed information on comparative performance currently available. Its continuing subscribers believe that, when used in the context of other internal and external information (including discreet informal conversations with peers in the scheme), it provides a much fuller understanding of comparative costs, returns, trends and possibilities than is otherwise possible. It allows them to make and justify longer-term investments with far greater confidence.

But arguably Fundratios has a wider significance. It both represents and reinforces, in the particular world of charities, a broader long-term trend in management towards the wider, more frequent and more detailed use of performance measures (Eccles, 1991). As one interviewee pointed out:

> I now have my own management accountant in the fundraising department. In the old days we only had quarterly figures – and they came in two months late. We were navigating in the dark. There has been a major shift over the last five years.

The largest charities may be leading the way, but the medium-sized ones will gradually follow. Data-handling costs continue to fall; accounting and reporting systems become friendlier *and* more sophisticated; the staff skills are still developing; and the environment increasingly expects measurement. Even if small charities are unlikely to be drawn in, the trend towards more measurement still has a long way to run.

This trend has many longer-term implications, not least for the competences required for fundraising staff and Trustees, which those who teach and recruit for these roles will need to consider. But it is also the main reason why it is a safe bet that, in one form or another, Fundratios will continue to grow and develop. In what way this will happen is the next question; a range of interesting possibilities exists.

References

Camp, R. C. (1989) *Benchmarking The Search for Industry Best Practices that Lead to Superior Performance*, ASQC Quality Press, Milwaukee, WI.

The Charity Commissioners (1995) *Accounting by Charities – Statement of Recommended Practice*, The Charity Commission, London.

Eccles, R. G. (1991) 'The performance measurement manifesto', *Harvard Business Review*, Jan.–Feb., pp. 131–37.

El-Mahgary, S. (1995) 'Data envelopment analysis', *OR Insight*, Vol. 8, No. 4, pp. 15–22.

Greenfield, J. M. (ed.) (1994) *Financial Practices for Effective Fund Raising: New Directions for Philanthropic Fundraising*, Jossey-Bass Inc., San Francisco, CA.

Hunter, T. and Hill, R. (1998) 'Prediction of donor lifetime value and the development of true segmented donor strategy', *Non-profit and Voluntary Sector Marketing*, Vol. 3, No. 4, pp. 312–20.

Kaehler, J. and Sargeant, A. (1998) 'Financial-based measures of performance for UK charities', in *Performance Measurement – Theory and Practice*, Centre for Business Performance, University of Cambridge, Cambridge.

Luksetich, W. and Hughes, P. N. (1997) 'Efficiency of fundraising activities: an application of data envelopment analysis', *Non-profit and Voluntary Sector Quarterly*, Vol. 26, No. 1, pp. 73–84.

Pharoah, C. (1997) 'The numbers game – counting voluntary income after SORP', in C. Pharoah (ed.) *Dimensions of the Voluntary Sector*, Charities Aid Foundation, West Malling, pp. 163–9.

Reed, A. (1991) 'A management accounting dilemma', *NGO Finance*, Vol. 1, No. 2, p. 10.

Rooney, P. M. (1997) 'A better method for analyzing the costs and benefits of fund raising at universities', 26th Annual ARNOVA Conference, Indianapolis, IN.

Sargeant, A. (1998) 'Donor lifetime value: An empirical analysis', *Non-profit and Voluntary Sector Marketing*, Vol. 3, No. 4, pp. 283–97.

Wood, D., Jones, J. and Barrar, P. (1997) *Benchmarking the Finance Function – A Practical Approach for Small and Medium-sized Enterprises*, The Institute of Chartered Accountants, London.

Zairi, M. and Leonard, P. (1994) *Practical Benchmarking: The Complete Guide*, Chapman & Hall, London.

Zaleski, P. A. and Zech, C. E. (1997) 'Efficiency in religious organizations', *Non-profit Management and Leadership*, Vol. 8, No. 1, pp. 3–17.

Chapter 13

Jenny Harrow and Sue Douthwaite

FUNDRAISING REGULATION:
FOR WHOM AND BY WHOM?

Introduction: the prominence and significance of fundraising regulation

REGULATION IS A PROMINENT issue in fundraising circles. As charity fundraising is increasingly successful and gains public attention, so public and governmental wariness of its practices seems to grow. Many fundraisers dislike or regret the apparent lack of trust in charities, which regulation implies, and the resource demands, which it imposes. Arguments about the 'burdens' of regulation are commonplace. Other fundraisers see regulation as unavoidable in charity contexts, as in any other industrial sphere, and point to its role in maintaining donor confidence. Both these approaches reflect outworn notions of regulation; either as just another government activity, to be deplored routinely, or as a persuasive panacea for the sector's problems. This chapter argues that new and enduring modes of regulation are here to stay and are likely to increase, as they will do in other industries. As regulation modes grow in prominence, the responses of fundraisers towards them become significant.

Fundraisers need to recognize that engagement with fundraising regulation is a central part of professional practice, affecting both specialists and managers in an organization that uses fundraising. Readiness to participate in debates on regulation in informed ways will be required. This may involve challenging particular proposals, their forms and means of implementation or supporting their introduction and enforcement. Any sense of indifference towards regulation by fundraisers will damage fundraisers' professional standing. Equally, intolerance of regulation is not an option, whether this is presented as well-meaning ('we really are too busy to pay attention to this') or wilful ('this can't possibly apply to us').

Fundraisers' decisions, then, in the light of the regulatory frameworks within which they work or actively advocate, will be critical; especially as new and changing regulatory forms offer opportunities in which credible fundraising will thrive.

This chapter begins with a discussion of the concept of regulation and especially the new forms emerging during the past twenty years. This background is important because regulation is a 'cluster' concept, with multi-layered forms and expressions. Groups and organizations which are the focus of attention have opportunities to influence the nature, direction and enforcement of particular regulatory forms. The chapter continues with an account of the development of and the rationales for regulation in charity fundraising, identifying three consecutive regulatory modes which have now been woven together to form a complex pattern of regulatory rules and frameworks. A composite view of the coverage which fundraising regulation now offers – the 'to whom, by whom and for whom' issues – then follows. Finally, the chapter examines the kinds of choices concerning regulation which charities and their fundraisers face, and revisits the purposes of such regulation, and the tensions arising from regulation, which fundraisers must be seen to be managing pro-actively. In a situation of multiple regulatory oversight of charity fundraising, it is possible to see charity fundraisers as high-profile scapegoats for wider charity failings. Here the professionalization of charity fundraising as an outcome of and a response to complex and demanding regulatory regimes is central.

The modern concept of regulation

Regulation may be defined as 'the standards, rules and instructions concerning what can and what cannot be done by individuals, businesses or other organisations' (Dudley, 2005, p. 9). Within this description multiple meanings of the concept emerge, suggesting wide variations in response, from active welcome to downright hostility. These meanings include regulation as a rule or a principle that customarily governs or prescribes behaviour, as an authoritative (i.e. governmental) rule, as the state of being controlled, and as the act of bringing uniformity to a situation or of controlling activities according to rules. As such, regulation is inherently controversial, capable of being described simultaneously as 'protecting' a field and 'stifling' its activities.

Agencies (normally governmental but also non-governmental in some circumstances) are necessary for the oversight and implementation of regulation; and these institutional arrangements may become targets of criticism if regulations are too strongly (or too weakly) enforced. A whole series of dependency relations is then developed – between governments and agencies delivering regulatory implementation, between agencies and those who are regulated, and between government, the agency and the public, especially where the purpose of regulation is presented as protective of public interests.

From exploration of these complex sets of relations, two key ideas have emerged as modern expressions of regulation. The first is that of regulation as a 'decentred' set of activities, away from a central controlling state or single body; and the second is that of self-regulation as an appropriate and reliable means of contributing to regulatory objectives. Within both ideas, the role of organization and individual norms and values remains critical, both demonstrating that the expressions and outcomes of those values can no longer be taken for granted. Hence both decentred regulation and self-regulation are increasingly underpinned by professionalization in industries under regulatory scrutiny.

Where regulation is decentred, regulatory activities are diffused throughout society, linking formal and informal sets of values and reliant on multiple sites of regulatory authority. This idea is proposed by Black, since command-and-control regulatory practice may be easily critiqued and since a 'government-telling-others-doing' approach has numerous cases of failure (Black, 2002, p. 2).

A decentring account of regulation therefore makes assumptions about the importance of interactions between a variety of actors and between actors and governments. Regulation is thus a multi-directional process, sometimes co-produced between governments and the regulated group or industry. This degree of complexity makes regulation best-understood as a 'cluster concept' (Black, 2002, p. 2).

Decentring and self-regulation go hand in hand, the latter an expression of the former. Thus, for example, as global fundraising increases, this may be regulated by the ethics of the funded organizations themselves as well as by national and supra-national governmental requirements. Charities' decisions to accept or refuse donations from apparently tainted sources would be a further example. Rosenman (2006) discusses this bluntly in the case of a range of well-known US charities' acceptance of funds from legislators implicated in legal proceedings against a well-known US lobbyist, asking, 'Have charities become money-launderers, knowingly accepting stolen goods?'

Within a decentred approach, the encouragement by government and agencies of compliance, using incentives rather than overt control, is an important feature. It is likely to be a major strand in governments' regulatory strategy; that is, encouraging co-operation in a general steer towards good corporate conduct rather than seeking and punishing wrongdoers (Parker, 2000). Parker considers that 'compliance based regulation can be seen as weaker, perhaps less expensive and certainly less aggressive than other styles of regulation' (Parker, 2000, p. 560). This view emphasizes the risk that compliance rhetoric will be used to manage appearances rather than deliver sound conduct. In fundraising, this is a continuing concern of critics of voluntary codes of ethics, arguing that 'signing up' may be far more of a marketing than a governance aspect of fundraisers' practice.

Taking action *ahead* of governmental imposition of regulation rules, and acting under self-regulation principles, is a regulatory option in industries where there are shared values, where there is a degree of field maturity and where its occupants endorse degrees of regulation to gain credibility for their work. This may take a number of forms. One such, with mixed social and economic goals, is the development since the late 1980s of the self-certification of products meeting 'fair trade' principles. Since 1997, an international body, Fairtrade Labelling Organizations International (FLO), has become the main worldwide certification body, with some twenty national affiliates, including the Fairtrade Foundation UK and TransFair USA. Although coffee provides an example, where the fair trade movement has made inroads into the marketplace, the movement continues to face challenges as its activities 'run counter to the historical concerns of coffee production and trade' (Rice, 2001).

It is also possible that government support for self-regulation may reflect a chronic lack of government interest, willpower or capacity to proceed further. DeMarzo *et al.* (2005, p. 688) assert that 'self-regulation has always been subject to public criticism [since] self-regulating organisations have inadequate incentives to enforce the rules that protect the public'. Newman and Bach (2001, p. 6) present a worst-case scenario, where 'many fear that self-regulation benefits from image while actually permitting the wolf to guard the sheep'. Nevertheless, self-regulation may also represent a badge of 'coming of age' in an industry where regulatees are acknowledged as trustworthy, able and willing to self-monitor in the best interests of their users/customers/clients. This is certainly the tone being presented in a government-funded and charity-sector-hosted initiative for the self-regulation of fundraising in England, Scotland and Wales (Home Office, 2005; Institute of Fundraising, 2006), set up following public and sectoral consultation.

'Regulation', then, is a complex set of governmental, quasi-governmental and non-governmental actions with an essentially protective intent – for citizens, communities, organizations and governments. When regulation is seen as de-centred, this challenges the widespread view that regulation is a distinctive activity only of the state. It may be seen as a cluster or as a continuum of state-directed *and* self- or voluntary-directed or sanctioned, and rules and frameworks which seek to affect, if not control, practices and behaviours in specified fields. As in other industries, regulation of charity fundraising may be seen as simultaneously supportive of the field's best interests and drawing attention to its failings.

The development of charity fundraising regulation

Perspectives on fundraising regulation must reflect the general accountability climate and governance demands facing charities (Cornforth, 2003). Garton (2005) argues that four of the traditional justifications for regulation apply equally to charities: (1) the prevention of anti-competitive practices, (2) the prevention of externalities, (3) the prevention of information deficits, and (4) the co-ordination of the sector. Of these four, regulation around competition may become problematic as fundraising techniques increase in sophistication (or desperation); and 'sectoral co-ordination' may point to state pressure, for example, in mandating organizational merger. However, these developments will vary according to the 'favourability or unfavourability' of the legal frameworks within which nonprofit organizations operate (Salamon and Toepler, 2000). These authors note that 'regulatory action that seeks to suppress or prevent the emergence of nonprofits can simply push nonprofit actors towards informal, legally unrecognized forms of organizing' (ibid., p. 2). Where legal frameworks experience major change, fundraising regulation will be subsumed in wider regulatory issues but continually under pressure. For example, Remias (2000) notes that, in post-Soviet Central Asia, NGOs are generally unable to generate revenue without the same tax liability as for-profit bodies; with Kazakhstan's pro-NGO reform of taxation unique in the region. Edele (2005) describes how restrictive procedures for NGO registration in China since 1998 have 'probably led to an increase in the number of informal groups that do not bother to register', making these in principle illegal.

In charity fundraising, then, the regulatory space is crowded. Informal constraints may be influential alongside formal ones, stemming from cultural norms (for example, those affecting ways in which gift requests are made, the expectations of and requirements for donor publicity, or societal views which sanction or frown on particular fundraising methods, such as charitable gambling). Furthermore, the mix of regulatory approaches suggests that there are three major modes of regulation, each with their characteristics, rationales and opportunities to work well or to work badly, in particular sets of circumstances. These are the modes of 'minimal oversight', 'state supervision' and 'distributed regulation', as set out in Table 13.1.

The three modes of regulation in operation

The 'minimal oversight' mode

In this mode, thriving, high-commitment organizations will operate alongside those where malpractice may go undetected. Here the 'badge' of charity is seen less as an entrée into tax exemption or vital service provision, and more as designating altruism and good behaviour. Means of coping with personal aggrandizement in charities are very limited, and sanctions, if applied, will invariably disappoint. Operating on a values-based rather than rules-based approach presumes 'other-seeking' behaviour, reducing the costs of state oversight apparatus. The approach mostly also assumes relative benevolence from regulatory bodies. Minimal oversight may also occur where charities are initially unknown or appearing with external support (for example, in the European transition economies). It may be limited but restrictive (for example, 'social organizations' in China being unable to work in areas other than the region where they are registered). Moreover, there may be some areas where minimal oversight is the only feasible approach. For example, notwithstanding the increasing profile of web-based fundraising, the inability of nation states to 'control' the geographically unbounded Internet is very evident. However, the reappearance of minimal oversight as a prevailing regulatory model for charity fundraising is unlikely to occur, even where apparent glimpses of a deregulated operating climate appear. Thus the promising title (for minimalists) of the UK report in November 2005, *Better Regulation for Civil Society*, with its yet more intriguing subtitle *Making Life Easier for Those Who Help Others*, belies recommendations which adjust regulation at the margins of charities' work.

The 'statutory supervision' mode

This mode develops from a variety of factors, including states' changing awareness of the growing power and accomplishments of charities. (It is arguable that *any* mode of regulation beyond the minimal approach reflects attempts at performance

Table 13.1 Three modes of charity regulation

	Regulatory system		
	'Minimal oversight'	'State supervision'	'Distributed regulation'
Characteristics	Limited legal framework supported by small-scale and low-profile regulatory apparatus. Sanctions, seldom applied – and exercised with considerable discretion.	A more elaborate set of statutory rules, upheld by a specialist workforce operating a system of obligatory reporting, backed up by investigation and intervention.	Developments at national and supra-national levels, across different regulatory arenas, and in new forms of self-regulation give rise to a shifting mosaic of regulations with multiple lines of reporting and accountability.
Rationale and benefits	Charities seen as private or local bodies, not requiring supervision. Low costs for all parties. Appropriate where charity sector relatively small and homogeneous, and underpinned by informal community oversight (e.g. through the social standing of those involved).	Aims to solve the problems arising when 'minimal oversight' is seen to fail; and to safeguard public confidence by visibly using actual and implied legal processes to stimulate improved charity functioning. Appropriate where a unitary state is accepted as protector and dominant actor, and where the sector is more important and varied, but not subject to very rapid change.	Aims to solve the problems arising from costly, inappropriate and overloaded state regulation in an era of rapid change and multi-level governance. Benefits lie in less costly and intrusive regulation that is more flexible and dynamic, targeting investigative effort more intelligently. Appropriate where complexity and pace of change warrant fine-tuned approaches; and where professionalization and public understanding can support forms of self-regulation.
Limitations and pitfalls	Reliance on normative controls leaves it open to abuse, with little risk of exposure or sanctions.	Insufficient or outdated supervision skills in the regulator. Incremental increases in the regulatory rules irresistible to governments and regulator, making for increased costs for all parties. Inflexible and protracted nature of legal processes.	Multiplicity of regulation sources leads to inconsistencies and public confusion. Overall load increases (though with more costs now internalized by charities). Sudden changes in political situations (e.g. terrorism) lead to impromptu legislation, with uncertain effects.

management of charities, by stakeholders, whether governmental or within the charity sector.) Under this mode, expansion in overall supervision and legal rules occurs. Where states are constitutionally complex, awareness of significant differentiation within areas arises, sometimes together with calls for unification or commonality of codes. In Australia, for example, all Australian States and Territories except Northern Territory have legislation which 'regulates various aspects of fundraising', although to date 'only regulators in New South Wales, Victoria and Western Australia have included requirements that make mandatory the proportion of income generated from public fundraising that is spent on fundraising' (Flack, 2004). Moreover, in this regulatory mode, laws and systems applying to other areas of jurisdiction may be applied inappropriately to non-profits. For example, Lyons (2003) argues that, while the Australian Securities and Investment Commission is 'not particularly interested in nonprofit companies, the law requires that it applies the same regulatory rigour to them as to publicly listed corporations', and notes that 'several medium size nonprofits have been thus bankrupted for minor infringements' (ibid., p. 96).

Complexities occur where there are multiple levels of statutory authority, to the point where some regulatory frameworks are evidently more lax than others, with varying consequences for charity practice. Fishman and Glenn (2005) show that organizations in US states with 'poor government oversight' have managerial compensation more highly correlated with inflows of donations and allocate a smaller percentage of donations to endowment for future work, relative to organizations in 'strong oversight states'. Where overarching legislation also applies, such complexities are compounded. In the US, with charity regulation at state level, supra-state jurisdictions also exist (for example, the role of the US Federal Trade Commission, given jurisdiction over for-profit telemarketers, calling on behalf of charities, by the US Patriot Act). Proposals to extend 'national do-not-call lists' from the FTC to charities cut across developments in some states and raise the issue of the appropriateness (and feasibility) of applying this to volunteer fundraisers.

In general under this mode, the expectation is that state bodies which exist to regulate will do so, notwithstanding arguments that independence or privacy may be entailed. Moreover, in such environments, anti-disclosure (anti-regulation) lobbying may encourage suspicion where there is no cause. The very existence of the US coalition American Charities for Reasonable Fundraising Regulation, looking to mount court challenges to excessive and costly regulation instances, draws attention to the mosaic-like nature of the regulatory environment in the US, but also begs the question as to what is 'reasonable' in US fundraising contexts, to and for whom.

'Uniformity' within and across state borders is no less straightforward. In Canada, where provinces vary in their approaches, practitioner and academic exploration of challenges in charity regulation has identified extensive concerns about Federal regulatory inadequacy and Provincial lack of regulation. More-over, Oosterhoff (2004, p. 8) draws attention to 'the inability, because of confidentiality rules, of regulatory agencies to keep each other informed of allegations of wrongdoing and of investigations into such allegations'. Subsequent draft legislation was drawn up in 2004 by the Uniform Law Conference of Canada, creating a universal series of regulations on fundraising that all Provinces would adopt. However, Provinces are not required to approve or abide by these proposals.

In the post-'new public management' world, it is almost axiomatic that statutory supervision of charity fundraising will be seen as costly, inflexible and slow in response to changes in a fast-moving charity world. Hence an overarching emphasis on state regulators as arbiters makes for frustrations; not least where regulatory bodies also seek a developmental, supportive role. During consultation on charity governance reform in Ireland, one organization noted of a proposed regulatory body that it 'cannot be both pal and policeman' (The Wheel, 2004, p. 1).

The distributed regulation model

This mode inaugurates a mixed series of regulatory activities, frameworks and regulators, predicated on the argument that the interests of regulator and regulated are shared, and that good if not 'best' practice will result. For charity fundraising, this emphasizes that the sector has everything to gain from its own and public endorsement of regulatory activity. An increase in the profile and professionalism of fundraising is a marked feature, taking a positive and protective stance on regulation. Thus, in 2003, a major survey of Canadian fundraisers reported over half agreeing on the need for increased fundraising regulation, and for a government ombudsman regarding fundraising complaints (McMullen, 2003). The North American-wide Association of Fundraising Professionals has stressed both its detective and protective roles in evidence to the US Senate Committee on Finance, where it described that part of its work is 'to identify wrongdoers who hurt the charitable sector' (AFP, 2004).

This mode does not downplay the role of the state, more often increasing state interest in regulation while delegating authority for its practice. Its key characteristic, a variety of regulatory or would-be regulatory organizations, makes clear that charity fundraising has become a central focus of regulatory effort, in part due to its likely greatest degree of contact with the public. Such regimes are marked by growth in Codes of Conduct, to which individuals or groups of organizations adhere voluntarily, as a sign, variously, of their maturity, morality, and the marketing advantage which Code membership bestows. Organizationally, charities with shared interests seek agreement on working boundaries and 'good' (if not 'best') practice. Individually, fundraising employees (and some volunteers) commit to certain practice values, and seek to lead the professionalization of their work.

Such codes offer a basis for development of more explicit regulation narratives, and give a non-legal but moral edge to quasi-regulatory 'policing' of the fundraising sector. For example, 2004 marked the tenth anniversary of the 'Code of Conduct for the International Red Cross and Red Crescent Movement and NGOs in Disaster Relief'. For an international conference on the Code's possible future, Hilhorst (2005) explored the Code as regulator (for example, where beneficiaries should be able to use the Code to complain about poor aid provision). Here, an extension of the Code to relate more precisely to fundraising dilemmas in disaster scenarios could follow.

The importance of such codes for public reassurance and as a charity marketing device makes sense intuitively. There is some research evidence to support this. Bekkers (2003) analyses the development of an accreditation scheme for charity fundraising in the Netherlands, where membership extends to approximately 90 per cent of the fundraising market, and where the accreditation seal has become widely known and valued by a giving public. The introduction of such accreditation systems is not easy, however, requiring wide non-profit support, clear and strict criteria, and public knowledge of the scheme. These aspects are costly and the payback period for some charities may seem a long, uncertain one. Similarly, Bittner (2005, p. 4) analyses developments in the Austrian 'Seal of Approval for charities', where the two largest charities adopted a 'wait-and-see policy' because of their existing high credibility, and 'small organizations regard the mandatory audit as a burden'.

A central expression of distributed regulation is the growth in self-regulation schemes for fundraising (Douthwaite and Harrow [2005], Harrow and Douthwaite [2005] in relation to the UK) and for NGOs generally (Lloyd, 2005). The above discussion has suggested its snares and value. 'The particular blend of high behavioural expectations and limited institutional frameworks that make up the notion of self-regulation may be offered by governments and professional bodies as a regulatory "ideal type". Dependent on trust in professionals, apparently inexpensive in operation, self-regulation systems aim to confirm industry credibility, and perhaps limit government culpability' (Harrow, 2005, p. 1) Recent developments in the UK offer a mixed-sectoral approach, with government funding of a self-regulation of fundraising body, to be an independent body but hosted initially within the sector's (charitable) Institute of Fundraising. Such institutionally based solutions may be challenged, as a preference of the larger and largest fundraising charities, as the result of poor governmental judgement based on a media assertion of lack of public trust in charitable giving, and as likely to be less cost-effective as time goes on. However, as in the UK case, behind most self-regulation 'offers' lies the fall-back position of governmental intervention. In such cases, charity fundraisers are under pressure – some of it of their own making – to make self-regulation work, and to do so quickly.

It is within this mode that contradictions in regulatory demands are likely to be strong. The argument for concentrating regulatory powers in charities most potentially culpable or at risk is one which could benefit charity fundraisers. Thus Irvin (2005, p. 175), in the context of the '50 permutations of regulation' in the US for non-profits, argues convincingly for changes to the costly multiple reporting and recording systems: 'the resulting state deregulation could – paradoxically – lead to a reduction in charitable solicitation fraud, as states will be relieved of the burdens of record processing, and will be better able to concentrate their efforts on monitoring and prosecution of suspect operations'. There is also the case made for regulatory anticipation by charities. Johnston (1999, p. 51) has argued for pro-activity concerning Internet regulation:

> it is inevitable that there will be on-line solicitation fraud. If non-profit organizations do not plan to deal with the regulatory reactions now,

they will find themselves dealing with regulatory regimes imposed from above that will be onerous on small organizations soliciting on the Internet.

Regulatory interaction

These modes reflect a developmental progression, emerging one after the other, with the later ones subsuming earlier modes. As a result, they all now co-exist. They may also be seen as operating in an interrelated form, sometimes in conflict, sometimes in concert. It is quite possible for one organization's practice to exemplify all three modes – fundraisers who adopt self-regulation codes of practice to enhance their work, chief executives who report in the light of governmental stated rules, and boards which fondly believe that they are under 'minimal oversight', and can (in a spirit of charitable goodwill) do as they like.

Fundraising regulation is then found both within the wider parameters of governmental decisions about the control of the sector generally and highly contextually based, in the fine-grain detail of seeking, winning and sustaining incomes. Especially since the three modes are not hermetically sealed, their consequences may be unexpected and unwelcome (for example, donors' non-comprehension of charities' regulatory reporting costs). External and internal expectations for regulation are then not abating. Overtly, these may take dramatic forms, for example, concerning responses to control infiltration of legitimate charities, accessing fundraising for terrorist ends, the creation of bogus charities to 'fundraise', and the concealment of sources of illicit funds, moved through charity accounts (money laundering). Less dramatic but persistent issues include those of disclosure of costs of fundraising campaigns, the implications of fundraising through forms of charitable gambling, the opportunity to divert funds raised for one purpose into another (for example, following solicitation for disaster relief), the dissipation of fundraising effort into excessive managerial compensation, fraud protection in off-street public collections, and perceived donor harassment or privacy. Taken together, these instances confirm the growing expansion and complexity of regulatory frameworks, whether or not they represent abnormal or normal occurrences.

Cross-national state regulation remains especially problematic, likely to lead to ever more detailed reporting requirements, within increasingly tight time frames. This appears to be the case especially in relation to international responses to terrorist financing and associated argument for non-profit and charity control. The July 2005 European Union's draft recommendations for member states on a code of conduct to 'promote transparency and accountability best practices' among non-profit organizations, with apparent inherent suspicion of the sector and its potential for criminal activity, is a case in point (EU, 2005a, 2005b). In other transnational jurisdictions, proposed regulatory responses to malign organizations' practice indicates varying cultural or social expectations (for example, the recommendation from the Middle East and North Africa Financial Action Task Force that '"charitable associations"/institutions should cease the raising and spending of funds in cash' (MENAFATF, 2005, p. 6).

The specifics – the 'why', 'what' and 'how' questions

Within these inter-related modes of regulation, the specifics of fundraising regulation – the 'why', 'what' and 'how' questions – need to be addressed. An overview of what a composite account of charity fundraising regulation might look like may be drawn from the existing patchworks of national schemes (for example, Lee's [2004] account of UK legal and social regulation perspectives). A more useful approach is to ask questions concerning what might be included in a particular national or transnational regulatory framework. Figure 13.1 demonstrates the extent to which such questions are numerous and overlapping, taking its inspiration from the argument that regulation is a 'cluster concept'.

Figure 13.1 is designed to demonstrate the kinds of choices that face developers and implementers of charity fundraising regulation. It illustrates the scope and nature of the regulatory remit as it interlinks with the core questions of governance and performance in charities, and as it focuses on the behaviour of individuals. The first question – should there be regulation – is taken as a given. The final issue identified – that of consultation with the VCS (using the British nomenclature of the 'voluntary and community sector') – begs further questions, notably, which kinds of organizations with charity fundraising activities might be expected to speak for the sector; and the extent to which grant-making as well as fund-seeking non-profits should have a voice in the regulatory debates. (Private foundations and public grant-makers have also been prey to fundraising 'scams'.)

Overlapping circles may also be seen as a shuffled pack of cards. This suggests the extent to which much debate concerning fundraising regulation commences at issues 5 and 6 (forms of regulation and enforcement) where, for example, disappointment or a drive for reliance on internal pressures leads on to the self-regulation case. The figure is drawn together from a range of ideas within the fundraising literatures. It does not reflect those literatures where regulation may be seen as repressive, harsh and criminalizing, rather than benign, supportive or encouraging. That is, it assumes the best of motives in securing fundraising regulation and shared interests between fundraisers, the charities they underpin, the giving publics and governments which gain directly or indirectly from charities' work.

Choices in regulation

It seems unlikely that there was ever a golden age of minimal regulation where charities, naturally answerable to local communities, were never exploitative of donors' propensity to give, nor operated beyond their altruistic calling. The chances of minimal regulation being regained are very unlikely. However, calls for co-ordination across jurisdictions, to abolish unfair advantage or lax practice, may also reflect an urge to 'tidy up', legally speaking. In the latter case, the interests of non-profits may become secondary to those of lawyers and public servants. It is important to note that charity fundraisers are not passive creatures in these ongoing debates, but often lobbyists as well (particularly where professional fundraiser bodies gain in stature). Yet the volunteer fundraiser (often no less professional or professionalizing) may lie consistently outside the scope of many regulatory systems owing to diminished visibility or intermittent operation. So much of the regulatory systems presume a continuing fundraising presence, and this may not be so for many smaller groups, or for some volunteers who may come and go in their fundraising roles.

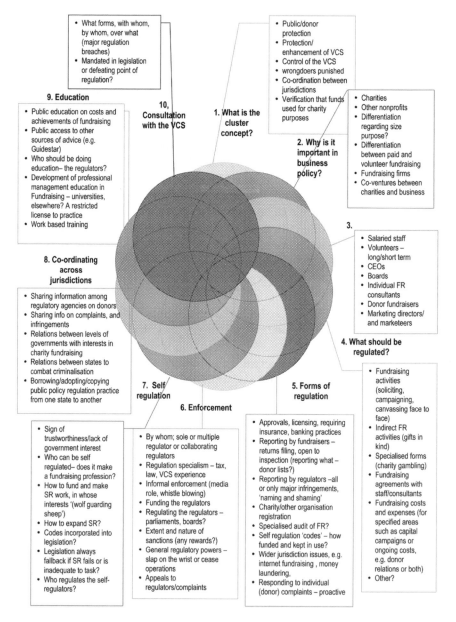

Figure 13.1 Regulation as a cluster concept, the core issues for charity fundraising

Charities have choices to make over fundraising regulation without waiting to be asked or coerced. There is no reason to suppose that charity fundraisers will look any less cynically – or purposefully – at regulatory rules than others. But nor is it safe for the regulators to assume that most organizations which break regulatory ranks will be those that are already becoming allied to illegal activities or those where key individuals set out to instigate fraud to their own benefit. The 'rotten apple' theory is often a comfort in other areas of public misdeeds and this is no less true for charities and their fundraisers. Yet the very mission-driven nature of charity work and the thoroughgoing emphasis by its staff and volunteers on its vital work may encourage regulatory lapses, or activities outside the codes of individual professionals. When ends justify means, charity fundraising can be presented as a good case in point. The backgrounds of charity fundraisers may also be important. Many organizations look to their fundraisers for fundraising innovation, to match their own innovative work. If fundraising is regarded primarily as a marketing activity, with practitioners' roots in creative industries, rather than non-profits generally, these are arguably areas where innovation and risk-taking are at a premium but regulatory instincts are not paramount.

Charity fundraising regulation needs to operate at 'high-tech' and 'low-tech' levels simultaneously. International concerns over and responses to terrorist financing may have done charities and non-profits a gross disservice, to the extent that they imply their openness to 'takeover', or their naïvety as they work on the margins of community life. At the same time, the spotlight placed on non-profits is one that will not be wholly unwelcome; and one which gives an increased stage for governmental lobbying by non-profits for governments to understand fully the sector's shape, scope and promise.

Conclusions: revisiting the purposes of fundraising regulation

Regulation may be variously understood as a 'badge' of sectoral expertise, a licence to practise or be legitimated, a framework for delivering public (donor) trust, a reputational safeguard, and a small part of the story of the expanding regulatory state. Multiple regulation is an inevitable outcome of the blurring of sectors in post-welfare states. With the increasing profile – and power – of non-profits come sets of expectations of regulation from different stakeholders. Of these, governments may be the most important. If partnering with non-profits continues to grow as a major plank of public policy, then a trustworthy, transparent non-profit sector is vital, to confirm that policy's rationale. From this perspective alone, over-regulation and under-regulation are not in governments' interests.

There remains the question of the extent to which public trust can be delivered by refining regulatory structures, redesigning reporting forms and creating new collaborative oversight bodies. Fundraisers may assert that donors mainly do not seek close encounters with their charities through accessing donors' charters or other such codes; also, that many will not share general criticisms of the sector when applied to their charities. (It is also possible, moreover, that in some circumstances and in some kinds of charities, donors will be willing to forgive charities coping with financial problems and scandal.) Charities' abilities to make discussion of the costs of fundraising for different purposes and in different ways an open and public one are, however, critical for the regulatory climate; an issue of public education of the extent to which and ways in which fundraising is not a cost-neutral exercise. Without this, charity fundraisers may increasingly become high-profile scapegoats for non-profit failures generally, with their likely loneliness within their organizations and relative isolation from their boards making them clear regulatory targets.

Thus discussion of regulatory principles — such as proportionality and consistency — may be accepted at the level of generality yet not implemented organizationally. How much regulation, then, is symbolic, and how much improvization in the face of fast-moving events? Regulatory systems will always be dynamic and evolving, not simply through the kinds of systems interactions described above, but because of the co-evolution of regulation and regulated behaviour. Fundraisers' behaviour, then, is central to the ways in which these systems progress. It is argued here that fundraisers should be willing to confront rather than just 'live with' the regulatory contexts in which they work. Regulation and fundraising share a key common element; and that is that they are centrally about communication. Fundraisers need to communicate the narratives of fundraising experiences, good and less good, in the public domain, as an educative action, and be open to accepting the risks and rewards which regulation brings.

Acknowledgements

The authors are indebted to Professor Rob Paton for his incisive commentary and supportive development of their work, including, especially, his idea for the developmental framework concerning modes of charity regulation.

The authors are very appreciative of the technical assistance given for this chapter by Mariana Bogdanova, Research Assistant in the Centre for Charity Effectiveness, Cass Business School.

References

Association of Fundraising Professionals (AFP) (2004) *Charity Oversight and Reform Roundtable, Oral Comment and Statement for the Record,* Paulette Maehara, President and CEO, Senate Committee on Finance, 22 July: AFP, Alexandria, VA.

Bekkers, R. (2003) 'Trust, accreditation and philanthropy in the Netherlands', *Non-profit and Voluntary Sector Quarterly,* 32: 4, pp. 596–615.

Bittner, G. (2005) *Austrian Seal of Approval for Charities,* Workshop on Certification Systems for Non-profit Organizations, Prague, Czech Republic, 23–24 May, 1–4, www.oefse.at/Downloads/veranstaltungen/Prag2005.pdf.

Black, J. (2002) *Critical Reflections on Regulation,* Centre for Analysis of Risk and Regulation, London School of Economics and Political Science, London.

Cornforth, C. J. (2003) *The Governance of Public and Non-profit Organisations – What Do Boards Do?,* Routledge, London.

DeMarzo, P. M., Fishman, M. and Hagerty, K. M. (2005) 'Self regulation and government oversight', *Review of Economic Studies*, 72, pp. 687–706.

Douthwaite, S. and Harrow, J. (2005) 'Am I my sister's keeper? Perspectives on impending self-regulation in charity fundraising', *Proceedings of the National Council of Voluntary Organisations/Voluntary Sector Studies Network 'Researching the Voluntary Sector', Tenth Annual Conference,* The University of Warwick, 30 August–1 September.

Dudley, S. E. (2005) *Primer on Regulation*, Mercatus Center Policy Resource Series, Paper 1, George Mason University, www.mercatus.org/regstudies/article,php/1415. html, 1–49.

Edele, A. (2005) *Non-governmental Organizations in China*, Programme on NGOs and Civil Society, Centre for Applied Studies in International Negotiations, Geneva, Switzerland.

European Union (EU) (2005a) *Draft Recommendations to Member States Regarding a Code of Conduct for Non-profit Organisations to Promote Transparency and Accountability Best Practices,* Directorate-General, Justice, Freedom and Security, Directorate D, Unit D2, Combating economic, financial and cyber crime.

European Union (EU) (2005b) *Commission Communication to the Council, the European Parliament and the European Economic and Social Committee: The Prevention of and Fight against Terrorist Financing Through Enhanced National Level Co-ordination and Greater Transparency of the Non-profit Sector*, 29 November.

Fishman, R. and Glenn, H. R. (2005) 'Precautionary savings and the governance of non-profit organisations', *Journal of Public Economics,* 89: 11/12, pp. 2231–2243.

Flack, T. (2004) *The Mandatory Disclosure of Cost of Fundraising Ratios: Does It Achieve the Regulators' Purposes?, Working Paper CPNS26,* Centre for Philanthropy and Non-profit Studies, Queensland University of Technology, Brisbane, Australia.

Garton, J. (2005) 'Justifying the regulation of charities and civil society: the relevance of traditional economic theories of regulation', *Socio Legal Studies Association Annual Conference*, University of Liverpool, 30 March–1 April.

Harrow, J. (2005) 'Institutional and policy perspectives on self-regulation in charity fundraising', *International Research Colloquium on Accountable Governance/ESRC Seminar Series on public accountability in the new institutional environment,* Queen's University, Belfast, 20–22 October.

Harrow, J. and Douthwaite, S. (2005) 'All grown up now? Policy maturity or infancy in UK fundraising self-regulation', ARNOVA Research Conference, Washington, DC, 17–19 November.

Hilhorst, D. (2005) 'Dead letter or living document? Ten years of the Code of Conduct for Disaster Relief', *Disasters*, 23: 4, pp. 351–369.

Home Office (2005) Written Ministerial Statement, Regulation of Fundraising Scheme, www.homeoffice.gov.uk/docs4/WMS-self-regulation-March 05.

Institute of Fundraising (2005) Funding for Self-regulation, www.institute-for-fundraising.org.uk/self_reg.html.

Irvin, R. (2005) 'State regulation of nonprofits: accountability regardless of outcome', *Non-profit and Voluntary Sector Quarterly*, 34: 2, 161–178.

Johnston, M. (1999) 'The Internet and the regulation of the non-profit sector', *New Directions for Philanthropic Fundraising*, pp. 39–56.

Lee, S. (2004) Developing alternate fundraising regulatory frameworks', Fourth Annual Charity Law Conference, London, 26 February.

Lloyd, R. (2005) *The Role of NGO Self-regulation in Increasing Stakeholder Accountability*, One World Trust, London, July.

Lyons, M. (2003) 'The legal and regulatory environment of the third sector', *Asian Journal of Public Administration*, 25: 1, pp. 87–106.

McMullen, K. (2003) *A Portrait of Canadian Fundraising Professionals – Results of the AFP/CPRN Survey of Fundraisers, 2002*, Canadian Policy Research Networks, Research Paper W/20, July.

Middle East and North Africa Financial Action Task Force (2005) Best Practices issued by the Middle East and North Africa Financial Action Task Force Concerning the Charities, 1–7, www.policylaundering.org/archives/MENAFATF/best_practices_ charities.pdf (the Policy Laundering project is a joint project of the American Civil Liberties Union, Statewatch and Privacy International).

Newman, A. and Bach, D. (2001) *In the Shadow of the State: Self-regulation Trajectories in a Digital Age*, Annual Convention of the American Political Science Association, 30 August–2 September.

Oosterhoff, A. (2004) Charitable Fundraising Research Paper, The University of Western Ontario, *Uniform Law Conference of Canada, Civil Law Section*, 15 April.

Parker, C. (2000) 'Reinventing regulation within the corporation: compliance-oriented regulatory innovation', *Administration and Society*, 32: 5, pp. 529–565.

Remias, R. (2000) 'The regulation of NGOs in Central Asia: current reforms and ongoing problems', *Harvard Asia Quarterly*, 4: 3, n.p., www.asiaquarterly.com/content/ view/75/40/.

Rice, R. A. (2001) 'Noble goals and challenging terrain: organic and fair trade coffee movements in the global marketplace', *Journal of Agricultural and Environmental Ethics*, 14: 1, pp. 39–66.

Rosenman, M. (2006) 'Money laundering and moral leadership', *Stanford Social Innovation Review: Forum*, 30 January, www.ssireview.com/forum/archives.2006/01, accessed 10 February 2006.

Salamon, L. M. and Toepler, S. (2000) *The Influence of the Legal Environment on the Development of the Non-profit Sector*, Center for Civil Society Studies Working Paper 17, Johns Hopkins Institute for Policy Studies, Baltimore, MD.

Wheel, The (2004), Submission on 'Establishing a modern statutory framework for charities', Consultative Paper, 27 May , 1–20, www.cnm.tcd.ie/dialogue/forum/ Wheel.pdf.pdf.

Chapter 14

Marilyn Fischer

THE COLOUR OF ETHICS

Edited from: Fischer, M. (2000) 'Conceptual tools for ethical decision making', in *Ethical Decision Making in Fundraising*, Chapter 1, John Wiley & Sons, Inc.

Introduction

'IT'S SUCH A GREY AREA', we often hear, when difficult ethical situations come up. Grey is the colour of fog, of cloudy dull skies without clarity or edges. In ethical reflection, we sometimes feel as if we are navigating in a fog with no landmarks and no sense of direction. Grey is also a colour made by mixing black and white. Sometimes, in our ethical reflections, we see no clear, right answers; every alternative is tinged with negativity, evil taints the good.

'Ethics as grey' is a potent metaphor, and as with all things potent it needs to be used with great care. Some ethical choices are clearly right or wrong and to call ethics 'grey' in these cases is a way of hiding from ethical truths and ethical responsibilities. But in other cases choices are not so clear, and it is important to identify and acknowledge the ways in which ethics can be grey. In some cases, it may be true that no alternative course of action is ethically pure, and all alternatives require uncomfortable compromises. A second type of greyness arises when ethically decent people prioritize their values differently. Some members of a social service agency may want to emphasize relieving immediate needs for food and shelter; others may want to stress education and job training as long-term self-sufficiency skills. A third type of greyness arises from the way that the same acts can accomplish both ethical and unethical purposes. For example, in the early twentieth century, the Phillis Wheatley Home in Cleveland offered shelter, safety, friendship and job training to young black women. Many white women contributed financial support to the Wheatley Home, but historian Darlene Clark Hine sees a racist underside to their generosity. It gave them a way to keep the Young Women's Christian Association exclusively white and to get more highly trained maids for themselves. Non-profit fundraisers, educators, and facilitators of the gifts that build community must sort through such strings and complications every day.

When ethical situations look grey, it is important to sort out just which sense of greyness applies. If the real difficulty is that morally decent people prioritize their values differently, but those involved think the greyness results from good mixed with evil, organizations may become needlessly polarized.

When an ethical quandary feels grey, thinking of ethics as story-telling can be helpful. When the full story of the ethical dilemma is told carefully, with sympathetic understanding of each person's perspective, this sort of polarization can be minimized. In this chapter, a method of ethical decision-making is presented that will help fundraisers construct stories in a way that clarifies the greyness and brings basic ethical commitments to the foreground. The method encourages sympathetic understanding and imagination as tools for resolving ethically troubling situations.

The ethical decision-making model

Most daily decisions have an ethical dimension, and much of the time we instinctively function as competent ethical decision-makers. We may not be directly conscious of it, but much of our 'common-sense' decision-making incorporates concern for basic ethical values such as honesty, establishing trust with others, and showing concern for their well-being. Usually, we are kind to children, fair to our colleagues, and decent to strangers.

A story will illustrate how we insert ethical concerns into our everyday lives. By examining this story, we can draw out the ethical dimensions of everyday thought, and then apply the same pattern to ethical decision-making in fundraising.

After work, you pick up a 4-year-old (your child, your grandchild, a neighbour, or some other youngster to whom you are attached) from day care and stop by the supermarket to find something to serve your second cousin twice removed, who just happens to be passing through town this evening. At the store you bump into a friend and stop to chat for a few minutes. You talk about the fact that if it does not rain soon your shrubs will die, about the sale on avocados in the produce department, and about getting a haircut before the fundraising gala next week. All the while, the 4-year-old is wandering about examining boxes of granola bars.

This may look like a rare moment of idyllic calm in your over-stressed life, but what is really going on inside your head is some remarkably sophisticated ethical decision-making in which you link moment-by-moment decisions to your most basic values. You let the 4-year-old wander (although always in sight) because you want him to grow up to be curious and independent. Your friend has been an important source of strength and support for years. She is the one who did your laundry for a month when your father was dying of cancer. You know her daughter has a drug problem, so as you chat through a guacamole recipe you watch her face and listen to her tone of voice, judging if this is the day she needs for you to take an extra five minutes communing about produce sales. It has little to do with avocados, and everything to do with sustaining the friendship.

Suddenly, right when you are getting to the part about adding the lemon juice, you break off in mid-sentence and dash madly after the 4-year-old, as he gets perilously close to the pyramid of glass pickle-jars. Keeping him alive and reasonably intact is also something you care about.

Here, your decisions about pickles, granola bars, and guacamole revolve around your basic values of caring for the child and sustaining your most important relationships. Much of getting through the day is a matter of negotiating life's little details in ways that support these basic values. Most of the time, at least in familiar surroundings, we successfully integrate basic values with life's minutiae, without even being conscious of it. When troubling or unusually complex issues arise, however, or when we have too many responsibilities to juggle at once, it is helpful to articulate these values and deliberate about what courses of action are most consistent with our basic value commitments.

In this story, caring for the child and sustaining the friendship are basic value commitments. For fundraisers in their professional capacity, three basic value commitments can be identified:

1   The organizational mission that directs the work
2   Our relationships with the people with whom we interact
3   Our own sense of personal integrity

The fundraiser, acting with integrity, has the task of creating and maintaining a supporting network of relationships in order to further the mission of the organization. We bring ethical sensitivity to decision-making when we place particular decisions in the context of these three basic value commitments. The ethical decision-making model takes these three value commitments and uses them to conduct stories about alternative ways of resolving ethically troubling situations. Here, each of the three value commitments will be described briefly, and then a sample case analysis using the model will be given. Then I will point out how using this method incorporates (different) dimensions of ethics: sympathetic understanding, social and temporal context, and sustaining the gift economy's vitality.

1 Organizational mission

Every philanthropic organization has a mission – a social need it is trying to meet, a human good it is trying to achieve. Such purposes range from providing disaster relief to preserving rainforests; from meeting basic survival needs to enriching our spirits through artistic excellence or religious devotion. The mission justifies and directs daily tasks and decisions.

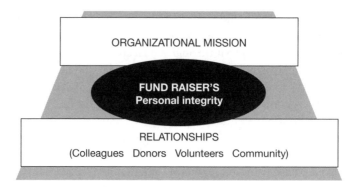

Figure 14.1 Fundraisers' three basic value commitments

Ethical difficulties often involve misalignments between the organizational mission and daily decisions. Decisions about a university athletic programme may bring glory to the school, while the athletes remain poorly educated. Professors may favour outside consulting to the point of neglecting their students. In some organizations, when glamorous fundraising events net little income, one has to ask if their primary function is to serve the organizational mission or to provide high-class entertainment for the organization's supporters.

Many organizations have more than one fundamental purpose. A hospital, for example, may define its mission in terms of patient care, medical research, and educating future medical practitioners. While a given daily decision may not further all three goals, we can at least take care that a decision furthering one purpose does not unduly slight or injure another. Soliciting funds for long-term basic research is fine, as long as that emphasis does not diminish the quality of patient care.

Each non-profit's specific organizational mission is embedded inside the larger framework of philanthropy. Although it is good to review and revise the mission statement periodically to make sure it advances philanthropic values, it is also helpful to assess even small-scale decisions in light of their impact on philanthropy as a gift economy. Does a particular decision revitalize the spirit of giving and move the gift along its way?

2 Relationships

The slogan goes that fundraisers raise friends as much as funds. Networks of relationships with donors, colleagues, volunteers, and community members are the medium through which organizational missions are furthered. The second basic value commitment, then, is concerned with the character and quality of our relationships to each of these groups. Many ethically troubling situations are caused by or may cause fractures in workplace relationships.

Think of the qualities that characterize healthy, long-term professional relationships. Respect, honesty, and open communication are high on the list. Sensitivity, caring, and a good sense of humour also figure prominently. And trust, no doubt, is a central value – trust in the goodwill and integrity of the other, and trust that one is respected and that one's basic concerns are taken seriously. When thinking through alternative ways of resolving ethical difficulties, try to enter imaginatively into other people's way of experiencing the world. How do others, with their own idiosyncratic concerns, priorities, and values view this alternative? How would it strengthen or weaken the relationship? Not all relationships can or should be preserved; even in ethically sound decisions, some relationships may still get bruised. The point is to incorporate sympathetic understanding as much as possible, and maintain the possibility of a future healthy relationship.

3 Integrity

The third value commitment is to preserve and strengthen one's own sense of integrity, to express basic values in everyday actions with courage and compassion. 'Ethics' comes from *ethos*, the ancient Greek word for character. Aristotle defined an ethical person as someone with a virtuous character, in whom virtues reside as deeply internalized personality characteristics. Virtues, like skills and habits, are acquired through practise. Just as a pianist acquires habits of skilful playing through daily practice, so we can practise being generous, fair, brave, thoughtful and honest. Through using daily decisions as opportunities for practice, we gradually nurture and develop the ethical qualities of our character.

Often, a sign of ethical trouble is that gnawing feeling that a given path of action would compromise one's integrity. You know that few of the clients in your drug rehabilitation clinic achieve the glowing success portrayed in your TV spot. Your stomach turns a bit when a donor tells you he was so moved by the spots that he wants to double his pledge. Is your fundraising success based on dishonest portrayals? To maintain a long-term perspective it is helpful to think of integrity as a lifetime project, always in the making. In a sense, we are continually engaged in writing our own autobiographies. Each decision, each encounter adds a few lines. The question 'How should I act now?' is layered inside the larger question 'How would I like this page of my autobiography to read when I look back at it many years from now? What sort of a person will this decision incline me to become?'

Using the ethical decision-making chart

Ethical reflection is an activity, carried out through conversations. Because ethically troubling situations generally involve several people, practising ethics as a social activity enables the participants to hear the others' perceptions and ways of dealing with the difficulty. It also creates the space for collaborative decision-making. Even when done alone, ethical reflection often takes the form of conversations with oneself, in which other voices are imagined and projected. Using the ethical decision-making chart shown in Table 14.1 can guide us in constructing stories and using our imaginations to think about the characters and the setting of the workplace dramas.

Making a good ethical decision rests, in part, on whether the participants have asked enough good questions. Placing daily decisions in the context of these three basic value commitments is one way of ensuring that enough good questions are

Table 14.1 Ethical decision-making chart

Alternatives	1	2	3	4
Organizational mission How does this alternative promote or detract from the organization's mission? Basic philanthropic values				
Relationships How does this alternative affect long-term relationships with colleagues, donors, volunteers and community members?				
Personal integrity In what ways does this alternative help or not help you develop into the person you want to become? How does it strengthen or weaken your own integrity?				

asked. After gathering all relevant information, you are ready to use the chart, 'Ethical decision-making: evaluating the alternatives'. Begin by writing in a few alternative ways of resolving the case. It is all right to start with alternatives as obvious as 'do it' and 'don't do it'. Include alternatives with which you are pretty sure you disagree. Analysing obviously unethical alternatives often brings out insights that can be applied to less clear-cut solutions. Participants often find that additional and often more creative resolutions arise as they discuss the case.

Now work your way down the chart. For each alternative resolution, ask yourself:

- How does this alternative promote or detract from the organization's mission? How does it promote or detract from basic philanthropic values?
- How does this alternative affect long-term relationships with colleagues, donors, volunteers, and community members?
- In what ways does this alternative help or not help me develop into the person I want to become? How does it strengthen or weaken my own integrity?

There is no equation or formula that, if applied correctly, will yield an 'ethically correct' decision. This is not a flowchart; you do not insert facts, add values, push a button, and wait for a correct solution to emerge at the other end. Ethics always involves judgement, and people of goodwill often disagree on how to interpret the facts or assess the values of a given situation. For many situations, there may be no one right answer; the ethics may be 'grey' in one of the senses discussed above. But there are plenty of wrong answers, and the hope is that after reflection the wrongness of the wrong answers will be clear. One will then be able to choose among the others with sensitivity and good judgement. If an alternative supports all three basic value commitments, you can be assured that it is ethically sound.

Sample case analysis: the wildlife painting case

Consider this scenario:

> A college fundraiser has been working with an alumna, a famous wildlife painter. She agrees to do an oil painting of a nostalgic campus scene. Alumni who donate at least $100 to the college annual fund will receive reprints of the painting. After a highly successful fundraising programme, the artist presents the fundraiser with one of her original oil paintings, valued at more than $2,500. Is it ethical to accept the painting as a personal gift?
>
> The obvious alternatives are: (1) accept the painting or (2) reject the painting. We can start by analysing just these two (see Table 4.2).

Alternative 1: Accept the painting

Organizational mission. The college's fundamental purposes include educating students, contributing to the growth of scholarly knowledge through research, and serving the community. None of these is compromised in a direct or immediate way if you accept the painting. However, because you accepted the painting as a personal gift, the artist may feel you have an obligation to her. In the future, she could put you in an awkward position, which could have detrimental effects on the organizational mission. For example, she could pressure you to use your influence to get her a position on the college board of trustees. Or, she may want to establish a scholarship for students interested in studying an esoteric art form, even though the art department lacks the necessary personnel and the resources to support this study.

Should the artist use her influence in these ways, students and the college community could be adversely affected. She may not be qualified to be on the board, she may compromise the autonomy and good judgement of the art department, and so on.

Encouraging values such as generosity and gratitude helps to sustain philanthropy as a gift economy. If you accept the painting, you acknowledge the artist's generosity and gratitude. However, you also remove the painting from circulating within the gift economy.

Relationships. From the preceding discussion, it is clear that your relationship with the artist may be compromised. Instead of a professional relationship in which

Table 14.2 The wildlife painting case

Alternatives	1	2	3	4
	Accept the painting	Reject the painting	Ask the artist to donate the painting to the college	
Organizational mission How does this alternative promote or detract from the organization's mission? Basic philanthropic values?	Mission of education, research, service. No effects unless artist feels you owe her favours that are detrimental to the college. Acknowledges artist graduate, but removes painting from gift circulation.	Little immediate effect; you avoid being compromised in ways that might hinder the college's organizational mission. Keeps the college's mission consistent with philanthropic values.	Contributes to aesthetic education; may encourage other artists to support the college. Acknowledges artist's gratitude and keeps the painting with the gift economy.	
Relationships How does this alternative affect long-term relationships with colleagues, donors, volunteers, and community members?	You may have compromised your relationship with the artists. Relations with colleagues may become strained.	Strengthens relations with colleagues if they see you refuse a personal favour. Artist may be offended at your refusal, but keeps open the possibility of good future relationship with the artist.	Rewards colleagues who worked on the project. Maintains a positive and proper professional relationship with the artist.	
Personal integrity In what ways does this alternative help or not help you develop into the person you want to become? How does it strengthen or weaken your own integrity?	It may be difficult to exercise independent judgement in the future.	You maintain independent judgement and exercise courage.	Increases your effectiveness as a fundraiser while maintaining your integrity.	

mutual concern for the well-being of the college is foremost, personal ties of obligation may have been formed. Your relationships with colleagues may also become strained. Your colleagues worked with you on the fundraising project, yet they did not receive personal paintings. They might wonder if you have received personal gifts or favours from other donors as well. These suspicions would weaken the trust that underlies the long-term health of collegial relationships.

Personal integrity. You have compromised your own integrity and your ability to act with independent judgement by placing yourself in such a position with the artist. She did not merely offer you a personal gift, as between friends. By mixing personal and professional roles, the artist brings with the gift the expectation of future professional favours. By asking her to do the painting for the alumni in the first place, you gave her a lot of publicity. Alumni may like the print and want to obtain more of her work. The artist could use the personal gift as a way of pressuring you to open additional future opportunities for her. Accepting the gift this time may make it more difficult for you to act independently in future dealings.

Alternative 2: Reject the painting

Organizational mission. If you reject the painting as a personal gift, you avoid putting yourself in this compromised position. You will not be in a position to detract from the college's fundamental purposes, and you further its purposes indirectly by remaining the sort of professional best able to work for the institution.

The college's mission is consistent with the purpose of philanthropy as serving the public good. Although the artist's own sense of generosity may be dented if you refuse the painting, you keep the college on firm ground to encourage philanthropic giving from others.

Relationships. If colleagues knew you had been offered and had rejected the painting, this would strengthen the trust and respect they have in you, and thus strengthen your working relationships. Your relationship with the artist may become strained, but she has placed you in a position in which a healthy relationship is impossible. The strain may be temporary; rejecting the painting may be the only way to make a future good relationship with her possible.

Personal integrity. You have used this experience as practice for strengthening your own integrity, even though it may have been difficult.

By the time you work through these two alternatives, it is likely that someone will suggest, 'How about asking the artist to donate the painting to the college? It would look great hanging in the college theatre lobby'. So let us add this alternative to the chart.

Alternative 3: Ask the artist to donate the painting to the college

Organizational mission. One aspect of educating students and serving the community is to enhance people's aesthetic sensibility. Displaying the painting in the college theatre serves this purpose and also acknowledges the artist's generosity and gratitude. The painting remains within the philanthropic gift economy so that visitors and members of the college community can enjoy it.

Relationship. Accepting the painting for the college rewards all your colleagues who worked on this project, rather than giving special recognition just to you. This would strengthen the spirit of camaraderie among you and your colleagues, which would have a positive effect on future endeavours. Other artists and potential donors may also feel encouraged to support the college in analogous ways.

The artist may not have had ulterior motives in offering you the painting. She may simply have appreciated the opportunity to work with you and help the college. She may not have realized that in offering the painting as a personal gift she is placing you in a compromised position. By suggesting she donate the painting to the college, you offer her a way to show her appreciation, without the sense of embarrassment she may feel if you simply refuse the painting as a personal gift.

Personal integrity. Part of your own sense of personal integrity is to be an effective, diligent professional. Encouraging the artist to donate the painting is well in keeping with your role as a fundraiser. Rather than placing a block in the cycle of giving, you have facilitated its movement.

In this case study, the strongest alternative is to encourage the artist to donate the painting to the college. If she refuses, then you should refuse to accept the painting as a personal gift.

While working through this case, someone may ask, 'Suppose it's a lousy painting?' That is a good question, and it gives you a new case to analyse. So take out a fresh copy of the chart and begin anew.

The model, ethics as narrative and philanthropy as a gift economy

One rarely hears inefficiency praised as a virtue, but in thinking through ethically troubling situations thinking slowly has its advantages. One virtue of the chart is that by following it through systematically one is forced to think slowly and attend to reasons and details that might otherwise be overlooked. Also, by going through the chart one alternative at a time, the polarizing effects of a debate format can be avoided. Sometimes, debates about ethics are fruitful, but too often the effect is to further entrench disagreement. For good ethical reflection, it is important not to be defensive about one's own position and to be willing to enter into others' ways of thinking and feeling. Even people who initially advocate, and may continue to advocate, different alternatives will be able to uncover areas of agreement as they work their way through the chart, instead of simply arguing back and forth about their own preferred solution. Articulating areas of agreement may encourage creating compromise, enabling people to come up with new resolutions that all can endorse.

Thus, focusing first on the organizational mission is a good strategy, as people probably agree on its content and importance. Starting from clearly expressed, shared commitments, rather than polarized differences, bodes well for a healthy decision-making process.

There are several ways in which using the chart encourages sympathetic understanding. Articulating the organization's mission and its relation to the goals of philanthropy, and affirming shared commitment to those goals, gives an initial basis for sympathy and goodwill. Also, because the goal of evaluating the effect of each alternative on the fundraiser's relationship with various groups is to strengthen long-term relationships, sympathetic understanding emerges as one enters imaginatively into the perspective of office colleagues, board members, volunteers, donors and community members.

Social contexts will be articulated as the stories are told. Good ethical reflection involves careful attention to both factual details and basic values (remember the supermarket). As you work through the chart slowly, it is likely that different interpretations of the facts will emerge, along with value differences. In some discussions, ethical differences evaporate as people realize that apparent value clashes are really just different interpretations of facts, or different collections of facts relevant to the case.

The temporal dimension is present throughout. Placing the organizational mission in the context of broader philanthropic values is a good way of checking whether the mission stays true through time or whether it has drifted. By focusing on long-term relationships, the bumps caused by immediate disagreements are more easily recognized and kept in perspective. Finally, thinking about integrity in terms of our continuing autobiographies better equips us to accept temporary discomfort with serenity. 'If I don't say just what I think the donor wants to hear, we won't get this gift this time' will not seem so compelling as a reason to cheapen one's sense of integrity.

Finally, this method helps us to remember that what is important about philanthropy is that it serves public purposes by keeping the philanthropic gift economy functioning. Reviewing the mission clarifies the public purposes being served. Keeping philanthropic values firmly in mind helps us resist those short-term gains that compromise long-term consistency with philanthropic purposes.

Chapter 15

Nikki van der Gaag

IMAGES IN FUNDRAISING

'The most political decision you make
Is where you direct people's eyes.
In other words, what you show people,
Day in and day out, is political.'

Wim Wenders, *The Act of Seeing* (1997)

FUNDRAISERS TODAY FACE stiff competition in their use of images. The total global image market is estimated to be worth US$6.5 billion (Clark, 2004). The image industry has seen huge changes in the past ten years – photos are sent across the world in a matter of seconds, people can take digital photographs with their mobile phones, and the media can summon the film or the image they want at the touch of a button. Linda Royle, Managing Director of the British Association of Picture Libraries and Agencies, comments: 'There is a phenomenal change going on in the market at the moment. I really think people will look back at this period in the same way people now look at the changes from agricultural to industrial' (Clark, 2004).

At the same time, just under two-thirds of the British public gives to charity, with international aid and development organizations being the most popular recipients. In 2004, there were 166,129 charities in England and Wales and 17,684 in Scotland (Charities Aid Foundation, 2004).[1] To succeed in this context, a fundraising appeal has to be different. It needs to catch the imagination as well, appeal to the emotions, challenge the intellect – and often have a memorable and arresting image.

Traditionally, appealing to the emotions has often meant images portraying people as victims – whether this is a woman farmer in Sierra Leone caught up in the conflict or a disabled person in the UK. But this has also led to problems for the organizations concerned. First, it demeans the person in the photo. Second, it often takes them out of context. Third, it can reinforce the very stereotypes that the organization is often trying to counter. Fourth, it may well be a distortion of the way the organization actually spends its money. This chapter examines the issues around the use of images for not-for-profits working on development and disability, and asks: What has changed over the past decade?

The media

In 2004 O'Brien found that most people gained information about developing countries from television news (82 per cent), followed by newspapers and magazines (45 per cent) and television other than news (21 per cent). They are bombarded by up to 10,000 images a day through advertisements, magazines, television, the Internet and their mobile phones. Even the largest not-for-profit cannot compete with the power and sheer number of images put out by the media. Barbara Stocking, Director of Oxfam, speaking on Radio 4's *Today* programme, noted that not-for-profits today did not need to use images of starvation, as the media were often there first (18 October 2005).

But what if donations to not-for-profits become dependent on such media appeals? Neil Townsend, Oxfam's humanitarian co-ordinator for southern Africa, noted in September 2005:

> Niger was forecast six months in advance, yet rich countries did almost nothing until the 11th hour. People died as a direct result. Now there is an impending crisis in southern Africa. If rich countries wait to give money, once again, until television crews show children dying, people in southern Africa will pay the price of their neglect.
> (quoted in Meldrum, 2005: 14)

The tsunami in Asia in 2004 was another example of media images leading to an outpouring of generosity on the part of the general public which then forced governments to increase their own contributions. Coverage of development issues on television has dropped considerably in the past ten years: 'The amount of factual international programming on the four largest terrestrial channels was 40 per cent lower in 2003 than in 1989/90' (3WE, 2003).

The result is that the most powerful images of developing countries generally occur in the context of a disaster. They make good news stories, they may raise money, but they do little to promote further understanding of the people involved, their lives, the reasons why the disaster occurred or the political situation. And they are overwhelmingly negative.

This negativity applies not only to images of people in other countries, but also to many of those with whom not-for-profits work. Asylum seekers, the homeless, people with disabilities – how often is there a positive story about such people? In 1992, Colin Barnes noted that the mass media put disabled people into ten categories:[2]

1   As pitiable and pathetic;
2   As an object of violence;
3   As incapable of participating fully in community life;
4   As atmosphere or curio;
5   As a burden;
6   As sinister and evil;
7   As super-cripple;
8   As an object of ridicule;
9   As their own worst and only enemy;
10   As sexually abnormal.

There was a final category too – absence. A report for the Department of Work and Pensions in 2005 noted that disabled people were now largely missing from advertising altogether. They have started a campaign to include them in government materials.[3]

The first five of the above categories, and the final one (absence), could equally be applied to portrayals of people in the South. A study by the Glasgow Media Group for Britain's Department of International Development (DFID) noted that: 'In news output, developing countries were either not covered, or were mentioned only in the context of visits by westerners, sports events, wildlife or bizarre/exotic stories'. It found that 'the developing world was perceived very negatively and media images (especially news) were cited as the major source of this view. Most respondents used words like "poverty, famine, drought, wars and disasters" in the third world and began initially to speak about Africa' (DFID, 2000). In 2001, NOP's research for Voluntary Service Overseas (VSO) found that '80 per cent of the British public strongly associate the developing world with doom-laden images of famine, disaster and western aid' (VSO, 2002).

The historical context

Much of this has changed very little over many decades. Although the technology may be new, the images often aren't. European missionaries collected money with pictures of starving black babies. The founder of the Spastics Society, a father of a child with cerebral palsy but also a marketing person by profession, sold the image of the attractive, blond, not very disabled child that became an iconic begging box in the 1960s. More often than not, the images that raise the public's emotion and encourage them to give to 'worthy' causes continue to be those of children and babies because they pull at the heart (and purse) strings the most.

The October 2005 edition of the *New Internationalist* magazine did a brief trawl through the images used by not-for-profits in overseas development to raise money for the famine in Niger. Most of these are children, sometimes emaciated, with their eyes raised in supplication (*New Internationalist*, October 2005). The text alongside read:

> The use of emotive images, particularly children in distress, to raise funds has long been a contentious issue. They ignore the context and

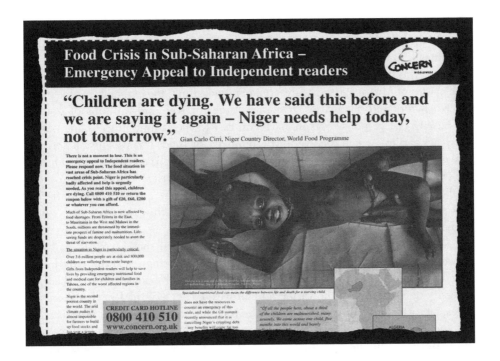

Food Crisis in Sub-Saharan Africa –
Emergency Appeal to Independent readers

CONCERN WORLDWIDE

"Children are dying. We have said this before and
we are saying it again – Niger needs help today,
not tomorrow." Gian Carlo Cirri, Niger Country Director, World Food Programme

CREDIT CARD HOTLINE
0800 410 510
www.concern.org.uk

exploit the subject. The children appear as passive and helpless – and, by extension, so do the societies in which they live. The question is why we still respond to them.

In 2002, the Africa–Canada Forum (ACF) brought together NGOs, churches, unions and solidarity groups from across Canada that 'have a specific interest in development issues and social justice in sub-Saharan Africa'. Amos Safo, in an article for *News from Africa*, noted that 'It came to light during various sessions of the G8 and G6B summits that, in their fund-raising activities, some NGOs present false images about Africa in order to attract donors'. He continued:

> The ACF said these false images of Africa, if not curtailed, paint a bleak picture about a continent that has no hope, save depending on charity from the west. In the end, some donors, rather than sympathizing with Africa, become reluctant to release funds for humanitarian activities.
>
> (Safo, 2002)

In the 1990s, there was much talk of what was called 'compassion fatigue'. It was feared that people would become so inured to such images that they no longer felt like giving. There does not seem to be much evidence of this. And there was a period in the 1990s when fewer images of starving babies and emaciated children were seen in the not-for-profits' materials. Funds did not drop as a result, though no detailed research study was undertaken of the link between images and income.

The images disappeared not because there were fewer famines or disasters, but because there had been a big debate after the first Live Aid in 1985 as to whether such images in the long term did more harm than good.

Live Aid, the original Live8, in 1985, which came into being after the famine in the Horn of Africa, started a new trend in fundraising: the big, high-profile event where singers and celebrities give their time for free and millions of pounds are raised. The response was in stark contrast to the famine in the same region ten years earlier, which received little publicity or funds but was just as serious. The difference may be attributed almost entirely to media attention. In addition, the crisis in 1984/85 was viewed very differently in Africa. While the European public perceived it as a 'dramatic and catastrophic event', in African countries it was seen as a 'process over an extended period of time, not an immediate happening'.[4]

Subsequent research[5] on images of Africa showed that Live Aid had also boosted the public's image of Africa in the West as a single starving continent, raised arms holding a begging bowl. The public in the UK had no sense of the huge diversity of countries, of the variety of cultures, or even of the fact that there are cities, factories and industry in Africa. The research also showed that international aid and development charities had played into this image in their fundraising materials, thus helping to reinforce these messages. 'The mobilization of emergency relief for the starving Africans serves to reinforce the European's self-image as saviours and heroes. The true image of the people affected by the food crisis is in diametric opposition to the passive and fatalistic picture diffused by the European mass media. Rural people reacted to the crisis by using it as an impetus for developing new solutions and alternative systems for combating hunger and its causes' (Images of Africa, synopsis of African reports, 1988). This was corroborated by Tony Vaux, a former Oxfam worker and author of a book about the aid world, *The Selfish Altruist*: 'Ninety per cent of the people saved are saved by their neighbours and family and about 10 per cent by people rushing in from round and about, and about 0.01 per cent by people who come in from the other side of the world' (Gidley, 2004).

The research sparked a lively debate among international aid NGOs throughout Europe. Images of starving babies and of women and victims were very effective for pulling the public's heartstrings and raising money, but they did not relate to the way that money is generally spent by those same NGOs, nor to the Africans' own perception of the problem, which was that the famine was allowed to develop because of 'political considerations'. These factors were largely ignored, both by African and Western governments and donors, and in the coverage of the famine itself.

This debate led to a mushrooming of 'codes of conduct' on fundraising images, the most notable of which was the European Code of Conduct on Images and Messages Relating to the Third World, and the Red Cross/Red Crescent Code of Conduct.[6] The keywords were 'respect' and 'dignity'. The European Code noted that: 'The images and messages projected of the Third World by the media or NGOs themselves can undermine the work of development organizations for the quality of development co-operation and solidarity with the Third World is dependent upon the type of images and messages used by NGOs in their public awareness raising activities'. It called for NGOs to avoid:

- Images which generalize and mask the diversity of situations;
- Idyllic images (which do not reflect reality, albeit unpleasant), or 'adventure' or exotic images;
- Images which fuel prejudice;
- Images which foster a sense of Northern superiority;
- Apocalyptic or pathetic images.

For a number of years after this, fundraisers in international NGOs were very aware of the kinds of messages they were putting out – there was more emphasis on equipping people with the tools to make them self-sufficient: 'Give a man [*sic*] a fish and he can eat today; teach him to fish and he can eat for a lifetime'. But research which looked at the changes in images used by British NGOs in their communications over the decade revealed that, although 60 per cent of the organizations surveyed in 2003 claimed they had changed the way they use images over the past ten years, there was very little statistical difference in how they used images in 2003 compared with 1993 (Clark, 2004).

Negative images, says Lynne Roper of Stirling Media Research Institute,[7] are also present in telethons such as the BBC's Children in Need, which, she says, have been criticized for being 'the 20th-century version of the beggar in the streets. Even the begging-bowls are no longer in our own hands'. She then goes on to examine if this is true:

- 'Telethons use images of brave, smiling and grateful recipients of charity. They ask us to donate out of relief that we don't have their problems.
- They create the impression that it is not the job of the state to provide essential funds for disadvantaged groups, and do not question why people are disadvantaged. By making certain people dependent on charity, we create beggars.
- Emotive images push other images out. Those who look fit and well are assumed to be able to look after themselves, which is not always the case.
- Telethons could help us to understand, but usually don't. People donate because they're being entertained. There is a conflict between the way you raise money, and the way you raise awareness. They are not necessarily the same thing.
- Who will give disabled people a job when they see such images? The implicit meaning is that we should help disabled people, not that we should integrate them into society.'

But there is one crucial difference between images of disabled people and images of people in the South; there is a vibrant and radical movement of disabled people in the UK which over the past ten years has had a voice within the disability organizations. And this, says Richard Brewster, former CEO of SCOPE, has made a difference to the images that many such organizations are using (personal interview with author). SCOPE's current statement says that it is 'committed to working in alliance with disabled people and disabled people's organizations to advance the goal of disabled people's equality'.[8] It also says that it is committed to what it calls 'co-production' as a way of working: 'That means that disabled people should lead the campaign and Scope will use its resources to support their leadership'. Disabled people are more likely to veto images that they think do not respect their dignity.

The self and other

By becoming involved in the organizations that are funding disability projects, disabled people also blur the distinction between the 'watcher' and the 'watched', the 'self' and the 'other'. And, as French philosopher Michel Foucault noted, such distinctions define our discourse and are inseparable from power relations (Foucault, 1980). In this very real sense, then, image-makers are setting the boundaries of what is considered 'normal' and what is not.

This 'otherness' is not just about difference, but also implies moral judgements that relate to the power one group in society feels it has over another. Edward Said (1978) said that 'the construction of others is bound up with the fluctuation of power and powerlessness'.

Lamers (2005), in a study of a poster campaign by the Belgian NGO NCOS, found striking dichotomies between the 'self' viewing the posters and the content of the posters, portrayed as follows:

The 'other'	The 'self'
Child	Adult
Ignorant	Wise, knowledgeable
Passive	Active
Helpless	Helpful

David Campbell (2003) notes that emergency appeal images for development NGOs

> portray a particular kind of helplessness that reinforces colonial relations of power. With their focus firmly on women and children, these pictures function as icons of an infantilized and feminized place. A place that is passive, pathetic and demanding of help of those with the capacity to intervene.

In the analysis of the coverage of Live Aid 1985, findings showed that 80 per cent of the *Daily Mirror*'s and 43 per cent of the *Guardian*'s images of the situation were of women and children. The report concluded:

> All these pictures overwhelmingly showed people as needing our pity – as passive victims. The photos seemed mainly to be taken from a high angle thus reinforcing the viewer's sense of power compared with their apathy and helplessness. The 'Madonna and Child' image was

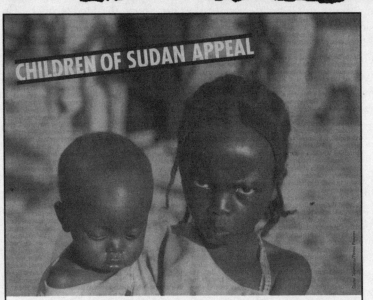

CHILDREN OF SUDAN APPEAL

The children of Darfur, Sudan are caught up in a horrific conflict which is having a devastating effect on their lives.

Nearly 2 million people have fled their homes as the fighting continues. Entire villages have been destroyed and thousands of lives have been lost. Water and shelter are in short supply.

UNICEF has been working tirelessly to protect children's lives since the emergency began: providing medical supplies and access to safe water and sanitation.

However, as the humanitarian crisis continues, more and more vulnerable children desperately need our help. Without access to clean water and medical supplies, more lives will be lost. UNICEF urgently needs to provide this essential aid.

£30 will provide emergency health supplies to treat 86 children for 3 months

Children in Sudan are depending on UNICEF to stay alive. And we depend on you. Please give as much as you can today.

THE CHILDREN OF SUDAN APPEAL
0800 037 9797
24-HR FREEPHONE CREDIT CARD DONATION LINE

unicef

www.unicef.org.uk/sudanobs
UNICEF, FREEPOST CL885, Billericay CM12 0BR.

particularly emotively used, echoing the biblical imagery. Women were at the same time patronised and exalted.

(Images of Africa 1987)

Disabled women are simply removed from the picture: 'in film and TV drama . . . women do not have to be portrayed as disabled in order to present an image of vulnerability and dependency . . . therefore most disabled characters in film and television in recent years have been men' (J. Morris in Pointon, 1997).

This dichotomy has come home to haunt us. In societies today, the positing of the 'self' in this context – often seen as white Western – and the 'other' – often portrayed as black – bears no relation to the ethnic and cultural mix at home but does have a role to play in the complex mire of racism and racist attitudes. There are increasing numbers of migrants and refugees in countries where not-for-profits are located. Since the events of 11 September 2001, and the resulting increase in prejudice against Muslims, there are also issues for fundraisers about how and when to use images of veiled women or bearded men, especially in a context in which refugees and asylum seekers receive such a bad press in the media.[9]

Jenny Morris (1991) argues that cultural portrayals of disability are usually about the feelings of non-disabled people and their reactions to disability, rather than about disability itself. Disability thus becomes

> a metaphor . . . for the message that the non-disabled writer wishes to get across, in the same way that 'beauty' is used. In doing this, the writer draws on the prejudice, ignorance and fear that generally exist towards disabled people, knowing that to portray a character with a humped back, with a missing leg, with facial scars, will evoke certain feelings in the reader or audience. The more disability is used as a metaphor for evil, or just to induce a sense of unease, the more the cultural stereotype is confirmed.
>
> (Morris, 1991: 93)

Charity vs. partnership?

Some of this is in sharp contrast to the language used by not-for-profits today. They talk of 'partnership', and of 'capacity-building'. This is not the place to do an analysis of how this matches their work on the ground, but there is a cognitive dissonance about using the language of partnership while at the same time portraying people as passive victims. During the famine in the Horn of Africa in 1985/85, it was argued that such images made it more difficult then to put across more complex developmental messages in subsequent fundraising. Portraying women as passive victims on a continent where they make up the majority of farmers also cut across messages that the NGOs generally wanted to be putting out that women are economically active as well as socially productive. 'The quality of development co-operation and solidarity with the Third World is dependent upon the types of images and messages used by NGOs in their public awareness raising activities', says the preamble to the 1989 Code of Conduct.

In an isolated context, it might be argued, why is it a problem to show a starving child if that is the situation on the ground? The problem is that an image of a child or a baby cannot be seen in isolation, but relates to a whole iconography that may well be subconscious but which feeds back into ingrained colonial attitudes. There is also an issue of double standards. Oxfam's Pete Davis said:

> picture editors would usually think at least three times before publishing photographs of naked children, unless they were African famine victims. But naked famine's okay, it seems . . . Using pictures of bare-breasted women in a society where the only other place we see that is salacious tabloids is not acceptable.
>
> (quoted in Gidley, 2005)

Comments from respondents in NGOs (Campbell and Clark, 2003) revealed some of the dilemmas they face:

> 'As our DM [Direct Marketing] area has expanded, we have started to use more emotive photos which, to an extent, are sometimes at odds with our main image – portraying people positively rather than as victims. We are currently doing tests to establish the different impacts positive and negative images have on DM response rates.'

> 'When we (or rather, our predecessor organizations) started, we tended to use images that would appeal to the donors, more or less without regard for the people who were being photographed. But, gradually, we have gone over to a policy that is more acceptable from a development point of view, one which considers the rights of those being photographed (especially children) and which doesn't any longer treat them as victims. But it's been a struggle, as there is always a tension between the kind of image that brings in the money and one that doesn't demean the subjects of the photo. I could write on this at length.'

Many in the not-for-profits are well aware of the dilemma; there have always been heated debates between fundraisers and educators, between overseas department staff and those in donor relations. Few of these are voiced publicly; it would be seen to be washing your dirty linen in public.

But there have been changes in the climate and context which have affected the way the not-for-profits use images. First, there is increasingly intense competition for funds between different NGOs. This means that if one agency uses an emotive image, others feel they have to do the same. Competition has had other impacts on images as well. One member of a fundraising events team noted that: 'All the people who want to give are probably already doing it. So we need to think: how can we find different ways of interesting people in giving?' (personal interview with the author). Some of these new ways do not use images of the South at all, but to get people involved in fundraising themselves by travelling or walking or being sponsored to do something they find exciting.

The other change has been the digital revolution, which means that more and more staff of these organizations are taking photos that are now of useable quality. This cuts down costs, but in general the photos seem to be taken by staff visiting from the West rather than local staff.

The voices that have been largely missing in this debate are those of the 'partners' themselves. While disability organizations have tackled this by bringing disabled people into their governance structures, many organizations working in overseas development who have 'decentralized' their operations and employed local people to run offices in Southern countries still have not found ways of consulting Southern people on the images they use in the North.

Eva Von Oelreich, head of disaster preparedness at the International Federation of Red Cross and Red Crescent Societies (IFRC), said that NGOs 'have spent a lot of time on building up financial and legal accountability towards our donors, including the general public, but it's much more difficult to find an appropriate way of being accountable to the people who are affected by a disaster' (Gidley, 2004).

Some would argue that materials for a Northern audience are best produced by Northern 'experts'. There is some truth in this: in the summary of the report of the African countries participating in the Images of Africa project, the participants noted 'that misinformation about Africa in European countries is essentially a European problem' (Images of Africa, synopsis of African reports, 1988). But, unless the balance of 'us' and 'them' is redressed, little is likely to change. '"We'll know we've broken the colonial mindset when we start importing African photographers to cover stories in Europe", said Colin Hastings of Kijiji Vision, which promotes African photographers' (Gidley, 2005).

In addition to a focus on partnership, not-for-profits are increasingly focused on influencing policy. Most of these kinds of images do not encourage people to campaign as well as give money. But in terms of longer-term change and the alleviation of poverty, this again contradicts the general trend. The NGOs must take some responsibility for the fact that, in 2004, 60 per cent of respondents to a survey said that donating to charities was the most common way in which individuals felt they 'could help to reduce poverty in developing countries', followed by fair trade (46 per cent), paying taxes (32 per cent) and finally putting pressure on politicians (30 per cent).

New contexts

Today, in the year of Live8, there is a whole new generation working in international NGOs who have never heard of the Code of Conduct and who are not aware that there were ever any debates. But research would seem to indicate that the public are looking for change. The study for VSO noted that:

1   55 per cent of British people say they want to see more of the everyday life of the developing world, particularly on television. They want to see the positives as well as the negatives and they want context and background.

2   Any dilution of the powerful giver/grateful receiver model would have a positive impact on racial tensions and misunderstandings. Breaking down stereotypes forges stronger associations with individuals rather than an amorphous mass of victims. In turn, this is likely to lead to a more informed population able to engage in real global issues – such as trading laws, environmental policies and debt relief – while working with other countries can bring economic benefit and cultural enrichment.

3   78 per cent of adults agree that our future security depends on us understanding other cultures and countries better.

A qualitative survey of disabled viewers and listeners concluded:

> Many of the changes that viewers and listeners would like to see take place in broadcasting can be described as 'respect' issues: respecting the diversity of disability and portraying those varied experiences; respecting the views of disabled people and consulting with them to provide more authentic and credible portraits; respecting the abilities of disabled people and actively involving disabled media professionals in all aspects of programme production across all genres. . . . Crucially, what disabled audiences want is an acknowledgement of the fact that disability is a part of daily life and for the media to reflect that reality, removing the insulting label of 'disabled' and making it ordinary.
>
> (Ross, 1997)

Not-for-profits too are examining their emphases: Disability Awareness in Action says:

> We must make sure we place the emphasis firmly on full human rights and not on charity. Inappropriate images of disability have been a major barrier to the understanding of disability issues by the general public and policy-makers. Disability organizations need to ensure greater awareness of these issues in the media and through them, among people everywhere.[10]

There are a number of new initiatives looking at images and messages in international NGOs, including a Europe-wide initiative to launch a new Code of Conduct, fronted by the Irish NGO Platform Dochas and supported by Concord through the Development Education Forum. The Make Poverty History Campaign has a 'Messages Actions and Campaigns Working Group'. A number of not-for-profits are currently re-examining their guidelines on images. (While more than 50 per cent of the development NGOs in Britain claimed to have their own picture policy, only 15 per cent had a written policy [Clark, 2004].)

Internationally, too, images are an issue. The Evangelical Council for Financial Accountability in the US, which, among other things, monitors relief agencies' communications, has 'Seven Standards of Responsible Stewardship'. According to these, fundraisers must make sure that their narratives about events are current, complete and accurate, and that the material they create is free of omissions, exaggerations or 'any other communication which would tend to create a false impression or misunderstanding'.[11] The Australian Council for International Development (ACFID) has a Code of Conduct for NGDOs which is binding. To be a member of ACFID, agencies must sign the Code. Lizzie Noone, who is working on the European Code, said, 'top executives of NGOs need to give their backing to the code, and that signing up should be compulsory. "It's too serious to be a voluntary code"' (Gidley, 2005).

Others argue that a code would be impossible to enforce, and that what is needed is agreement on images across the fundraising industry.

Ways forward

Donors and fundraisers alike have new opportunities to look at the messages they put out, and to challenge the public's perception, while at the same time successfully raising the money they need. The drive for change needs to come from the top of the organizations and from those who raise the money.

Ways forward might include:

- The Association of Professional Fundraisers has its own Code of Ethical Principles and Standards of Professional Practice. These could be extended to include guidelines on the images used and how the people in the images feel about this.
- CEOS could commission longitudinal studies on different kinds of advertising to see whether they change the amounts of money raised. If 'negative' images are believed to raise more money, is the short-term benefit worth the long-term impact on people's dignity?
- Not-for-profits might want to look at the 'match' between the languages of partnership that they say underpins their work and the images they are using. Are they treating these people as partners?
- This could be taken one step further: if, as part of that partnership, people from the South or people with disabilities are being employed to run the organizations, how could they be given a stake in the images and messages that are being put out?
- Above all, the debate on images needs to continue.

Fundraising is essentially an ethical occupation, encouraging generosity and fostering understanding. The ethical use of images is simply an extension of this spirit – and a challenge to all those who work in the field.

Notes

1   http://www.cafonline.org/default.aspx?page=7236.
2   Quoted in Demos http://jarmin.com/demos/course/awareness/05.html.
3   www.disability.gov.uk.
4   Images of Africa, synopsis of African reports, 1988. Available at www.imaging-famine.org.

5   *The Images of Africa project*, 1987, United Nations Food and Agriculture Organization. Available at www.imaging-famine.org.
6   http://www.dochas.ie/Documents/Code_images_98.htm.
7   www.mediaed.org.uk/posted_documents/DisabilityinMedia.htm.
8   www.scope.org.uk.
9   'What's the story? Results of research into media coverage of refugees and asylum seekers in the UK', www.article19.org.uk.
10 http://www.independentliving.org/docs2/daa3.pdf.
11 http://www.christianitytoday.com/ct/2001/015/5.50.html.

References

Campbell, D. (2003) 'Salgado and the Sahel: documentary photography and the imaging of famine', in Francis Debris and Cynthia Weber (eds) *Rituals of Mediation*, University of Minnesota Press, pp. 69–96.

Clark, D. J. (2004) 'The production of the contemporary famine image: the image economy, indigenous photographers and the case of Mekanic Philopos', http://www.djclark.com/change/format./html.

Clark, D. J. and Campbell, D. (2003) Pictures for change: photographing the majority world, international development and the other Live Aid legacy, http://www.djclark.com/change/.

Department For International Development (DFID) (2000) *Viewing the World: A Study of British Television Coverage of Developing Countries*.

Department for Work and Pensions (2005) *Missing from Advertising: Images of Disability – Improving the Representation of Disabled People in UK Advertising*.

Dover, C. and Barnett, S. (2004) *The World on the Box: Factual International Programming on UK Television*, a report for Third World and Environmental Broadcasting Trust (3WE).

Foucault, M. (1980) *Power/knowledge: Selected Interviews and Other Writings, 1972–1977*, ed. C. Gordon, New York: Pantheon Books.

Gidley, R. (2004) 'NGOs still fail standards on appeal images', Reuters Foundation, AlertNet, 14 January.

Gidley, R. (2005) 'Aid workers lament rise of "development pornography"', Reuters Foundation, AlertNet, 14 September.

Lamers, M. (2005) 'Representing poverty, impoverishing representation? A discursive analysis of NGOs fundraising posters', http://66.102.9.104/search?q=cache:wLro9sJ-5zyJ:www.gis.ond/documents/journal_issue_3/lamers.pdf+Representing+Poverty+Impoverishing+Representation%3F+A+Discursive+Analysis+Of+a+NGOs+Fundraising+Posters&hl=en&ct=clnk&cd=1.

Meldrum, A. (2005) 'UN appeal for southern Africa draws a blank', *Guardian*, 10 September, p. 14.

Moeller, S. (1999) *Compassion Fatigue: How the Media Sell Disease, Famine, War and Death*, New York and London: Routledge.

Morris, J. (1991) *Pride Against Prejudice: Transforming Attitudes to Disability*, London: The Women's Press.

New Internationalist (2005) 'The Return of the Poster Child', October.

O'Brien, M. (2004) 'Public attitudes towards development: based on data for the National Statistics Omnibus Survey', DFID.

Pointon, A. and Davies, C. (eds) (1997) *Framed: Interrogating Disability in the Media*, London: BFI Publishing.

Ross, K. (1997) 'Where's me in it?', *Media Culture and Society*, Vol. 19, pp. 669–677.

Safo, A. (2002) 'NGOs present false images of Africa', *News from Africa*, August.

Said, E. W. (1978) *Orientalism (Western Conceptions of the Orient)*, Harmondsworth: Penguin.

van der Gaag, N. and Nash, C. (1987) *Images of Africa: the UK Report*, Oxfam.

Voluntary Service Overseas (VSO) (2002) *The Live Aid Legacy: The Developing World Through British Eyes – A Research Report*.

Chapter 16

Richard Brewster

FORMULATING AN INCOME STRATEGY TO FUND THE MISSION

What mix of funding streams? A strategic issue

TOP OF THE LIST OF QUESTIONS that keep most non-profit leaders awake at night is: 'Where and how can I find the resources that my charity needs in order to continue its work, and preferably to grow?' A critical role of a charity's leadership is to make decisions about which sources of funds they should pursue. This a demanding challenge because non-profits have available to them a considerable range of potential sources of funds (see Table 16.1). Each source requires its own relationships, skills and knowledge, and operations. Each additional source therefore requires additional investment and management time. How many sources should a charity attempt to juggle at any one time? In addition, some of these forms of contribution are restricted – the resources provided may only be used for the purposes which the funder specifies. How does a charity decide how much restricted income it should accept? Finally, there can be interrelationships between revenue generation and other activities: a charity shop can provide work opportunities for the charity's clients and therefore be part of its services as well as a fundraising venture. How do these relationships affect a charity's strategy?

In the light of this complexity, how does a non-profit decide what are its best sources of support, and what mix or combination of these to aim for? Despite the importance of this strategic question, the advice available to those seeking an answer is limited and problematic. The academic literature contains useful cases, theory and some helpful guidance; but it is fragmented and generally inaccessible to practising non-profit managers. The more thoughtful pieces of guidance offered

Table 16.1 Range of sources and types of support available to voluntary organizations

---

Private contributions
Individual financial contributions
• Small donations
• Major donations
• Bequests
Individual gifts of time-volunteering
Individual gifts in kind
Fundraising events
Giving by foundations
Giving by/partnerships with companies

Earned income
Fees for service
Fees for service paid for by third parties
Trading/commercial ventures (including commercial arrangements with companies)

Government income
Local and central contracts
Local and central grants

Membership dues

Investment income

Borrowing

---

to the practitioner only address a US context and do not reflect all the useful ideas contained in the academic literature.[1]

This chapter introduces an approach to income strategy development that integrates the relevant insights from the academic literature – but sets them within a decision-oriented framework. This does not mean that thinking through these complex issues can be reduced to the application of a formula – far from it. But a useful framework is one that challenges you to ask the right questions, and thereby cover all the important angles, even if these are sometimes difficult to answer and produce less certainty than one would like.

Presenting an analytic framework for strategy formulation involves a dilemma. Either one concentrates on the abstract ideas, keeping to a realm that is tidy, clear and logical – but leaves the meaning and application of those ideas untested; or one plunges into long, complicated case studies each of which is likely to illustrate only some of the important points. The solution chosen here has been to introduce the framework through a realistic but contrived example. That example – of a notional UK cancer charity reviewing and making decisions about its sources of income – is constructed precisely to illustrate a wide range of issues. Having told the story of a strategic review of income sources, the chapter then 'unpacks' its different elements to explain the underlying rationale.

As well as drawing on the literature, the story and the framework are underpinned by many years of personal experience both as a director of fundraising and as a chief executive of a large complex charity – experiences that stimulated the author's interest in the subject in the first place.

Cancerve in search of an income strategy

Background

Cancerve is a young national cancer charity with a mission to support cancer patients as whole people, not just as the carriers of a disease, and especially to alleviate the psychological effects of cancer. Historically, it has engaged in five programme activities: counselling of cancer patients, some of which is provided by cancer survivors; provision of hospice care; provision of physical aids for people with cancer; information provision; and funding research into specific ameliorative drugs. It has also recently begun to engage in campaigning for considerably increased resources from the government for research into the alleviation of the psychological effects of cancer. The organization has been funded by private contributions particularly in the form of bequests, though it also receives sponsorships from several companies. Cancerve has no significant reserves over and above its national and regional offices and hospice properties. The charity has recently decided to create three new hospices; to find ways to secure the future availability of its hospice services; and to find ways to meet high unmet demand for counselling. These are ambitious goals, but fortunately government health care agencies have recently been instructed to invest more systematically in the provision of counselling services. The leadership of Cancerve understand the value of the support they currently receive from so many individuals, but it is clear that the charity is missing funding opportunities. It establishes a planning group to identify these and to develop an income strategy.

Identifying likely funding sources

The members of the planning group decide to start by identifying the more promising sources of funds. This turns out to be more complicated than they expected and the discussion runs over three rather unfocused meetings, surfacing a wide range of issues. This is partly because they agree to consider all possibilities and to have clear reasons for ruling out the ones they deem 'unlikely'. But it is mainly because they gradually realize they have to consider potential sources of support from a number of different perspectives.

The resources that the charity needs. Cancerve's income strategy will have to take account of the different types and timings of expenditure that are anticipated, some of which will be susceptible to particular forms of support. If the charity can exploit these, it can increase the overall amount of support it receives. Thus:

* Its campaigning, information and direct services incur salaries and related personnel costs. Generally, these ongoing kinds of expenditure need to be covered by ongoing cash support.
* The capital investment required to stock the personal equipment service and to build three new hospices planned across the country can be financed from gifts-in-kind of land or equipment, or by debt, as well as by cash contributions.

- The charity has decided to protect its hospice services over the long term. This means creating an endowment, the prime sources for which are usually individual major donors or foundations.

Thus the group estimates the amount of money required to deliver Cancerve's planned programmes. This will provide an important foundation for detailed market research that will underpin the decision-making that will follow the group's work.

The current cancer support 'market'. The planning group identifies the main sources available to support organizations addressing cancer issues in different ways. For all the main cancer charities, individuals are the dominant sources of funds, in particular through bequests, and donations prompted by a wide variety of activities from direct mail through to special events. A small number of organizations have government contracts for services, for example, in-home nursing support; and charity stores remain a critical part of two large organizations' income profiles.

The type of good provided by Cancerve. In the course of the discussion, the group realizes that it is providing two very different sorts of 'goods'. In the context of developing an income strategy, the most obvious characteristic of the organization's counselling, hospice, personal equipment and information services is that Cancerve could charge fees for them all – though of course this might exclude some people in consequence. Cancerve's campaigning, however, is for research whose results will benefit everyone. A fee cannot be charged for campaigning, and government will not fund it; so, whatever else happens, Cancerve will need donations to sustain this activity.

Who benefits? The discussion about goods has led on to thinking about who benefits from the work of Cancerve and how this might be relevant to identifying potential contributors. They brainstorm answers to the question: Which individuals, groups or institutions do, or could, derive some value from paying for what Cancerve does? This involves lateral thinking about the meaning of 'benefits'. Their conclusions include these potential supporters:

- Individuals with cancer and with sufficient means who can experience greater psychological well-being and possibly alleviation of symptoms as a result of Cancerve's direct services, and may be willing to pay fees for these services. They may also get a sense of satisfaction that support is available for others with the same challenges and be willing to donate.
- Family and friends of people with cancer who can find value in the recovery of the morale of a loved one or the alleviation of the condition, and if the patient cannot pay for the service may be willing to do so on his or her behalf. They may get a similar sense of satisfaction that support is available to others, and want to invest in future services in case they experience cancer themselves, and therefore be willing to donate.
- Government health and social service agencies that will benefit from the availability of Cancerve's direct services since they are responsible for

delivering politically popular assistance, and there are few services of this type within the government's own direct service provision, which is concentrated on diagnosis and treatment. Budget constraints and multiple priorities will constrain how much state agencies will pay, and the need to demonstrate accountability will mean they are more likely to pay through contracts than grants.

• The very large number of individuals who do not have cancer but who may want to take out an 'insurance policy' against their contracting the disease in future and to help ensure that Cancerve's types of support will continue and that their campaigning will be successful. These people may donate and volunteer.

• The unknown number of people who derive strong personal rewards from donating. This and the previous group include Cancerve's current individual benefactors. However, it also includes private foundations with a specific remit to support people with cancer.

• Organizations that may get benefit from secondary services or products generated from the assets of the charity which is another form of earned income. The planning group concludes that there are opportunities provided by Cancerve's specialist counselling expertise, its comprehensive knowledge about cancer's effects, and even the property it owns.

The institutional environment. Cancerve then identifies players in the field, their interest, and their relative influence and power.

• Government health care agencies have no infrastructure of their own for counselling services, and they are therefore likely to be dependent on external suppliers.

• In addition to Cancerve, there are significant numbers of much smaller for-profit and non-profit general counselling organizations.

• Cancerve is the only supplier of comprehensive information about the psychological effects of cancer.

• Local authorities are the dominant suppliers of personal equipment. However, their equipment is generic and not specific to people with cancer and their service has a poor reputation in many areas.

• Hospice care is very fragmented. Only a few localities are willing to provide public funds for these. There is no dominant funder.

Beliefs of the voluntary organization. The planning group has identified a much wider range of potential sources of support than the individuals on whom Cancerve depends now. Some of these, however, have provoked debate and anxiety in the charity. Concern focuses on two particular beliefs of Cancerve. The first relates to the charity ethos: the Good Samaritan did not charge a fee for his services. The members of the group decide that, while they will recognize well-documented evidence that charging a fee for counselling leads to better results, nevertheless, Cancerve should not charge people from particular disadvantaged groups. The second concern is that taking on government money or debt may compromise Cancerve's independence. The group makes both of these concerns points of reference as they identify Cancerve's necessary and most likely sources of revenue.

The interim report

The planning group prepares an interim report which highlights four promising sources of funds.

Government funds, they report, have now become a real possibility for the charity. Their analysis of the institutional environment has made it clear that local decisions on the contracting out of counselling present the charity with a major opportunity to secure funds for a core service and to exercise a degree of control over the funder by influencing the standards for such services. However, in order to establish this control, the charity will need to co-opt private counselling providers. There is also a worry about whether the funding offered will meet the full costs of provision. The charity also feels there may be an opportunity to secure money from local social service departments for physical aids by negotiating to supply them on the local department's behalf. It is unsure about this, however, because these departments are its competitors.

Private contributions will remain a fundamentally important source and will need to grow: analysis of the type of 'good' delivered by the charity and of the activities for which it requires resources point to donations as an absolute necessity to cover its campaigning expenditure; if the fear that government funds will not cover the full costs of counselling are borne out, then donations will be required to fill the gap, at least for those who cannot afford to cover this themselves through fees; an increase in the number of hospices entails more private contributions – government will not provide this kind of capital; Cancerve's conviction that hospice services must be protected for the future also points to donations and other kinds of contribution from individuals and foundations in the form of endowments. Fortunately, the planning group believe that the analysis of who benefits confirms that the number of potential contributors is huge; they also believe that the charity can use the analysis to craft messages that appeal more powerfully to different motivations than those it delivers now to recruit more individual donors and enhance the value of each.

Gifts in kind are familiar to the charity but their analysis of the types of resource they need particularly for their new hospices have pointed them towards a more systematic approach to this kind of contribution.

Earned income makes the charity feel uncomfortable. However, the analyses of goods delivered and who benefits convince Cancerve that it must at least consider charging fees to those who can afford them for direct services. The justification for this will be that these fees can enhance the ability of Cancerve to subsidize disadvantaged groups among the cancer patient population, and enhance the impact of the service through a greater buy-in by clients. There are also opportunities to use Cancerve's sponsorship relationships with companies to develop sales of information on alleviation as a service to their staff and to earn more from property rentals.

Discarded options. Perhaps just as significantly, the planning group decide specifically *not* to recommend any investment in charity shops, because of the very high start-up costs and the complete lack of any retail experience within Cancerve. They also argue against using debt to fund capital investment because of concern about the charity's independence.

Enter: the Trustees

When the Trustees discuss it, they welcome the report, acknowledging that it significantly expands their perception of possible sources of income. This is exciting, but presents a new challenge: how to decide which of these new sources to pursue, and to what extent it should further develop individual contributions. At this point, the Treasurer is emphatic that she will want to see a serious business case with forecasts of the costs, direct and indirect, and the income streams, that may be expected from any new investment in income generation. When the Chief Executive mutters that the huge uncertainties will make this very difficult, the Treasurer accepts the point, but urges him to try to treat the main risks as additional costs wherever possible. And the Chief Executive is further reassured by the Chair insisting that the analysis should not just be about the finances – they also need to include any non-financial benefits in the appraisal.

The planning group now engages a number of staff in extensive research and analysis in order to define as precisely as possible the value to Cancerve of each of these new investments, and the associated incremental costs over the next five years. Three months later they are ready to present their main conclusions.

Income and benefit estimates

The group include in their spreadsheets the net values of any financial contributions to the achievement of Cancerve's mission, and also the values of non-financial contributions. In their commentary on the staff work the planning group highlight the following prospects:

- Significant increases in individual contributions, driven by Cancerve's greater awareness of the numbers who might give and in particular of the motivations identified in answering the question 'Who benefits?' As well as increasing the number and value of donors of smaller gifts, Cancerve intends to develop major donors and foundations for endowment.
- Gifts of land from board contacts for hospices.
- Funds from new government sources for counselling in amounts that exceed Cancerve's total current expenditure on this activity, but on a fee-for-service basis at a rate that is unlikely to cover the full cost. As feared, each extra client will generate a need for a modest subsidy from other sources.
- New unrestricted funds that result from imposing fees for counselling, personal equipment and hospice services on a limited number of those who

can afford these fees. The charity find this a challenging prospect both emotionally and technically.

- The additional 'mission value' that will arise from the increase in the number of cancer patients who will develop skills and earn a wage as counsellors if Cancerve takes on government funding to expand its services.

Estimating the full range of costs

Mindful of the Treasurer's strictures, the planning group have been particularly concerned to think through the incremental financial and non-financial effects that taking on new forms of income generation will have, and the costs of managing risks. In this connection, they decide to count threats to income as a cost. In their report they highlight the following costs:

- The expenditure on a major development office of five staff, until this begins to pay for itself, and the cost of the extra working capital that this requires.
- A 'substitution' cost corresponding to 10 per cent per annum of the current annual value of gifts from its present high-value donors. This represents the amounts that the charity fears those donors will switch from funding ongoing expenditure to supporting capital and endowment needs.
- An amount that reflects the difference between the price government agencies will pay per patient for counselling and its full costs. This cost will vary depending on how many new clients Cancerve decides to support, and how many of these clients agree to pay a fee.
- An amount that represents the 'volatility cost' of taking on a government contract for counselling. This takes the form of a new reserve equalling three months of the potential annual value of the government contract. This will enable Cancerve to maintain some level of services in the face of a loss of part or all of the government contract. Cancerve treats all this as a cost, because it will have to raise this money to make sure it has the reserve (it intends to do this by adding it to the target for its endowment campaign) and because this money could otherwise be used on a mission-related activity.
- The costs of the new technology system and management structure required to cope with the increase in the scale of counselling operations entailed by the government contract, and the net cost of the extra working capital required by this increase.
- Another amount corresponding to 10 per cent per annum of the current annual value of the government contract, this time to cover the possible withdrawal of donor support in response to the introduction of this government funding.
- Estimates of costs of the time that the Chief Executive and senior management will not be able to spend on their current activities because they need to manage the considerable changes and disruption in Cancerve created by the reporting and business systems required to support government contract work and individual fees, and the consequent changes in how staff work with

clients. Putting a value on these kinds of costs is challenging but Cancerve decides on a crude estimate of 20 per cent of the salary costs of the Chief Executive and four senior managers.

The Trustees' discussion

The leadership's first conclusion is that they have the opportunity to 'scale up' Cancerve's activities substantially: the combined extra net value of all these sources to the organization is considerable. It is very comfortable with the prospect of pursuing significant increases in donations. This is not simply because the charity's familiarity with this type of fundraising reduces the opportunity costs of making the investment, and the future value of the source is high; in addition, this kind of revenue may be used to cover unexpected shortfalls in other sources, because it is unrestricted. This is also true of any extra monies from fees for direct services and rents – these will go straight to the 'bottom line', though their value is much lower. Any combination including donations is therefore that much more valuable than, for example, the combination of the same total value but comprising only estimated government funds, which will be restricted to the services specified in the contract.

The Trustees are surprised at the relatively high cost of the government contract, but this is a specific result of the fact that this will not cover the full costs of the service, and of the decision to create a large reserve to match the perceived risk of volatility in a source that is brand new to them and that entails considerable responsibility. It is still extremely valuable to the charity, however, and the value to the mission of the considerable number of cancer patients that will get the opportunity to develop skills and a future career adds previously unrecognized value to the benefits of this source.

To the delight of those who are hostile to the introduction of fees, the start-up costs are surprisingly high, though once these are recovered the extra unrestricted funds newly available to Cancerve would be significant.

Logically therefore the Board concludes that Cancerve should pursue all the options before it. What gives the Board pause for thought is the realization that most of the Chief Executive's time (and by implication therefore the time of several other senior managers) *would be entirely consumed by the new ventures*. This represents a bottleneck that they do not know how to clear. They therefore begin to consider the pros and cons of focusing principally on the government contract.

'Unpacking' the Cancerve story

What has Cancerve been doing here? What kinds of frameworks have its leaders adopted and what concepts have they applied to their situation and work? In fact, the Cancerve planning group has followed a relatively orderly three-stage process as it works its way towards making decisions about how to increase its income. Table 16.2 summarizes this process.

In working its way through the first stage of this process – identifying sources of support with the most potential – Cancerve has used ways of thinking from

Table 16.2 Stages in developing an income strategy

---

1   Identify the most promising sources of support

Define what resources are needed for, and in what quantities: by programme activity and types of expenditure (e.g. human resources, equipment, buildings, grants) and by timing of different types of expenditure, including present versus future obligations. Identify the sources of income that can supply these resource needs.

Identify the main sources of funds *currently* in the charity's field.

Consider the implications of the non-profit's type of 'good' for its income strategy.

Identify who might benefit from paying for each of the principal activities of the charity.

Assess the likely levels of dependence between funder and funded organizations for each of the principal activities of the charity.

Decide which sources of support may be precluded by the beliefs of the non-profit, or for other reasons (e.g. lack of capability).

2   Develop investment cases for new and expanded income sources

The value and costs of each of these likely income sources for a selected/required time period:

Value

- amount of mission/programme impact and other organizational activity that the income source can 'buy',
- mission/programme value of 'crowd-in' effects [Cancerve is not the beneficiary of this effect];
- direct mission/programme value of any revenue generation activity.

Costs

Financial costs of investing in a new source, of expanding, if current.

Direct financial costs of taking on a new source when source does not cover full costs of funded activity.

Costs to the non-profit associated with:
- the value of revenue lost through 'crowd-out' effects;
- developing, maintaining and monitoring relationships with sources of funds;
- managing internal change;
- mitigating risk associated with goal displacement;
- mitigating risk of volatility and unpredictability.

Any additional benefits and costs of different *combinations* of these likely income sources:
- the benefits of diversification – the extra value of unrestricted sources;
- leadership opportunity cost.

3   Use these calculations to inform debate and to make judgements

---

economics and sociology that are often overlooked, though of course once spelt out they may seem quite obvious. The main insights on which they draw are as follows.

- Charities can access a uniquely varied range of funding sources that includes gifts in kind and volunteers. Cancerve are aware that if they are to benefit fully from this variety they need to define their resource needs in non-financial as well as financial terms. This enables them more easily to spot the opportunity to pursue gifts of land for their new hospices.
- The missions of some non-profits include obligations to future generations and the corresponding need to guarantee income to discharge these obligations. Cancerve could see that its decision to secure hospice care for the long term *required* an endowment – and the greater need therefore for individual and foundation donations (on top of what they will need to *build* the hospices).
- The likelihood of securing support is greater if in a given field (in this case helping people with cancer) there are well-established organizations already present, and ways of giving and receiving money are institutionalized. The cost of entry for a newcomer is low and familiarity with the field predisposes organizations and individuals to give to this cause. *These factors can often outweigh the risks of competition.* Cancerve already benefits from the pre-dominant form of funding in the cancer charity field, namely private contributions, and is very comfortable with the prospect of investing in growth. On the face of it, the government funding they are thinking of pursuing is relatively unusual for cancer non-profits. However, non-profit–governmental relationships are extremely common and highly institution-alized. Only a small number of organizations will adopt a different pattern, as is demonstrated in the cancer field in the case of charity shops.
- Goods that are 'excludable' can be financed through a fee. Most of Cancerve's services fall into this category. Other non-profits deal in non-excludable goods. These may be funded through taxation if they benefit a large enough proportion of the population to attract political support ('public goods') or through various forms of collective funding by the particular group that benefits ('club goods').
- Activities that produce benefits of different kinds for a variety of individuals, groups or institutions will be able to attract funding for the non-profit from a variety of sources. This is an extension of the economists' insight about types of goods, developed specifically with non-profits in mind. Cancerve asks the question 'Who benefits?' and comes up with a blend of funding for its counselling services:
    - individual fees because of the specific benefits that service users receive (private benefits);
    - donations from those who get value from giving specifically to help people with cancer (group benefits);
    - government funding because of the new political mandate to spend on ameliorating the psychological effects of cancer (public benefits);

— funding companies which want to help employees affected by cancer
    and get the most value by using an expert organization like Cancerve
    (trade benefits).
*   Fundamental to the charity sector is its belief- or value-driven nature. In
    Cancerve's case, these beliefs help determine income strategy in precluding
    debt and determining that it will subsidize services for some users.

For the second stage of this process, Cancerve explores different investment
cases in considerable detail. They take an unusual approach to this, however.
Boards and senior management, when considering investment in a new income
source, often examine an organizational budget with the income and expenditure
figures for the new source included. The leadership of the charity can then look at
the difference the new source makes. Also common is the use of a discounted cash
flow (DCF) calculation. This allows a board of trustees to judge the real extent of
the financial rewards they will get for their investment in a new funding stream.
Cancerve's Board will at a later stage of their decision-making ask for both the
budget and a DCF for each new form of support. Staff initially, however, want the
Trustees to focus on a comparison between the *overall* value that the charity will
receive from a new income source and the overall impact on the organization. This
reveals costs and value that remain hidden in the other types of analysis. This type
of investment case is summarized in section 2 of Table 16.2. It draws on the
principles of cost–benefit analysis and other insights from economics, sociology and
non-profit management studies:

*   Non-financial as well as financial benefits should be accounted for. Cancerve
    makes sure that the value to cancer patients of the skill development and work
    experience provided by their employment as counsellors is added to the
    financial value of the potential contract with government agencies for
    counselling services.
*   Transaction costs are critical. The introduction of a new source of support
    will entail expenditure on the mechanical aspects of doing business, but also
    require the chief executive and senior managers of Cancerve to develop and
    maintain relationships with new funders while also controlling and limit-
    ing the effects of the new relationship (for example, government agency
    reporting requirements) on the quality of the relationship between coun-
    sellor and client in Cancerve, and on the charity's independence. This means
    that Cancerve senior staff will not be undertaking their current activities.
    Cancerve chooses to express this in its investment case as an opportunity cost
    in the form of a proportion of senior management salaries.
*   For most non-profits donations go down when government funds increase.
    This 'crowd-out' effect has been demonstrated by a large number of studies.
*   Unrestricted income is worth more than restricted income because it may
    be used for any purpose, including covering shortfalls in other sources.
    Cancerve goes as far as to add some extra value to the unrestricted income
    in its investment case.
*   The Chief Executive's effectiveness is the main determining condition of
    success in securing and maintaining a new source of funds for non-profit.

As it moves towards a decision on which sources of funds to develop, Cancerve begins to understand that this may present a major bottleneck.

Conclusions

In this fictional example, the complexities that had to be considered were all ones that will often be relevant – even if all the ones referred to seldom appear in the same case. Cancerve followed a structured and rational approach to formulating an income strategy. Of course, it may be said that such decisions are rarely entirely rational: charities, like other organizations, have to deal with internal political dynamics, and personal preferences can loom large. A planning tool cannot prevent this, though it may help channel and contain such undercurrents. Moreover, the approach described cannot generate either certainty or 'solutions'; its role is to inform discussion and to support the exercise of judgement. As such the approach can raise the level of debate and stimulate important insights – but one should not expect answers. Final decisions will require several iterations and the organization has to keep its feet on the ground: it needs, for example, to consider the cash-flow aspect, and make sure the books stay balanced.

The approach is not only structured. It also brings together and applies to a practical situation the implications of research and thinking about non-profit income that have so far only been available piecemeal. This framework now needs further testing-in-use in a range of different settings. This will result in new insights and hopefully encourage non-profit leaders to seek out and reflect further on ways of thinking that enable them to develop robust funding strategies in pursuit of their cause.

Note

1   For those who wish to explore the ideas of this chapter in more depth, there are three main publications that address the formation of income strategy. *Understanding Non-profit Funding* by Kirsten Gronbjerg (Jossey Bass, 1993) emphasizes the role of the institutional environment and transaction costs; *Financing Nonprofits: Bridging Theory and Practice* edited by Dennis R. Young (Rowan & Littlefield, 2006) introduces the theory of types of benefits; and Michael Selzer's *Securing Your Organization's Future* (2nd edn, Foundation Center, 2001) provides the most thoroughgoing practical guidance.

Index

Page numbers in *Italics* represent Figures and page numbers in **Bold** represent Tables.